THE WAITING FATHER

THE WAITING FATHER

Sermons on the Parables of Jesus

HELMUT THIELICKE

Translated with an Introduction by
JOHN W. DOBERSTEIN

the Attic Press, Inc.
GREENWOOD, S. C.

This book is a translation from *Das Bilder Buch Gottes*
Copyright ^c Quell-Verlag

First published in Great Britain 1960
Reprinted 1964
Reprinted 1966
Reprinted 1978

ISBN 0 227 67634 3

Published by James Clarke & Co. Ltd.
7 All Saints' Passage, Cambridge CB2 3LS, England

Printed in Great Britain by
Redwood Burn Limited, Trowbridge & Esher

Contents

Translator's Introduction

The addresses here presented in English dress represent in my judgment the greatest preaching being carried on anywhere in the world today. Paul Althaus once said that people today are not tired of preaching, but tired of *our* preaching; and the response to Helmut Thielicke's preaching bears this out.

Here is a university professor, steeped in the lore and language of theology and philosophy, who nevertheless, because of his closeness to life and his passionate concern to communicate to men in real life, can draw, without benefit of public relations techniques and high-powered promotional build-up, thousands of people, young and old, men and women, sophisticated students and ordinary shopworkers, filling the largest church in non-churchgoing Hamburg (capacity four thousand) on Sundays and again during the week with a repetition of the same sermon. This is phenomenal, and the explanation for it, it seems to me, lies in this preacher's concern to speak the language of our day. His success is due not only to a great native gift of speech and imagination, but to the devoted, painstaking efforts he makes to translate his message into contemporary, colloquial terms. The native gift commands admiration, but the diligent effort is exemplary and is a challenge and a comfort to the ordinary preacher.

But vivid, pictorial, poetically perceptive power of speech is not the only excellence of these addresses. Their profoundly evangelical insight into the meaning of Jesus' simple, but frequently baffling, parables; the sensitive, empathetic knowledge of contemporary life which they betray, all the way from James Dean's movies, the plays of Sartre and Dürrenmatt (one of which recently opened on Broadway), the novels and poems of Bernanos, Brecht, and Benn, the philosophy of those mentors of our age, Pascal, Heidegger, and Kierkegaard, to the agonies of the beat and off-beat generation (nothing in this world is alien to this preacher!) ; but above all, their constant, personal, compelling address to the hearer and reader, whether he be the regular occupier of a pew, or the dweller on the fringes of the Christian fellowship, or the soul saturated in all the bitter juices of skepticism, secularism, and nihilism —all this, along with the gospel of God's judgment and grace drawn in a steady bead upon our real situation in this world and before God, this

7

is great preaching. This is "existential" preaching, in the Christian, Kierkegaardian sense of that much-abused word. Dr. Wilhelm Pauck, who shares my regard for these sermons, said to me recently, "*There's a man who takes you by the scruff of the neck!*"

The clue to Thielicke's power as a preacher and a theologian lies in his constant concern to speak to modern man as a person in his peculiar predicament, and in this he may be compared with Schleiermacher in his "addresses on religion to its cultured despisers," though the comparison soon breaks down, for Thielicke's message is far more solidly biblical and realistic than Schleiermacher's, and the modern "cultured despiser" has been leached in waters far more disintegrative than rationalistic skepticism. In 1934 Thielicke published his dissertation on *History and Existence,* in which he dealt with the problem which ever since he has considered the central problem of life. As he says in his book, *Encounters,* an autobiographical essay, this is the problem of

how the vertical dimension of the revelatory event relates to the horizontal ranges of the life in which we live by nature, to the state, to culture, and to personal life. The question that always interested me most was whether and to what extent a whole new understanding of life comes to expression in the Christian faith. For me the leitmotiv became Luther's dictum, *Persona facit opera,* "It is the person that performs the works." In everything that man thinks, wills, and does, no matter in what province of his life, he is realizing himself. I was never interested in political, economic, and cultural programs and performances as such; but I have been extremely concerned with the question of what the person looks like who betrays, expresses, and realizes himself in all these areas. I cannot even see a movie or watch a tightrope dancer without asking myself what this person, who is here manifesting himself, really thinks of himself, and to what extent therefore all these things are fragments of a great confession. Correspondingly, I have then been interested in the theological question of what change takes place in a man, and naturally also in the forms in which he expresses himself, when he finds God and so also finds himself. For of one thing I was always sure, that when a man seeks himself, he fails to find himself, and that he gains and realizes himself only when he loses his life in God.

Helmut Thielicke was born in Barmen in 1908. Following the German custom, he studied at a number of universities, Greifswald, Marburg, Erlangen, and Bonn. Upon recovering from a severe illness which was a turning point in his life, he completed his doctoral dissertation as an assistant at Erlangen. In 1936 he was called to a professorship at Heidelberg, where he taught until 1940, when he was summarily dismissed because of his bold criticisms of Nazi policies. The dismissal came just as he and his wife returned from their wedding trip and he was obliged even to return the month's salary check he had just received. They were left destitute. The Nazi official in charge of university affairs gave the reason for his dismissal in these words: "As long as there are any faculties of theology left—and it won't be much longer, sir—I shall see to it that only sucking pigs and no wild boars are given professorships. But you belong to the younger generation of theologians who are pugnacious in their cause. We can't use these people. The old ones we'll soon wear down." For the rest of that year he served in the army. Returning to civilian status in 1941, he was ordained by Bishop Theophilus Wurm and became a pastor in Ravensburg, where he had his first real taste of preaching to a congregation. During this period he also made extensive lecture tours throughout the country until, like Dietrich Bonhoeffer and other fearless pastors and theologians, he was forbidden to travel or speak publicly. In 1942, again through the good offices of Bishop Wurm, he was called to Stuttgart, where he gave courses in theology for ministers and delivered popular lectures on Christianity which week after week attracted crowds of three thousand and more. This was in the midst of the bombing of the city by the Allied forces, and the meetings were moved from place to place as one auditorium after another was bombed out. After each address several hundreds of volunteer stenographers remained and took down dictated excerpts of the lectures, which they then duplicated privately. Printing was forbidden, but these copies of the Christian message, handed from person to person, found their way to thousands of eager readers. In June, 1944, at the request of Karl Goerdeler, leader of the German resistance to Hitler, he wrote for the proposed revolutionary proclamation the section on the new regime's attitude toward Christianity.

At the close of the war in 1945, Thielicke was called to the chair of systematic theology in Tübingen and in 1951–52 he served as rector of the university. From Tübingen he was called in 1954 to become the first dean of the newly founded faculty of theology in the University of Hamburg. In June, 1955, he was granted the honorary degree of Doctor of Theology by the University of Glasgow. (The address he delivered on that occasion was published in the *Expository Times* (LXVII, 154–157, 175–177) under the title, "Reflections on Bultmann's Hermeneutic.") In 1956 Dr. Thielicke was a guest professor at Drew University and lectured at Union Theological Seminary, Princeton Theological Seminary, the Chicago Federated Theological Faculty, and in Washington, D.C.

Thielicke's published output is prodigious in scope and erudition. There can be no question that he is one of the supreme Protestant theologians on the Continent today. The following is a partial list of his works with titles rendered into English, most of them now in their third and fourth German editions:

The Relation between the Ethical and the Esthetic, 1932; *History and Existence, Foundations of an Evangelical Theology of History,*

1934; *Reason and Revelation, A Study of Lessing's Philosophy of Religion,* 1936; *Between God and Satan, The Temptation of Jesus and the Temptability of Man,* 1938; *The Prayer that Spans the World, Addresses on the Lord's Prayer,* 1945; *Death and Life, Studies in Christian Anthropology,* 1945; *Questions Christianity Puts to the World, Studies on the Intellectual and Religious Crisis of the West,* 1947; *The Faith of Christianity, A Lay Dogmatics,* 1949; *The Theology of Anfechtung, Collected Essays,* 1949; *Nihilism, Its Nature, Form, and Conquest,* 1953; *Theological Ethics,* Vol. I, 1951, Vol. II, 1955; *Life Can Begin Again, A Passage Through the Sermon of the Mount,* 1956; *In America Everything Is Different, Encounters and Observations,* 1956; *Christian Responsibility in the Atomic Age,* 1957.

Of these the two volumes of Theological Ethics are of prime importance; the third volume, on the "theology of politics," has now appeared in Germany. An introductory section of his "Ethics" will be the next book of his to be published in English under the Harper imprint.

This present volume, entitled in German, "God's Picturebook," but given an English title which reflects the theme that runs throughout the addresses, constitutes a worthy and charming introduction to a great theologian and preacher whose appearance in English is long overdue. There is an Italian play on words which reads: *Traditore, tradutore*— translators, traducers. No translation ever quite escapes that accusation and all too many are libels upon the author. I have followed the old rule of translating "as literally as possible and as freely as necessary," keeping in mind what Luther said of his translation of the Pentateuch, "I endeavored to make Moses so German that no one would suspect he was a Jew." The challenge of making a highly original German stylist speak in idiomatic American has made the translation of these addresses a rewarding and memorable experience.

J. W. D.

August, 1959

Ah, there is only one problem, only one in all the world. How can we restore to man a spiritual significance, a spiritual discontent; let something descend upon them like the dew of a Gregorian chant. . . . Don't you see, we cannot live any longer on refrigerators, politics, balance-sheets, and crossword puzzles. We simply cannot.
—Antoine de Saint-Exupéry, *Letter to a General*

To the Reader

To characterize the parables of Jesus as God's picturebook[1] may be somewhat provocative. Are seedtime and harvest, home and the far country, birds and flowers, are all these figures and latitudes of our world actually images of the divine mysteries? Is everything transitory merely a symbol, as Goethe says? If this were so, then it would be possible to read all the mysteries of the eternal from this picture writing of our terrestrial world and perhaps there would be no need for the explanatory word.

And yet the teller of these parables indicates that the lilies of the field and the birds of the air are not simply runes which can be employed to unlock and, as it were, spell out the riddle of our existence. On the contrary, the parables themselves are surrounded with mystery. They can lead—and this may even be their intention—to the listeners' "hearing" but yet not "understanding"; indeed, they may actually drive him to deafness and impenitence. Their purpose can be to obscure rather than to illuminate, to draw a curtain rather than to open windows to eternity.

Someone has said that either there is a point from which all the contradictions and seeming absurdities of a book can be resolved or the book had no meaning in the first place. So it is with the parables. For anybody who does not see the world from the point of view from which Jesus Christ, the *teller* of the parables, sees it, the whole profusion of parabolic images turns into a confused labyrinth; for him the doors are shut instead of opened. Are the birds of the air and the lilies of the field really nothing more than pointers to the Lord of creation, who cares for all his creatures? Or are they not also figures of a world

[1] The title of the German edition of the book. (Trans.)

of nature that is dumb, nature that is silent to *me,* that goes on its way, careless of my concerns and my loneliness. Are the stars just symbols of an eternal order or are they not also a sign of orderly processes that go on quite indifferent to my lot? May they not chill me with the cold of cosmic space rather than make me feel the pulse-beat of a Father's heart? And one thing more; may not the picture language of this world lead us to gods and idols instead of to God? Do not all the pseudo absolutes and all the isms, the hubristic attempts of philosophy to attribute to a single phenomenon—whether it be spirit, matter, or an idea—the prerogatives of ultimate reality—do not all these have their source in this same attempt to interpret the picture language of this world and derive its favorite symbols from it? So where does this transitory which we elevate to the position of a parable lead us? May it not be a "poetical fraud" (Nietzsche)?

In the parables of Jesus the opposite way is taken. He first shows us his Father and points to the "heart of all things." Then from there the things themselves gain their meaning. We start with God and then learn to discover the world anew; but anybody who tries to discover God through the world sees only the distorted reflections of created things, a reflex of his own mind.

This is the reason why the picturebook of created things is in itself of no use at all. Indeed, it confines and limits us to this introverted creation. The mystery of our temporal and eternal destiny is disclosed to us only in the great textbook of God—the Word in which he speaks to us and tells us who he is and what his purposes are. But it is of the mercy of his condescension that in doing so he employs the images and figures of our world. And these images are helpful and comforting; they find us where we are at home. They are so homely that they make us feel at home and give us the certainty that God is not in some remote, inaccessible beyond, but that he gives to everything around us a relationship that leads to his heart, not only grain and fruit, but also the far country and the father's house, summer and winter, lamps and night, money and clothing, weddings and death.

When we read the parables we are surrounded by the scenery of a world that is very near, *our* world. But everything depends upon our finding the right entrance from which their meaning is discovered. We must remember that the pictures do not lead us to the textbook, but that the textbook interprets the pictures for us. The *heart* of all things discloses the things themselves; but the things themselves do not reveal the heart. We are dealing here not with just "any" picturebook but with *God's* picturebook.

The following addresses were delivered first in St. Mark's Church, Stuttgart; later—after revision—they were resumed in St. James's Church, Hamburg, and then continued, on account of want of space,

in the large St. Michael's Church in Hamburg. Always the listeners
were greatly varied, young people in large numbers and also the aged,
men and women of all stations and degrees of education, Christians
and non-Christians.

It is primarily for these listeners and at their request that these
expositions of the parables are published. For the author, to be sure,
another wish is involved. There were all kinds of reports and picture
stories concerning this series of sermons in the newspapers and magazines. Some were gratifyingly factual, but others were out after sensa-
tionalism. The talk that this produced did not really contribute toward
making clear what actually happened and what was said in the
sermons. As a matter of fact, the author has pursued exactly the same
course that he followed in his earlier books of sermons.[2] Nor has his
style of address changed in any way at all. It may be that some deeper
soundings have been opened up to him, as often happens when one
grows older. Quite certainly, however, the author has tried to dig
deeper into the texts and probably also applied the file much more
assiduously in order to achieve the right mode of expression. On the
other hand, he has frequently left the plane and the polisher unused.
The reader should know that this was done with intent. But that the
author has not scorned these tools may perhaps have been noted by
some of his friendly readers who have seen some of his works which
belong more in the atmosphere of the lecture room than the pulpit. The
language of preaching, which must dispense with all qualifying and
safeguarding clauses and is essentially thetical, has cost the author far
more effort and difficulty than the "carpentered" academic form of
speech. In one case we are dealing with an intellectual and more or
less homogeneous audience of listeners and readers; in the other we are
addressing a mixed crowd of people who come with many different
expectations and even more diverse presuppositions. And in the midst
of all this diversity we must bear witness to the "one thing needful." On
the other hand, however, this one thing must be said in many different
ways. Perhaps the reader will therefore understand that the author
wishes to acknowledge how far he has fallen short of the task with
which he was presented, but also that he has spared no effort to serve
the great cause.

The book is dedicated to my friend and co-worker,
the present student pastor at the University of Tübingen,
Hans Schmidt, D.Theol.

---

[2] *The Prayer that Spans the World, Addresses on the Lord's Prayer,* 6th ed.;
Life Can Begin Again, A Passage through the Sermon on the Mount, 3rd ed.

THE WAITING FATHER

Sermons on the Parables of Jesus

I

The Parable of the Prodigal Son

PART ONE

And he said, "There was a man who had two sons; and the younger of them said to his father, 'Father, give me the share of property that falls to me.' And he divided his living between them. Not many days later, the younger son gathered all he had and took his journey into a far country, and there he squandered his property in loose living. And when he had spent everything, a great famine arose in that country, and he began to be in want. So he went and joined himself to one of the citizens of that country, who sent him into his fields to feed swine. And he would gladly have fed on the pods that the swine ate; and no one gave him anything. But when he came to himself he said, 'How many of my father's hired servants have bread enough and to spare, but I perish here with hunger! I will arise and go to my father, and I will say to him, "Father, I have sinned against heaven and before you; I am no longer worthy to be called your son; treat me as one of your hired servants."' And he arose and came to his father. But while he was yet at a distance, his father saw him and had compassion, and ran and embraced him and kissed him. And the son said to him, 'Father, I have sinned against heaven and before you; I am no longer worthy to be called your son.' But the father said to his servants, 'Bring quickly the best robe, and put it on him; and put a ring on his hand, and shoes on his feet; and bring the fatted calf and kill it, and let us eat and make merry; for this my son was dead, and is alive again; he was lost, and is found.' And they began to make merry."

—LUKE 15:11–24

Several years ago I once set my little son down in front of a large mirror. At first he did not recognize himself because he was still too young. He quite obviously enjoyed seeing the small image that smiled at him from this glass wall. But all of a sudden the expression on his little face changed as he began to recognize the similarity of the motions and he seemed to be saying, "That's me!"

The same thing may happen to us when we hear this story. We listen to it at first as if it were an interesting tale with which we ourselves have nothing to do. A rather odd but fascinating fellow, this prodigal son. Undoubtedly true to life, undoubtedly a definite type of person whom we have all met at some time or other. And certainly we are all objective enough to feel a bit of sympathy with him.

Until suddenly *our* face may change too, and we are compelled to say, "There I am, actually. This is I." All of a sudden we have identified the hero of this tale and now we can read the whole story in the first person. Truly this is no small thrill. This is the way we must move back and forth until we have identified ourselves with the many people who surrounded Jesus. For as long as we fail to recognize *ourselves* in these people we fail to recognize the *Lord*. A landscape painter moves about from one spot to another until he discovers the right perspective for his picture. There is no value in his pedaling through the high country until he spies the outline of a snow-capped peak between two treetops and then says, "This is the Säntis," and immediately dismounts and sets up his easel. No. From this point the outline of the Säntis is so undefined that it might just as well be some other mountain. The artist must rather search for a long time until he has found the spot from which he can see all the characteristic features of this mountain. That is the only way it will be recognized and the only way to avoid the danger of people's saying that his picture is an imaginary landscape or confusing the painted Säntis with some other mountain.

So we too must search for the right vantage point from which we can see the Lord rightly and without distortion, and not in such a way that he can be confused with all kinds of other people, heroes, moral teachers, or founders of religions. Now, the best thing to do is always to take up your position at exactly the same spot where one of the persons who meet him or appear in his parables stands; to stand, for example, where John is in prison, addressing doubting questions to him, or the Canaanite woman, who desires nothing of him but the crumbs that fall from the Lord's table, or the rich young ruler, who will not forsake the god Mammon and so goes away unblessed.

When we do this we make a remarkable discovery: in all these figures we suddenly find ourselves gazing at our own portrait. In every one of these stories we find sketched out the ground plan of our own life. The prodigal son—this is I, this is you! And the father—this is our Father in heaven who is waiting for us. But now for a moment we must stand here before this mirror and get the image very clearly in our minds, so that we can say from the bottom of our hearts, "This is I."

The first thing we are told about this young man is that he is a "child in the house," a child in the house of his father. At first to the son this is far too natural and matter-of-course for him to be able to notice it himself. He accepts it as perfectly natural that he, the son of the lord of the manor, should be the leader in all the boys' games. He accepts the role almost automatically. But one day he hears one of his companions say, "Ah, if I were only a nobleman's son, a king's son— just for *one* hour! But I am only a poor boy and I never knew my father."

And when he hears this, all of a sudden it is no longer a matter of course to this son that he should be a child in the house. Suddenly he sees the house and his comrades and even the father with new eyes. After all, it might not have been so, it *need* not have been this way. There is no reason why I should deserve, he says to himself, to be the child in this house and not a servant. And exactly in the same way it is by no means whatsoever a self-evident thing that we as Christians should be the children of our Father in heaven and that we should have peace. It could very well be—indeed, according to the laws of our natural existence, it must necessarily be—that we should think of our-selves as being surrounded and imprisoned by the sinister serpent of Midgard, or pursued by the avenging Furies, or delivered over to nothingness. It is absolutely *not* a matter of course that all this should not be true and that we may have a home, an eternal security.

But for the young man in our parable this is only a passing mood. Often the old man gets on his nerves. Why can't a fellow be his own boss? Don't do this and don't do that. Always coming around with his everlasting "Thou shalt not"; always jerking the leash and whistling a fellow back. Even those "children" Adam and Eve may often have re-belled at this when they were still in Paradise, in the "Father's house." There, too, was the prohibiting sign, "Thou shalt not," and very specifically placed on the tree of life with all the dark allurements of its mysteries. There for the first time appeared that annoying limita-tion: so far and no farther. "And you call this freedom; always tripping over barriers and signboards; how is a person going to be able to de-velop and live his own life with the old man constantly stepping in with his house rules?" Just so have Adam and Eve and all their chil-dren and children's children sighed and groaned again and again.

The *Father,* of course, thinks otherwise about this. He does not bid and forbid in order to "play the Lord" (why should he need to?) or to play tricks on his children or even to give them "inferiority feelings." No, he knows that children need this kind of guidance and need to re-spect boundaries. We all know the educational product of parents who have trained their children in "freedom," and what unbearable brats they can turn out to be—not only unbearable to others but also a burden to themselves, sick of themselves and at odds with themselves, utterly unhappy in this fictitious freedom that knows no fear, no rever-ence, no limits.

Surely the father and son in the parable must have talked about this many times. The son would say, "Father, I want to be independent. You must give me my freedom. I can't go on listening to this everlasting 'Thou shalt' and 'Thou shalt not.'" And the Father replies: "My dear boy, do you really think you have no freedom? After all, you are the child in the house, you can come to me any time you wish, and you can tell me anything and everything that troubles you. Many a person would be happy to have such a son's privilege. Isn't that freedom? Look, my whole kingdom belongs to you. I love you and I give you your daily bread, I forgive your trespasses with joy whenever you bring to me the burdens of your heart. You are quite free and subject to no one; you don't have to account to anybody except me. And yet you complain that you are not free."

And the son flares up and says, "No, father, to be honest with you, I don't care a hoot about all that. I can't stand this constant training. For me freedom means to be able to do what I want to do." And the father quietly replies, "And for me freedom means that you should become what you ought to be. You should not, for example, become a servant of your desires, a slave to your ambition, to your need for recognition, your love of Mammon, your blasé intellectual boredom—oh, I could go on adding to the list. (For when it comes to a man's desires and drives, his physical *and* mental drives, he has a full inventory of them.) *That*'s why I forbid you so many things. Not to limit your freedom but just the opposite, in order that you may remain free of all this, that you may become worthy of your origin and be free for sonship, just because you are a king's son. Don't you understand that it is *love* that is behind my bidding and forbidding?"

But the son leaves the room grumbling and slams the door. Naturally, he knows that the father is right. But he can't use this rightness now. He has other plans and what his father says does not suit him now; it does not fit in with the way *he* wants to live. It is too terribly narrow for him. Outside the mysteries of life are beckoning, his pulses are beating and his passions are seething. The elemental force of a healthy vitality is straining to overflow its banks. Isn't it right to let all this get out and express itself?

The son has a dreadful fear that he will not taste life to the full, that he may miss something. "Is that bad?" he asks himself (for he is not a bad fellow at heart). He feels a tremendous urge to live and he is ready to fight for it and carry it out. "Even if it means stopping at nothing, so be it. I'll show them what I can do and what good there is in me, and bad too; I'll show them my creative powers, my passions, and my kingly urge to assert myself."

And as he is thinking all of this the face of his father appears to him again. And, though he thinks he is only affirming life by wanting all these things, he still has the vague feeling that his father's face would condemn him.

But he does not give in that easily. "I want all this just *once;* then I'll come back. Just *once* let my body have its fling, *one* ecstasy. After all, you must be able to do that *too,* otherwise a fellow is not a 'real man' and never develops his full potential. Then I'll come back! I know that a man has to have a home somewhere and that one can't separate oneself from one's roots. But now—now I need a break, where I can be beyond good and evil, where neither God, devil, father, nor mother matters; otherwise I'll miss the boat to life. Then, when I'm old and the wild oats have been sown, I'll come back; then I'll be good. But for the time being—thank God—I'm a long way from a coronary or any other kind of seizure."

So he says, and he still has no intention of being a rascal, but only a fellow who is alive to life. And now I ask for the first time: Haven't we all felt this at one time? Do we not hear our own voices in the bickering of this soul?

Again the son appears in his father's office. Resolutely he says, "Tomorrow I'm going away to be my own boss. Pay me my inheritance."

Perhaps at the next meal there is a family discussion of this "nasty business at the office." And perhaps the boy's uncle is there, or the kind of avuncular friend of the family who knows life and the world. He defends the young man. "After all, it's a good thing for a young man to sow his wild oats. A man grows up when he gets away from home. Sure, he'll get into some messes; you have to expect that if you're a human being with any adventure in you. But the main thing is whether he wriggles out of them. Then he'll know what life is and he'll be a man. You have to risk boys to get men. Better get into trouble—and out of it—than stay at home like a good, innocent mamma's boy."

"What?" breaks in the older brother, the one who appears at the end of the parable. "You say it's a healthy thing to leave one's father and go bumming around in all the sinks and dives of the world? Surely, it's the worst mistake a man could make to cut himself off from his roots, violently separate himself from what he is bound to with all the fibers of his being, and even cut loose from his *father!* God help him, if he really goes. But he doesn't want any help."

That is what the family says and that is what the children of this world say when they answer this age-old human question and never come to any agreement on it.

And now they all look at the father. How will he solve the problem? And the father says not a word. He goes to the safe, gets the money, and without a word pays out the boy's share of the inheritance. He does not force the son to stay at home. He must have his freedom. God forces nobody. He did not force Adam and Eve to refrain from snatching at the forbidden fruit.

Then, wordless, the father watches the departing son.

I imagine that as he stands there in silence a deep affliction shadows his face and that in itself is eloquent. I am sure he is not thinking that the boy will grow more mature in the far country. He is asking the anxious question: How will he come back?

The father will keep the son in his thoughts. He will wait for him and never stop watching for him. Every step he takes will give him pain. For the father knows better than this son who sets out, happy and lighthearted, on his chosen life. But the voice of his father in his heart will follow him wherever he goes.

So now the son can do what he wants.

He lives in grand style; he has friends, of both sexes. People turn around to look at him on the street when he appears in his brilliant new wardrobe. The house he rents has taste and is better than most. One day he sums up his new life: he has a following, he has developed taste and culture, he is making an impression—even though everything seems mysteriously to run through his fingers.

There is one thing about his situation, of course, that he cannot overlook (but he does!), and that is that everything he has came from his father. But he uses it all *without* taking him into account. His body, which he adorns and uses, which so many are in love with—that came from him. His possessions, money, clothes, shoes, food, and drink—they too came from his father, gained from the capital he gave to him. In themselves they are good things; otherwise the father would not have given them to him. But as he uses them they become his undoing, for he uses them for himself, he uses them *without* the father.

So all this becomes mysteriously changed. His body becomes a vehicle of uncontrolled passions; he becomes something completely different from what he expected from his former radiant vitality. And his inheritance, the dower of his father? It makes him soft, gives him delusions of greatness, diverts him, and makes him dependent upon the people he thinks he can "buy" with it. (For he knows very well that the love of his friends and the regard of his fellow men, which he values so much, would soon cool if he were obliged to cut down his standard of living and no longer had power, buying power, that is.) Somehow, puzzlingly and oppressively, everything is changed. Sometimes he even gets no pleasure from the delights he could secure with his father's capital.

After all, he can't keep on sipping tall cool ones from his refrigerator, that dream appliance of modern civilization. A man gets fed up. But then everything goes so horribly flat. Where will this aimless boredom lead me? A man can't spend all his time staring at a television screen.

Oh, the horrible hours afterward, the hideous emptiness which we have
tried to forget for a little while with these optical delusions.

Again this text catches at us and we feel that we are hearing a part
of our own biography. But it also grasps at our whole generation.

Is not Europe, is not the Christian Western world on this same road
of separation from its origin and the source of its blessings? Who today
knows the peace of the paternal home, of which Matthias Claudius
sang in his evening song, when the whole world lay at rest in the hand
of the Lord and he caught the vision of that "quiet room where you
may sleep away and forget the day's distress"? Are we not in danger of
being stuck with our freezers and television sets—not that they are bad
in themselves but because we have made them into a delusive kind of
stuffing to fill up our emptied and peaceless lives? And meanwhile we
are still impressed by all this blown-up nothingness and many even
indulge the illusion that when "X day" comes we shall be able to
impress the invading Communists with all these gimcracks. I am afraid
the Communists will hold their noses at the vile-smelling wealth of the
man who has squandered the Father's capital and goes blabbing around
a battlefield with a few decayed Christian ideas. Europe, the Christian
West, threatens to become something impossible to believe.

True, everything we have comes from our Father, our ability, our
industry, our technical know-how. But when we use it without him,
when we treat it as paid-out capital which we can use as we please, it
decays in our hands.

Take our *reason,* for example. It is the supreme gift with which the
Father has endowed us, the endowment which really distinguishes us
from the animals. By nature it is the organ of "perception" which is
attuned to his eternal Word. But when did that curious reversal occur
that made reason make us "more beastly than any beast"? Have not
all the arguments against God, philosophical and otherwise, been
financed out of this capital of reason, which has now become a DP in
a "far country"? Are not the torture methods of the GPU and Gestapo
simply excesses of this exceedingly acute reason which was given to us
by the Father and then misused?

And when the great physicists and scientists of our time repeatedly
conjure up in horror the vision of Goethe's sorcerer's apprentice, are
they not expressing something like what the prodigal son felt when his
capital had dwindled away? Isn't this what they are saying: We are at
the end of our reason and that which the Father once gave us—"Fill
the earth and subdue it!"—is now turning against us! God changed his
creative energy into substance and we are changing this substance back
into blind energy!

And what about our *art?* Cannot art, too, become a squandered
inheritance when the design of creation is no longer reflected and, as it
were, focused and concentrated in the work of art? How is the artist

to capture the mystery of being in form if he no longer knows the thoughts of the Creator and his very theme has escaped him? Is not what has been described with the (admittedly too prejudiced) catch-phrase, "loss of the center," an index to the fact that this theme has been squandered? Does not art then become merely the expression of dim dreams, the dreams of a man who seems to be saying almost out loud, "I must say something, but what is there to talk about?"

Are not these the dreams of a homeless man who has lost his Father, a man who goes plodding down the endless street because the windows of the Father's house no longer shine above him? A man who since he lost his wholeness no longer has a whole and healthy world?

But I should not wish to be thought only a negative critic of the artist. For the same thing could surely happen to this artist, who, even though he is on the wrong track as he stumbles confusedly down that street, may still be a great and honest artist, as happened when Jesus met the rich young ruler. What happened then was that "Jesus, look-ing upon him, loved him." But the very moment in which he would let Jesus look upon him so, he would suddenly realize how far away is the country he is dreaming in and what a home is awaiting him.

Of course, the artist dare not merely fabricate this whole and inte-grated world; he dare not be a hypocrite and act as if he were still at home in the world of Joseph Haydn or Adalbert Stifter. After all, the prodigal son cannot act as if he were still at home either. On the con-trary, he deserves all respect when he honestly despairs, when he calls the far country by its right name, as existentialism does, and when he fashions works of art in the far country. But how much he would gain if he would only allow himself to be told that the Father is waiting for him! Reason and art, too, can come home again and find fulfillment beneath the eternal eyes.

Every age has its own peculiar "far country," and so has ours. All these estrangements, in whatever age they occur, have certain common features. It is true that we work with the Father's capital, with our energy and ambition, our highly developed reason, our technical skills, our ability to be inspired by great things and great ideas—for, after all, these are all things which the Father has given us! But we use them *without him*, even though we may still have moments when we talk about providence and the Almighty. That's why we get nowhere. That's why our capital keeps constantly dwindling. That's why what we possess explodes in our hands. That's why it cripples us. That's why modern man has bad dreams as soon as he is alone and has a little time for reflection. That's why he *has* to turn on the radio or run to the movies to divert himself. It's true, isn't it: this is the portrait of us all that presents itself here; this is the portrait of our whole era?

And yet this is the way it is: the more unhappy and lost the son feels the more he celebrates, the more he throws himself into the company of his "friends," the more he diverts himself. "He diverts himself"—we know what that means. More than anything else it means that he can no longer be alone; he must have something going on around him. What did we say? He *cannot* be alone; he *must* have diversion. And one day this realization must have struck the prodigal son too. (It strikes us all at some time or other, when God is so gracious as to remove the blinkers from our eyes.) But when he *cannot* and therefore *must,* then he is no longer *free!* No, God knows, he is not free. This is the great new thing that suddenly dawns upon him—him who, after all, set out to be free, free above all from his father.

He is *bound* to his homesickness, so he *must* amuse himself.

He is *bound* to urges, so he *must* satisfy them.

He is *bound* to a grand style of living and therefore he *cannot* let it go. He would be prepared to lie and cheat and disregard every good resolution, so spellbound is he by his standard of living.

That's what freedom looks like outside the Father's house—to be *bound,* to *have* to do this and that, to be under a *spell,* to be *compelled* to pursue the path he has chosen by an inexorable law. His friends and others when they look at him think: "What an imposing, free man, so independent of his otherwise very influential old man! He pays no attention to principles or education; he's the very type of the sovereign 'superman,' the prototype of autonomy."

But he, the prodigal son, who sees his condition from the inside, knows differently. The world outside sees only the façade and what is put in the show window of this botched-up life. But *he* hears the rattle of the invisible chains in which he walks and they are beginning to make him groan. But nobody helps him and nobody really knows him. Only the distant father, who watched him go away, knows.

And so it goes on from bad to worse. He loses his possessions, falls into destitution, and finally has to hire himself out to a farmer—this fellow who never before was dependent upon any man, subject only to his father. He becomes subject to men. He has to work somewhere in the fields. His life is worse than that of the cattle whose feed he would be glad to share if somebody would only give it to him. Naturally he complains but nobody pays any attention. Now he is under a master, a "man," who has no interest in him, for whom he hardly exists. Now for the first time he begins to realize what it means not to be with the father, no more to be a son. So this is the end of his freedom, his autonomy, and whatever other glittering terms one may use.

The fact is, of course, that we are always subject to *one* master. Either to God, and then we are in the Father's house, possessing the freedom of the children of God, sons and not servants, with constant access to the Father. Or we are subject to our urges and therefore to ourselves, subject to our dependence on men, subject to our fears—with which our hearts are always well supplied—our worries, our Mammon.

There is no such thing as neutrality between these two masters. And we begin to surmise what Luther was saying when he spoke of our human life as a battlefield between these two masters. We are not masters at all, as the prodigal son wanted to be; we are only "battlefields" between the real masters. In other words, the question we face is whether we want to be the child of the one or the slave of the other.

"*I* wanted to be free," says the prodigal son to himself—perhaps he cries it aloud, "I wanted to become myself; and I thought I would get all this by cutting myself off from my father and my roots, fool that I am! I have found nothing but chains." And bitter laughter goes up from the pigsty.

That he should have wanted to separate himself from his father now seems just as ridiculous as that a person should fret over being dependent on air and then hold his breath in order to assert his freedom. We cannot with impunity—actually, without being utterly foolish—separate ourselves from the element in which we live and have our being. We can't take God off as we would take off a shirt. To separate ourselves from the Father is at bottom not merely "unbelief" at all, but simply the most monstrous kind of silliness. Does not mankind often present the spectacle of a Mardi Gras parade, reeling about like a man who has lost his balance and his bearings?

And now this is the point to which the prodigal son has come. Now comes the great crisis in his life. Now he is in a fever to get home. Now he is ready to turn around and look at himself.

I wonder whether we can visualize this turn in his life. Surely he must first have been disgusted with himself. And this disgust grew as he saw in his mind's eye the pinnacles of his father's house, which he had lost and upon which he no longer had any claim. He knows he has no right to sonship. But now, as he remembers his father's face when he left, suddenly, despite all the justified scruples, he knows that his father is waiting for him. And as he looks at his empty hands, even though he realizes that he is too ashamed even to lift up his eyes to his father, he knows, he is sure that his father is waiting for him.

In Wilhelm Raabe's *Abu Telfan* the wise mother, Claudine, says, "My son, there is one bell that rings above all the tinkling cymbals," above all the tintinnabulation of the far country. This bell had never quite ceased to ring in his life. And this bell he now listens to and follows.

The repentance of the lost son is therefore not something merely negative. In the last analysis it is not merely disgust; it is above all homesickness; not just turning away from something, but turning back home. Whenever the New Testament speaks of repentance, always the great joy is in the background. It does not say, "Repent or hell will swallow you up," but "Repent, the *kingdom* of *heaven* is at hand." When the son thinks he has come to the end of his road, then God really begins with his way. This end, from man's point of view, and this beginning, from God's point of view—this is repentance. Disgust with himself could never help him. It might perhaps have made a nihilist of him, but in no case would it have shown him the way back home. No, it's the other way round; it was because the father and the father's house loomed up before his soul that he became disgusted with himself, and therefore it became a salutary disgust, a disgust that brought him home. It was the father's influence from afar, a byproduct of sudden realization of where he really belonged. So it was not because the far country made him sick that he turned back home. It was rather that the consciousness of home disgusted him with the far country, actually made him realize what estrangement and lostness is. So it was a godly grief that came over him and not that worldly grief which produces death (II Cor. 7:10).

And now the lost son arises and goes home. In all his rags he dares to approach the father's house. How will the father receive him? But, more important, what will he himself say when suddenly he is there before the father again? Will he say, "Father, I grew more mature in the far country. Father, I've grown up, I have suffered and atoned for all my sins; I have a claim on your acceptance. I accepted the risk of life and in good and evil I have been a man. Now you must take me in; I'm at the end of my resources!" Is this the way the lost son will speak when he meets his father?

André Gide, the French writer (along with many other thinkers), takes this point of view. He invents another ending to the parable and has the returned prodigal sending his brother out into the far country so that he, too, can "grow up" and mature. What Gide is really saying is that it was good for the lost son to be lost for a while. It was good for him to sin. After all, a person has to go through this kind of thing. And one must have the courage to renounce God in order that one may be accepted by him afterward. The son has simply experienced to the full the fruitful polarity of life.

But Jesus' parable says nothing about all this. The son who came home says only, "Father, I have sinned against heaven and before you." What he is saying is, "Father, I have no claim on you whatsoever."

The fact that the lost son was taken back again is not attributable to his greater maturity, but solely to the miracle of God's love. Here a man has no claim whatsoever upon God. Here a man can only be surprised and seized by God. It is the amazing, gracious mystery of God's love that he seeks the lost and heaven rejoices over one sinner who repents.

But now we face one last question. Where does Jesus Christ appear in this story, or, if there are no direct traces in the story, where are we going to place him? Is not the Father, of and by himself, so altogether kindly and well disposed that he is ready to forgive? Why, then, do we need the Cross, why do we need any mediatorship and reconciliation and the whole of Christology? Does not this story, just as it stands, have about it a divine simplicity; and is it not a fact that there is no Christ in it?

We are not the first to ask this question.

In any case, there is one thing we have seen, and that is that it is only because heaven and the Father were open and receptive to him that the lost son was able to come home at all and be reconciled. Otherwise the best he could have done (that is, if he had not become utterly obdurate, a complete nihilist) would have been to pull himself together and assume some sort of attitude. But the torments inside would have remained. His conscience would have gone on accusing him beneath the cloak of his assumed attitude.

But Jesus wants to show us that this is not the case and that we shall be given a *complete* liberation. "You are right," he says, "you are lost, if you look only to yourselves. Who is there who has *not* lied, murdered, committed adultery? Who does *not* have this possibility lurking in his heart? You are right when you give yourself up as lost. But look, now something has happened that has nothing to do with your attitudes at all, something that is simply given to you. Now the kingdom of God is among you, now the father's house is wide open. And I—I am the door, I am the way, I am the life, I am the hand of the Father. He who sees me sees the Father. And what do you see when you see me? You see one who came to you down in the depths where you could never rise to the heights. You see that God 'so' loved the world that he delivered me, his Son, to these depths, that it cost him something to help you, that it cost the very agony of God, that God had to do something contrary to his own being to deal with your sin, to recognize the chasm between you and himself and yet bridge it over. All this you see when you look at me!"

So Jesus, who tells this parable, is pointing to himself, between the lines and back of every word. If this were just anyone telling us this story of the good and kindly Father we could only laugh. We could only say, "How do you know there is a God who seeks me, who takes any interest in my lostness, who, indeed, suffers because of me? Why do you tell such nursery tales? *If* there is a God, he has enough to do to keep the planets moving. And perhaps if he has nothing better to do, he may sometimes take pleasure in an upstanding man or a great heroic act. But run after the lost like the Salvation Army? Some God!"

Or another says, "What are you saying? God intervene with forgiveness and a new beginning? No, God does nothing but carry out the eternal law of sin and atonement. 'God' is only another word for the law of justice and retribution, because every sin has to be paid for on earth. *That's* what concerns God, my friend, not forgiveness!" And, indeed, this is what we should all have to say if just anybody were to tell us of such a Father.

But this is not just "anybody." This is Jesus Christ himself who is speaking. And he is not merely telling us about this Father; the Father himself is *in* him. He is not merely imagining a picture of an alleged heaven that is open to sinners; in him the kingdom is actually in the midst of us. Does he not eat with sinners? Does he not seek out the lost? Is he not with us when we die and leave all others behind? Is he not the light that shines in the darkness? Is he not the very voice of the Father's heart that overtakes us in the far country and tells us that incredibly joyful news, "You can come home. Come home!"?

The ultimate theme of this story, therefore, is not the prodigal son, but the Father who finds us. The ultimate theme is not the faithlessness of men, but the faithfulness of God.

And this is also the reason why the joyful sound of festivity rings out from this story. Wherever forgiveness is proclaimed there is joy and festive garments. We must read and hear this gospel story as it was really meant to be: good news! News so good that we should never have imagined it. News that would stagger us if we were able to hear it for the first time as a message that everything about God is so completely different from what we thought or feared. News that he has sent his Son to us and is inviting us to share in an unspeakable joy.

The ultimate secret of this story is this: There is a homecoming for us all because there is a home.

II

The Parable of the Prodigal Son

PART TWO

"Now his elder son was in the field; and as he came and drew near to the house, he heard music and dancing. And he called one of the servants and asked him what this meant. And he said to him, 'Your brother has come, and your father has killed the fatted calf, because he has received him safe and sound.' But he was angry and refused to go in. His father came out and entreated him, but he answered his father, 'Lo, these many years I have served you, and I never disobeyed your command; yet you never gave me a kid, that I might make merry with my friends. But when this son of yours came, who has devoured your living with harlots, you killed for him the fatted calf!' And he said to him, 'Son, you are always with me, and all that is mine is yours. It was fitting to make merry and be glad, for this your brother was dead, and is alive; he was lost, and is found.' "

—LUKE 15:25-32

Anybody who has even a modicum of appreciation of the art of storytelling senses a complete change of atmosphere in this second part of our parable. In the first half it is all dramatic movement. There is a struggle between father and son, until this son gets his own way and departs into the far country. After the young man has had his moment of freedom, everything that happens later happens as it must happen. It proceeds with fateful cogency and inevitability down to the last misery of the pigsty. And in it all I recognize myself, I recognize, so to speak, the blueprint of my own life.

At one moment we are free and masters of our own resolutions. But the door slams behind us and then of necessity we are compelled to walk down an endless corridor; or, like the lost son, we are caught in a snare of guilt and guilt repeated that we can no longer cope with.

But then in the very midst of this law of guilt and retribution a great miracle happens: the lost son is allowed to come home. He becomes free again. Again he becomes a child, a son. And as his chains fall clattering to the floor the house of the father is filled with exultant joy over this one who has come back.

And if you survey this course of the story's action you see that here we are confronted with passionate, dramatic tensions; the wild, headlong, catastrophic fall of a man and his being graciously caught up at the last moment. Here we see the wrongheadedness of our life, the many wrong turnings, and here we also see the everlasting arms that hold us up through it all. Here in a compass almost incredibly compressed practically all the ultimate problems of human life are plumbed.

The second part of the parable, on the other hand, in which the elder brother has the center of the stage, seems by contrast to be a bit dull and humdrum. The story actually has no proper ending at all. It seems—at first reading at least—to run on somewhat forlornly and endlessly.

The man who occupies the center here does not live "dangerously." Nor does he get what Sartre calls "dirty hands." When a man is good and remains faithful to the father he has played it safe.

Undoubtedly there are many people today, young and old, who live their lives quite differently from the elder brother and therefore would much more readily recognize themselves in the image of the younger brother. Perhaps they have no time, or in any case think they have no time, to devote to the ultimate things of our life. Each day they ride the carrousel of their round of business, disposing of this and calculating that. And when evening comes they hardly know where their heads are. And therefore they do not know where God is either; for to know this, one must have some time to spare for him.

But there are still others among us, perhaps young people especially, who are utterly in earnest about this question of the meaning of life. They study Nietzsche or Marxism or anthroposophy. And in doing so great tensions are created and often they are afraid of falling into the void. Often they want to become Christians and yearn for peace and some solid ground to stand on (after all, who doesn't?). But they forbid themselves a too-hasty homecoming, because they do not want to be weak and come crawling to the warmth of just any religion and because the question of God is far too serious for them to want to make a soft pillow of him.

These two kinds of people are quite different, of course. But there is one thing on which they certainly agree: they cannot stand this elder brother, because he gets his peace with the father a little too cheaply, because he never takes any risks, just because he "played it safe."

Well, who is this elder brother anyhow? What is the secret of his personality?

This elder brother—this seems to be characteristic of him—cannot understand why the whole house should be turned upside down, why there should be celebrating, singing, fiddling, and lights in every window, just because it pleased this irresponsible scamp of a brother to come back home, poor as a church mouse and badly compromised—when obviously there was nothing else for him to do. For his pockets are empty and he also looks pretty starved. In a desolate condition like that even sin is no longer any fun. The best thing to do in that case is to go back home and lead a respectable life after having properly sown one's wild oats.

That's how banal the whole conversion story looks "from the outside." A man goes roaring through his youth, but gradually he begins to age, so he turns to virtue because he has no other alternative. We are all familiar with this cynical explanation. From the outside a man's conversion very often looks as trivial as that. In other words, anybody who has not experienced in his own life what it means to have the whole burden of his past suddenly wiped out and his I.O.U.'s torn up; anybody who has not experienced what it means simply to be accepted and to be able to start afresh; who has not experienced the joy of realizing that the Father has never forgotten him for a moment, that his arms are wide open to draw him to his heart; anybody who has not experienced this himself cannot do anything else but look upon another's conversion as merely the miserable capitulation of a sinner grown impotent or the panic reaction of a desperate man, just as the elder brother did here.

One can never understand a conversion, one can never understand any divine miracle "from the outside." The fact is that there are certain truths which simply cannot be understood but which must be experienced. Therefore, it is quite natural that the elder brother simply cannot get it into his head *why* the father should be so terribly happy and *why* all heaven should begin to exult. He finds this unjust. This good-for-nothing has somehow contrived to get everybody around him in a dither over him. But nobody ever got excited over *him*, who never found it necessary to come back home because he had always *stayed* at home; nobody ever killed even so much as a kid to celebrate over him. It strikes him, this faithful Christian church member, this model citizen of the Christian West, the guardian and representative of tradition, that he is being pushed over to the shady side of life.

But is he really? Finally, the father assures him too of his love and says to him, "Son(!), you are always with me, and all that is mine is yours." This is, after all, a very considerable avowal, and the recognition and acceptance inherent in it are unmistakable. The father does not say: You are a dog in the manger; you are a stick-in-the-mud; you don't even have the courage to sin; you have stayed respectable only because you lack the spirit to be anything else. No. The father *honors* the son who has served him faithfully. And by telling the story in this way Jesus gives us to understand that what he means in the figure of the elder brother is the type of Pharisee who takes his ethical and religious duties in bitter earnest. True, he shows this Pharisee (and there are thousands like him in the church today) his secret shortcomings, but he by no means makes him contemptible, as we are wont to do, even deriving a malicious enjoyment from it, when we include the term "Pharisee" in our catalogue of especially attractive insults. After all, it is something when a person faithfully reads his Bible every day of his life, prays every day, and faithfully follows the commandments of God.

And, again, anybody who looks at this from the outside will probably say: This is just conventional religious morality; this is nothing but the well-tempered equanimity of people who never have an "urge" and consequently never act out of character, never kick over the traces. They are the dull, tiresome, prissy paragons.

But this is not the way the father thinks. He sees the life of the elder brother too from the *inside,* from the point of view of his heart, and he says to him, "Yes, you are my beloved son, you are always with me, and therefore we share everything."

There you have the infinite goodness of the Father. When to men the conversion of the lost appears to be only a cheap capitulation, *he* sees in it the blessed homecoming of an unhappy soul. And when to men the faithfulness of the elder brother seems nothing more than dull, Philistine respectability, *he* sees in it the dependability of a heart surrendered to him. How broad is this love of the Father! It spans the whole scale of human possibilities. And the wonder of it is that even you and I, with all our peculiarities, have a place in that heart and are safe there!

And yet somehow there must be something in the fact that the elder son feels that he has been disadvantaged, that he feels that his life is being deprived of any real fulfillment, that it never has in it a shining flight, never a tingling joy that sweeps a man off his feet, never a wild and consuming passion. There are no festivals in this life, but only tedious, tiresome, though highly serious, monotony.

Actually, this is very strange. One would think that if a person were thus privileged to be so close to the Father this would in itself be fulfillment. Then a man would certainly not be merely vegetating, but really *living.* Then life would have purpose and meaning and direction. But there must be something wrong somewhere. Obviously, there is a kind of piety, a kind of obedience that has about it a mildewed, numbing lack of freshness and vitality that never makes a person really happy. There are plenty of "good people" whose religion never makes them really warm and happy. And many times in hours of weakness they even have a certain secret longing for the "far country" where at least a person can have a bit of "experience." They are honest, serious people with integrity and good will. But there is no concealing the fact that sometimes God becomes boring to them. These people should take a look at themselves in the mirror of this elder brother. What is the cause of his boredom and his discontent?

Just visualize his situation. This elder brother has lived from his childhood up and still lives every day from morning till night in the atmosphere and protection of the father's house. Naturally he *loves* the father and his environment. But the fact that he loves his father and is loved in return is so taken for granted that he is hardly conscious of it and nobody even speaks about it. To him it would have seemed ridiculous to go up to his father and say, "Father, today I love you quite specially." We do not reflect upon what is as normal and near as the air we breathe. Nor do we give thanks for it. It is the same way with many long-married couples. They are accustomed to each other. It would not occur to them to express in words what they mean to each other. Each is hardly aware of what the other means until he or she has gone on a journey or one is left forlorn at an open grave. Something like this is the elder son's relationship to his father.

Is not the Christianity of many people very much like this relationship? From childhood on they have heard that there is a "loving God"; they have, as it were, merely "heard" something about forgiveness and the Lord's atoning death rather than actually experienced and realized the sinfulness for which they are to be forgiven. But when through habit forgiveness has become something taken for granted, it has been falsified in the process. Then you begin to think of this "loving God" as someone who could never really be angry with you, someone who surely doesn't take things amiss and is always willing to stretch a point. Heaven becomes a rubber band that always gives. It is quite impossible ever to get hurt by it. The wonder of forgiveness has become a banality.

It takes no great acuteness to see that this kind of "faith" is no longer a joy and a liberation. What it means to drag about a wounded, tortured conscience, to be tormented by emptiness and meaninglessness, beset by accident and fate, and shocked by unseen bonds and dependencies, and then to be able to lift up one's eyes again and have a loving Father and a living Saviour—none of this can ever be realized with *that* kind of faith. Actually, it can be the death of our faith if we forget that it is literally a miracle, a gift, an absolutely-not-to-be-taken-for-granted fact that we are able to say, "Abba, Father," and "My Lord and my God."

Of course we don't have to go into the far country and of course we need not first have gone out and lived and sinned with a vengeance in order to experience this miracle of homecoming. It is quite enough if every day the first thing we do in our morning prayer is to give thanks that we are even *permitted* to speak with God, that he has promised to listen to us, and that we may lay all the burdens of our heart before him.

If we want to learn to "thank" aright we must "think" about the miracle that is happening to us. For thinking and thanking belong together. Both are worship and they cannot be separated. Both are an exercise which we must perform every day.

And if we want to do something more, we ought to think about our fellow men who know nothing about Jesus. We ought to realize what efforts many of them must make to shut their eyes to the meaninglessness and emptiness of their lives and how they seek to console themselves with all the entertainment which the world has ready for this purpose. We should hear in it the secret, scarcely ever admitted cry: "Let us eat and drink, for tomorrow we die."

We should do well not to look with a feeling of Pharisaic superiority upon these driven and drifting "wicked worldlings," so called; but rather with hearts wrung by that sympathy with which the father looked upon his departing son. We should do well to realize with thankfulness what it means that we are delivered from this anxiety and the torments of unforgiven guilt and that God has allowed his great miracle to happen in our poor lives.

Let us remember this one thing: the worst thing that can happen to our Christianity is to let it become a thing taken for granted, which we wear around every day, just as the elder brother wore, and wore out, his existence in the father's house as he would wear an old, tattered shirt.

The marvel of God's gracious act upon our life never really dawns upon us unless we render thanks to him every day. Only the man who gives thanks retains the wonder of God's fatherly love in his thoughts. But one who has this wonder in his thoughts keeps the very spring and freshness of his Christianity. He holds on daily and nightly, to a living joy in his Lord and Saviour. He knows that all this is not mere ideas and habits, but life, and fullness, and joy.

How else can we explain why it is that Paul is repeatedly admonishing us to rejoice, even in the midst of the pain and anguish of imprisonment; how else explain the rousing, vibrant cheerfulness that runs through all his letters? The reason is that for him Christianity was not merely a general philosophy, but because he lived his life in the name of a miracle, something utterly not taken for granted, and never allowed this miracle to become a matter of course, "second nature." He had persecuted and hated this Christ; he had rebelled against him fervently and passionately. But then, suddenly, he was wrenched out of this devilish circle of hate when the persecuted Christ met him on the road, not with blows of retaliation but mercifully calling him home.

Not long ago a young student told me that he grew up without the slightest knowledge of Jesus Christ. He lived as a child in a village where the village fool was given the nickname "Jesus." The children would run after the poor feeble-minded fellow, calling him "Jesus,

Jesus." One may guess what it meant to this young man when later he learned the message of Christ and what tremendous adjustments he had to make in order to overcome these first impressions of his childhood and this caricature of Jesus. But would not one expect (and this is what actually did happen) that this young student, when he finally discovered who Jesus Christ is, would be able to praise his new Lord far more joyfully, far more originally, and in quite other tongues than many a tradition-minded church member for whom what burst upon this young student as the most fabulous of miracles has become only a matter of course?

This surely is also what the Book of Revelation means when it speaks of the "first love." The charm of this first love is that it has not yet become habit and second nature, but comes into our life as an amazing surprise. That there should be someone like Jesus, that he should gain the Father's heart for us, that he should rescue us from the frustration of our personal lives and snatch us away from this horrible vegetating on the edge of the void—all this is indeed a tremendous surprise. But one must have cried out from the depths, one must have been at the end of the tether, one must have realized the fragility of all human consolations to comprehend what it is when it comes.

For how many a soldier in a concentration camp, weak with hunger and smarting under the knout of the torturers; for how many a person huddling in the last extremity of ghastly dread in a bomb shelter; for how many on the endless gray road of a refugee trek was it not *the* great experience suddenly to know: I am *not* in the hands of men, despite everything to the contrary; another hand, a higher hand is governing in the midst of all man's madness and canceling all the logic of my calculations and all the images of my anxious sick imagination? I am being led to the undreamed-of shore, the harbor, the Father's house. And always when things grow dark, suddenly that marvelous helping hand is there. If there is anything that is really bombproof, then it is this, that God is there, on the spot, punctually and with the most amazing precision!

Another characteristic which we note in the elder brother is that he *judges* his brother. To be sure, he did not carry his judging so far as to debar his brother from coming back altogether. It is, so to speak, part of the Christian routine for the church to readmit, if they desire it, even the madcaps, humbugs, worldlings, and erstwhile Nazis or Communists.

But yet I ask myself why it is that so many "worldlings," even the very respectable and definitely serious ones, are so difficult to get inside a church. Many of them have said to me, "Sure, when you speak in the university or in an auditorium I'm glad to come. But I have the same horror of a church that the devil has of a holy water font."

Even though this must surely be a complex, there are nevertheless some serious reasons here which ought to interest us. And one of these reasons is certainly this, that many say to themselves, "I am a seeker; I'm not treating this thing lightly. But these people in the church have everything settled, and they ought not to look down on me."

Or here is another who said to me, "It's the respectable people who go to church [he was referring, of course, to the "elder brothers"]. But I have led a reckless life, because I have some vitality and I am anything but a goody-goody. I've got some wild nights behind me and during the day too I've cut some corners in my job. But these respectable sheep, who never faced the temptations I have, need not think they are any better than I am. And they certainly need not think, 'Ah, he's a latecomer, but he's coming. How nice that he finally caught on; we knew he'd come around sooner or later.' "

This may be unjust and prejudiced, but there is a grain of truth in it. And now I submit that both kinds are here today, the church Christians and also the "gate-crasher," the hungry and the thirsty. And now we so-called pious people are going to make a confession to our brothers and sisters.

So, here goes! It is true that the "good" people have been affected by the acids of Pharisaism. We know, of course, that God has accepted us through grace alone. But yet we think there must be something rather decent and nice about us that God should have cast an eye upon you and me of all people and drawn us into his fellowship. And quite naturally we look down on the nihilists who believe nothing; we despise the people who have nothing to hold on to and take refuge with such a "dubious character" as Nietzsche or Rilke or Gottfried Benn. We despise those superficial types who cannot even enjoy nature without having a portable radio blaring away or some other fribble to distract them. We delude ourselves a bit about the eternal foundations upon which *our* lives are built, even though we have absolutely nothing to do with the placing of those foundations. Oh, we are fine fellows! God may well congratulate himself for singling us out of the crowd. He knew what he was getting when he got us. Yes, we are the salt of the earth, we are the Old Guard of the kingdom of God. What would happen to the world if there were no solid Christian middle class!

And look, my dear companions in the pious bracket, our nihilist brethren catch these spiritual waves which we emit and they react against them. All of a sudden we are identified with the elder brother in our parable.

For now we must observe the subtleties in our text. The elder brother, we should note, actually *dissociated* himself from the poor prodigal. He does not say, "My dear brother is back again." No, he says with a clearly defensive reaction, "This son of *yours* has come back." He and we do not say, *"My* brother down-and-outers . . ." but rather "These down-and-outers are God's creatures too." And the elder brother goes on to say, "*I* was always with you."

Doesn't he see that in the very act of saying so he is *not* any longer with the father? The father is overjoyed to have this dreadfully endangered son of his back again. His heart is simply leaping with joy. Doesn't the elder brother see that with all his respectability and faithfulness he is estranging himself from his father just because his heart is not beating in tune with his father's, just because his heart is at odds with the father's heart? A person who cannot wholeheartedly rejoice with God when the icy crust about a torpid, empty heart begins to thaw, a person who is not himself inflamed by the glowing love of Jesus for the erring and the lost and is not impelled to rescue human souls— that person is alienating himself from God in a very subtle but dreadful way, no matter how consciously and determinedly he continues to dwell with him, even though he prays and reads the Bible and goes to church. Now do we see where the bleeding wound is located in this elder brother, and where perhaps it lies in you and me?

Further, the elder brother is outraged by all that the younger son has squandered. It simply enrages this dutiful, correct man when he thinks of the many wasted hours which this adventurous madcap has failed to make use of. He is distressed by all the wasted money, which might have been used so much more productively and for Christian purposes. To him it is altogether uneconomical that this young struggler and seeker, going through the throes of "storm and stress," should take such a tremendously roundabout way to get home. He could have done the whole thing much cheaper if he had stayed home in the first place. Why does he have to read Nietzsche and Marx, why does he have to go off on these perilous odysseys?

So the sight of this human wreck does not move him to sympathy but rather makes him wild and whips up a wave of reproaches. And, again, he does not see that all this takes him away from his father. For how differently the *father* receives his poor, misguided son! He has no thought whatsoever of the wasted goods and all that the son has lost, but is simply overjoyed that he has *him* back again. What matters to him is not the wasted goods at all, but the person who has been regained. Despite the rags, despite the marks of dissipation and the ravages of passion, he recognizes and accepts his *son*. That's the heart and center of the gospel.

In our lives we may have squandered what we would. Perhaps we have squandered and mismanaged our marriage. We may have squandered away our good reputation. We may have ruined our bodies or our imaginations. Perhaps our thinking has been corroded by envy and the heat of harmful passions. Perhaps we have dragged the faith of our childhood in the gutter and become nihilists and cynics. All this may be true. But right here comes the great surprise: God has not given me up. He still counts me his child. He tells me that he cannot forget me. When anybody has done as much for me as my Father in heaven has done, when he sacrifices his best beloved for me, he simply *cannot* forget me. And therefore I can come to him. God pays no regard to what I have *lost;* he thinks only of what I *am*: his unhappy child, standing there at his door again.

But what if this unhappy child is not myself, but some other person, my brother perhaps or my friend? How do I act then? Like the elder brother, who simply says, "I come first; for after all, God, am I not your old standby?" But wouldn't this be a terrible attitude to take? Don't we see that this just takes us farther away from God—the very people who are the old and perhaps tried and tested Christians? *When the Father accepts a man as his child, we certainly should accept him as our brother.* Do I want to exclude myself from the Father's joy? This would simply nullify what the Father says: "All that is mine is yours." Then I myself would be revoking what he says. Peace with God is taken away from us immediately we can no longer rejoice when God rejoices and sorrow when God sorrows, immediately our heart beats out of tune with the Father's.

But even more than this happens. Very soon we also begin to doubt the Father, just as does this elder son, who may have asked himself in all seriousness, "Is this really my father if he acts so strangely?" Yes, the elder son *doubts*.

Have we ever thought why it is that so many doubts enter our hearts?

How many things we doubt and how many things we men are at odds with God about! We doubt whether there is a loving, fatherly God when we think of the frightful things we saw during the war, or when we think of torments we suffered or saw others suffer in prison camps or sickrooms. We doubt the omnipotence of God and his ability to keep his hand on the helm of history in all this confusion between East and West, in this insurrection of the powers of darkness. We doubt that God really breaks the law of sin and retribution. We doubt everything—except our own worries, anxieties, and hopelessness. These we believe in unshakably. God is surrounded by a ghastly silence and we have not the faintest inkling of where he is or what he is doing.

Have we really understood once and for all that doubts do not have their roots in the intellect, in rational difficulties at all, but in something altogether different? Do we understand that these doubts (look at the case of the elder brother!) keep rising like a toxic fog from a heart that is not in tune with the Father's, a heart that is no longer always with the Father, even though it lives every day in the amosphere of Christianity? A heart that therefore not only loses God but its brothers too, and perhaps becomes cynical, seeing only the rags but not the lost children of God who are clothed in these rags and for whom Christ died?

Here is the source of our doubt and discord, here and nowhere else. The elder brother shows us how it comes about that we doubt the Father, that we question him and quarrel with him, that even in the midst of our churchgoing and Bible reading we still feed upon the food of swine.

So we shall not close this hour of taking stock of ourselves without asking ourselves whether as Christian men and women we are also really free and joyful people or whether we are Christian slaves. Only if we allow ourselves to be kindled by the love of the Father's heart and then this very day look around for those to whom we can apply this love: this colleague who is so strangely impersonal and is perhaps bleeding from some hidden wound; that neighbor who needs help and counsel; our teen-age children who perhaps have become so estranged from us and are grappling with so many things that torment them, things which we do not see and understand—only if we enter into this living circuit of divine love and let it warm us and flow through us will it suddenly become clear to us what it means and what a joy it is to know the fatherly heart in heaven and the blessed brotherly heart of our Lord and Saviour. Then our daily prayer, which perhaps before we rattled off slavishly like a burdensome duty, becomes a gladsome conversation with the Father. Then our reading of the Bible, which we performed as a conscientious but servile obligation, becomes the catching of deep breaths of the air of eternity.

What a wretched thing it is to call oneself a Christian and yet be a stranger and a grumbling servant in the Father's house. And what a glorious thing it is to become aware every day anew of the miracle that there is Someone who hears us. Someone who is waiting for us. Someone who wonderfully sets everything to rights and finds a way out for us when all we can do is to wear ourselves out with worry. Someone who one day, when our last hour comes and we go back home from the far country and the hectic adventure of life, will be waiting for us on the steps of the eternal home of the Father and will lead us to the place where we may speak with Jesus forever and ever and where we shall be surrounded by that joy which here we have only begun to taste.

III

The Parable of the Rich Man and Lazarus

"There was a rich man, who was clothed in purple and fine linen and who feasted sumptuously every day. And at his gate lay a poor man named Lazarus, full of sores, who desired to be fed with what fell from the rich man's table; moreover the dogs came and licked his sores. The poor man died and was carried by the angels to Abraham's bosom. The rich man also died and was buried; and in Hades, being in torment, he lifted up his eyes, and saw Abraham far off and Lazarus in his bosom. And he called out, 'Father Abraham, have mercy upon me, and send Lazarus to dip the end of his finger in water and cool my tongue; for I am in anguish in this flame.' But Abraham said, 'Son, remember that you in your lifetime received your good things, and Lazarus in like manner evil things; but now he is comforted here, and you are in anguish. And besides all this, between us and you a great chasm has been fixed, in order that those who would pass from here to you may not be able, and none may cross from there to us.' And he said, 'Then I beg you, father, to send him to my father's house, for I have five brothers, so that he may warn them, lest they also come into this place of torment.' But Abraham said, 'They have Moses and the prophets; let them hear them.' And he said, 'No, father Abraham; but if some one goes to them from the dead, they will repent.' He said to him, 'If they do not hear Moses and the prophets, neither will they be convinced if some one should rise from the dead.' "

—LUKE 16:19–31

Little children and grownups too like to hear this story. For a moment the curtain before the mysterious landscape of the world to come seems to be drawn aside and heaven and hell are revealed. It pleases a child's imagination and it particularly pleases the old Adam in us adults to see how this rich man, who had it so "good" in this life, gets thoroughly squeezed in hell, and how the poor man finally receives a recompense for all the pains he has suffered. It appears to be a story of the great squaring of accounts in the next world. And as we read it we have something of the warm, pleasant feeling we had when we

listened to fairy stories in our childhood. It's probably the same feeling
we have when we hear somebody talk about the "good and loving God"
we remember from our nursery days.

But then we grow older and very gradually this Saviour—and this
story too—begins to look at us with questioning eyes, eyes that have
become strange and unfamiliar. And we begin to ask ourselves: Is Jesus
of Nazareth really the same Saviour we knew as children, who once
entered so gently and protectingly into our lives? As adults we read
things about him which are so completely different. We read that he
came to bring a sword and not peace. And in fact we see that history is
filled with the clash of arms of conflicting armies set at variance because
of him. We see that wherever he appears or is seriously proclaimed the
Antichrist is immediately alerted to battle. We need not go far in time
or space to discover the strife and dissension of mind and spirit that
occur wherever Jesus of Nazareth appears. The truth is that this figure
is quite different from the one we knew in the days of innocent childhood.

And this touching "child's tale" of the rich man and poor Lazarus,
it too begins to look quite different. Isn't there something wrong about
this remarkable reversal of values and circumstances in life beyond the
grave? May it not be that the evil motive behind this invention of a
balancing of accounts in the hereafter was merely to reconcile the
miserable to their lot, since men had neither the energy nor the good
will to change it? May not, therefore, this idea of reversal be based on
what Nietzsche once called "this eternity corruption"? Or may not this
thought of the rich man in hell originate in the hatred felt by those
who have gotten the short end of the stick?

It would be quite wrong to interpret the story this way. In this story
particularly everything depends upon finding the key that unlocks it.
And this key is none other than the speech of Abraham in which he
says that a man must hear Moses and the prophets if he is to come to
terms with his eternal destiny. It all depends upon one's identifying oneself with one of the five brothers and taking the right attitude toward
the Word of God. This is the point of the story. Only as we start with
this point will the story be unlocked.

But then we are in for a surprise, for the secret and the fate of the
rich man is determined not by his moneybags but by his relationship
to this *Word*. Here is where the ultimate and real decisions of his life
and ours are made. So in the light of this ultimate question let us look
at these two figures in the parable.

"There was a rich man." These words themselves indicate that there
is something wrong in the life of this man. Not that it is bad and
godless to be rich or, conversely, that it is a sign of goodness and godliness to be poor. And yet it is a terrible thing if the only and the ultimate statement that can be made about a person is that he was "rich."

If I have to write an obituary for a deceased relative or friend I try to express in a single sentence that which is most characteristic of him. For example, "He was a good father, concerned for the welfare of his family." Or "He was a civic leader." Or "He was a loyal friend." Now just imagine that here is a case where there is nothing that can be said about a person except that he was very rich, that he feasted sumptuously every day, and that he possessed a magnificent wardrobe. Nothing else impressed itself on the minds of his fellow men. Obviously he himself had nothing else in his mind either. This was his whole life.

People whose whole life is absorbed in their wealth have to frolic and regale themselves in order to prevent themselves from seeing that right next door to where they live there is another world, the world of the slums, Lazarus with his sores and filthy rags. So the rich man shuts his eyes whenever his carriage is driven through the slums. He can't bear the thought that this could happen to him *too*. For there would be nothing left of him if he ever had to give up his style of living. He is so utterly hollow that he needs at least this shell of wealth to keep from turning into thin air. He cannot look at Lazarus' sores, otherwise his own well-bathed and perfumed body would begin to itch in its purple and fine linen. Therefore, keep Lazarus at the back door, so he won't be seen!

He probably also drew the curtains at his windows whenever a funeral procession went by. For the rich man doesn't want to be reminded of death because it means saying good-by to everything that sustains his life or, better, everything that blows up his empty life into a something.

Perhaps he also donates large sums to put the mentally ill into institutions. This looks like a very philanthropic thing to do. But actually, of course, he only wants to get them out of his sight. For in the midst of his splendor he is afraid of the dark, menacing contingencies that can happen in life. What if one day the deadly cancer should grow in *his* body? So, rather fecklessly, he shuts his eyes to all the misery.

And there is still another thing that he evades, and that is *God*. Sure, he has gained the whole world, this rich man; he has at his command estates, carriages, bank accounts, and above all, men. But he has become callous, egotistical, anxiety-ridden. He has every reason to believe that he has lost his own soul. So he evades him to whom he is answerable for his soul. And the man who reminds him of this responsibility, Lazarus, his neighbor, he relegates to the back door.

Now, there could be no worse way of missing the meaning of this story than for us, who have no such great bank accounts, to nod our heads contentedly and say, "After all, we are better people than that." That is to say, in one way or another every one of us is rich and therefore at some point in our life we too face the question whether we too despise our brother Lazarus and, in our thinking at any rate, banish him to the back door.

Perhaps we are gifted, intellectually rich people who enjoy good books and interesting characters and look down with contempt upon the "rock-and-rollers" in our acquaintanceship, the people who go mooching along in the flatland between movies and sex, magazines, comic books, and the stupidities of television. Have we ever thought of the misery and the emptiness in which they go on living and that by the chilly superiority of our own rich and perhaps even emphatically Christian mental attitudes we are only driving them further into misery and consigning them to a backdoor existence?

Perhaps we are rich because we are loved—loved by a husband, a wife, our children, our friends. But in the neighborhood there is a crotchety old maid with a bitter, tightly closed mouth, whom little children run away from. For us she is a welcome contrast to our own wealth of love. Well, we think there must be good reason why we are loved. We amount to something. And because the old maid senses this, because she sees herself being relegated to the seamy side of life by hundreds of little gestures of the people around her, she grows more and more bitter, and her bitterness will be our accuser on the day of judgment.

How often we are shocked by a suicide or a nervous breakdown in our neighborhood. Suddenly we realize that here was a person who broke down under the lovelessness of us all; here was a person living in the shadows. And we ourselves avoided him. We felt some fear and uneasiness in the presence of his poverty and his cold bitterness. So we simply drove him into deeper loneliness. And there was no one to love him out of his isolation and lostness.

In one way or another every one of us has this poor Lazarus lying at our door, since every one, even the poorest of us, is in one way or another a rich man. Therefore we should not be too quick to rob this parable of its point by calling the rich man a scoundrel, a grafter, an antisocial brute, and then contentedly conclude that *we* are none of these things. The rich man was perhaps none of these things either. He was only afraid to come into too-close touch with misery. He was afraid of the smell of poverty, for it was always a challenge to his style of life; it always took the gloss off his standard of living. He was always yearning for security, this rich man. But anybody who wants to be secure must always be on guard against having any doubts cast upon himself.

Very likely there were times, perhaps in the night hours whose loneliness even the best foam-rubber beds cannot banish, when the rich man felt clearly that there was something wrong about his life. And then the anxious images would loom up in his mind. The miserable wretches would troop past him, staring at him, and suddenly his fine villa became a dirty hovel. What he repressed during the day came out in his dreams and accused his hard, unfeeling heart. So he did what most people do in such cases: he looked for a moral alibi. He tried to prove to himself and to others that he actually *did* have a heart for the poor, that he really was an openhanded fellow. So he begins to contribute to charity balls, which produce not only a lot of high jinks but also considerable sums for charitable purposes. He also forks out considerable contributions from his bank account to the social missions and the organized charities of his city. And finally, he also allows himself to be chosen the chairman of a welfare committee, though he has one of his men represent him at the meetings. He likes to keep himself in the background as a contributing and supporting member of these social and humanitarian endeavors. This, people say, is attributable to his modesty. But in reality he wants a protective medium between himself and misery. He is evading any "personal" contact with Lazarus. After all, Lazarus and people like him can be helped much better through the superior planning of impersonal organizations. "The only way to help these people," he says, "is through social measures. It simply doesn't pay to help others directly and personally. That way you reach only a few poor suckers and your philanthropy is only a retail business, whereas by organizational planning I provide it wholesale." And when he sends a contribution each month to the welfare society (naturally by check made out automatically with a check-writing machine and sent through his office) he thinks he has done his charitable duty. For him this contribution is a kind of talisman against inner uneasiness. For it is a sure thing that the rich man has no peace.

In his car a little mascot dangles from the windshield to bring him luck. And his bank account will take care of his eternal salvation. Why shouldn't a man take advantage of his "good works" when he can? The main thing, after all, is to *do* them! So he thinks, and goes back to his duplex where sounds the tinkling laughter of his friends and the champagne sparkles in crystal goblets.

There you have the picture of the rich man of the Bible, rich inwardly and outwardly. He represents the rich. They are people with talents, to whom much has been given. Indeed, it often seems that the people who are rich inwardly and outwardly are the ones who are most in danger. For everything that makes our life spacious and fascinating—our money, our vitality, our happy temperament, the fact that we are loved—can come between us and God. All this we can enjoy selfishly. Even the friends we make and the help we give can be enjoyed selfishly. Even the greatest of all gifts, "goods, fame, child, and wife," can be the price for which we sell our eternal life. And this process of selling out can begin quite simply and very hiddenly with our ignoring of the Lazarus at our door.

But then the process goes on ineluctably. What happens is what must happen to every one of us with a mortal certainty: the rich man dies.

And when he thus quite literally "comes to an end" he sees that he is absolutely separated from God. Now it becomes apparent how dreadfully different are the standards by which *God* measures our life. How foolish was our own assessment of ourselves and how foolishly we allowed ourselves to be assessed by others!

There the rich man is in hell, and from there he looks at his own funeral. Often during his lifetime he had allowed himself to imagine in pleasant moments of vanity what a splendid affair it would be. How many charitable societies would be in the procession, and surely the best preacher in the town would praise him to the skies while the poor whom he had showered with a thousand benefactions were sobbing in their handkerchiefs. But now he actually sees his own funeral. He sees it, however, from the viewpoint of hell and, suddenly and mysteriously, this alters the whole thing. It's all so oppressively different from the way it appeared to his coquettish fantasy. True, it is a magnificent funeral. But it no longer pleases him. It only gives him a pain because it is in such screaming contradiction to his real state.

He hears a shovelful of earth come thumping down on his coffin and one of his best cronies saying, "He lived life for its own sake." And he wants to interject (though nobody hears him): "I failed to live; I am in anguish in this flame."

Then the second shovelful falls and again the clods of earth come thudding down on his mahogany casket. "He loved the poor in the city," says another voice. And the rich man wants to shriek, "Oh, if you only suspected what the truth is; I am in anguish in this flame."

Then the minister, the popular and beloved "abbé" of society, casts the third shovelful: "He was so religious. He donated bells, windows, and a seven-branched candlestick. Peace be to his ashes." And again the clods of earth come rumbling down on his coffin. Or is it the rumbling of the crater of hell? "I am in anguish in this flame."

How different, how dreadfully different are the judgments of God!

Then we come to the poor man. His name is Lazarus, which means "God is my helper." And the fact is that, apart from God, nobody pays any attention to him. He lives on the garbage dumped at his feet and he is stationed at the back door of the house. Externally, this is about all that can be said about him.

We know already that now we dare not go off on an unctuous homily about the blessings of poverty, any more than we were obliged in the first instance to speak of the curse of riches. It was not riches that brought the rich man to hell nor was it poverty that brought the poor man to heaven.

It is true that poor Lazarus did not have to meet many of the temptations which confronted the rich man in his life. But we must not oversimplify the situation. True, he had a lot of time for reflection, sitting there at the back door, and time for reflection on eternal things too. But could it not be that this very time of reflection would drive him into bitterness and cursing, just as Job in his misery was ultimately driven to cursing? Could it not be that with all this free time on his hands, time apparently spent so meaninglessly, he indeed had "time to pray," but simply made no use of it because he was far too weary and hopeless? Affliction teaches a man to pray; but it may also teach him to curse.

Now, the Bible when it speaks of the "poor" always means a special kind of poverty, which does not necessarily have anything to do with lack of money. It is thinking of the publicans and the harlots, and therefore of the people who have no merits and no accomplishments to boast of, people who live on the fringe and fag end of life and in this sense are poor. All of us at some time in our life have been at this end and thus have been utterly poor and helpless. All of us have had experiences in which all our securities have been pulled from under us, perhaps in an air raid, a prison camp, or when we have burdened ourselves with some great cause for guilt. And perhaps we have had the experience of learning that it is precisely in these situations that the blessing and the guarding of God are near just at the point when we could no longer rely upon things and men. These are the times when God's promise counts for something; when we have nothing left and can see no way out, we can cast it all upon him, utterly and absolutely, and let him take care of us.

Despite the human fault that permits such things to be, the insecurity and poverty of those who have no roof over their heads and no bread for the morrow can by God's grace become for them the realization that they have no stay in themselves unless God be their stay, but that the Lord who moves the clouds and clothes the flowers is opening a way for them too and waiting for them with his surprises. The insecurity of those whose conscience is smarting can by God's grace become for them a sign which points to the fact that there is no peace that man himself can create, but that God will not despise a broken and contrite heart and will give his love to every human being who stands before him with empty hands.

But now the scene changes. We are on the other side. And on this other side of the great chasm we are suddenly confronted by a completely different set of values. Much that we counted as nothing but shadow without substance begins to shine and much upon which we built our houses crumbles and collapses to nothingness.

Lazarus, for example, had nothing in life except this one thing, that he could count on the mercy of God. But this one thing accompanied him across the chasm and it never forsook him. He now rests in the eternal fellowship of his God. He breathes his presence and dwells in the shining light of his countenance.

The rich man, on the contrary, possessed everything that life has to offer, but which it offers only as a loan and demands back again when a man departs forever. Now he sits there in dreadful loneliness which he was so clever to conceal in life, and across the appalling distance he sees the transfiguration of Lazarus. What a contrast!

To see this is really what hell is. For to be in hell simply means to be utterly separated from God, but in such a way that one is compelled to see him, that one must see him as a thirsty man sees a silvery spring from which he dare not drink. This is hell: to be forced to see the glory of God and have no access to it. The opposite of the peace of God, and thus of the fulfillment of life, is not the silence of extinction, which may be what the poor suicide is looking for, or the stillness of the grave or of Nirvana. The opposite of eternal rest and security is to be compelled to endure that state in which everything is forfeited forever, in which the splendor of the eternal majesty no longer lights and warms but consumes us. "Just you wait. Wait for the first quarter-of-an-hour's silence," says Bernanos in his novel *The Diary of a Country Priest*. "Then the Word will be heard of men—not the voice they rejected, which spoke so quietly: 'I am the Way, the Resurrection, and the Life' —but the voice from the depths: 'I am the door forever locked, the road which leads nowhere, the lie, the everlasting dark.'"

But then we must ask ourselves, are not countless people far from God even now while they are living? And yet they are by no means aware that they are in hell. On the contrary, they exult in their dissoluteness and lack of restraint and at best have only a pitying regret for Lazarus, who trusts in God.

And yet the life of even the most godless man is different from hell in two important respects.

First, here on earth the rich man, the godless man, is able to hide from himself his true condition. Life provides all kinds of astonishingly effective anodynes and narcotics, all of which are nothing but misused gifts of God. But now in hell, that is, beyond a fixed boundary set by God, all the securities and safeguards disappear into thin air. What here is only a tiny flame of secret self-reproach that flickers up occasionally and is quickly smothered, there becomes a scorching fire. What here is no more than a slight ticking sound in our conscience suddenly becomes the trumpet tone of judgment which can no longer be ignored. Lazarus is permitted to see what he believed, but the rich man is compelled to see what he did *not* believe.

Second, inevitably comes the time when all the decisions have been made. Here God is still calling us, and *we* are the ones to speak. But one day God will open the books and *he* will be the one to speak. Here Jesus Christ is asking us whether we will have him as our "one consolation in life and death." But one day this pleading, comforting question will cease to be asked. The mercy of God is boundless, yes; but it is not offered indefinitely. Here we are still living by the grace of God and the merit of Christ; the sentence is still punctuated with a colon. We still have a reprieve, a season of grace; we still have time to live and turn back home. But one day comes—finality, period.

And then even Lazarus will not be able to come to us, and Father Abraham will not be able to send him to add one extenuating phrase or happy ending to this full stop. Lazarus once waited for the crumb of bread from the rich man's table; now the rich man waits for the drop at the end of Lazarus' finger. But the hour of visitation, the hour of the waiting, expectant mercy of God has run out. The "acceptable time," the *kairos,* is past. Now there is only the yawning chasm that none can pass over.

And here in the extremity of his need the rich man feels, for the first time, something like love. Of all places he feels it in hell, where at best he may feel it but can no longer exercise it, where it lies dammed up within him, incapable of expression and causing him only further torment. He is thinking of his five brothers and with horror he sees them going on living their lives, in innocence, stumbling along without the slightest notion that in this life nothing less than our eternal destiny is at stake. What a torment it is to be forced to think of them as the rich man is compelled to think of them and see them here in hell! It is the torment of the dead that they cannot warn the living, just as it is the torment of the mature that the erring young will not listen to them.

The brothers keep thinking: First we're going to enjoy our life and have it to ourselves; then we'll see what comes next. "That we shall die, we know; 'tis but the time and drawing days out, that men stand upon," says Brutus in Shakespeare's *Julius Caesar.* But this "seeing what comes when we come to it" is nothing! *Now* the field is ripe for harvest, *now* is the acceptable time, *now* is the fruit demanded of the fig tree. And when this parable talks about heaven and hell it is not concerned with the geography of the hereafter—what would that matter to us? Why should we be concerned about the molten core of the earth where some have thought they could locate the inferno? What matters is that all this erupts directly into this very hour of our life here. Then it means that this hour of my life is not determined by the fact that it contains sixty minutes, but by the fact that it is charged and loaded with all the gravity of eternity and that sometime it will run out—just as this world will one day run down and the last day dawn upon it.

You are one of the five brothers of the rich man—that's the focal point in this message. *You* are the one—you, who may perhaps be sauntering down the broad road of your life, still young and with so much of the future before you; you, who, it may be, considers the mysterious goal of this road to be no more than a figment of religious fancy and the crossroads where you now stand just any arbitrary point on the way.

Do not imagine that a messenger will come from the beyond and confirm what is said in Moses and the prophets, what seems to you to be so unverifiable, so mythological. Father Abraham will *not* send you any such occult confirmation. For anybody who has an interest in evading God will also consider an appearance from the dead an empty specter and delusion. Nor will the heavens open above us and God will perform no miracle to bring us to our knees. For God is no shock therapist who works upon our nerves; he loves you as his child and it's your heart he wants.

So there will be no one appearing from the dead, no voice from heaven will sound, nor will there be any miracle in the clouds. *None* of this will come to you—you, who are one of the rich man's five brothers. We have only the Word, the Word made flesh and crucified, that namelessly quiet Word which came to us in one who was as poor and despised as his brother Lazarus. For he really wanted to be his brother. And that's why there could be no brass bands to march before him. That's why he renounced all royal pomp and show. That's why he had to risk the effect of ambiguity and forgo the demonstration of his power.

He wanted to be the brother of the poorest and in *this* way show them his love. "We love you," said Hermann Hesse, "because you are one of us." And therefore, like his brother Lazarus, Jesus too lay at the world's back door when he was born in a stable in Bethlehem. No one would have believed his love and brotherliness if he had come in the splendor with which human imagination is accustomed to clothe the image of God.

So he came, because of love, in great stillness, and you can hear and see him only if you hold your own heart completely still. You must hear the good words he spoke to the poor, the quiet people. But you cannot listen to them as you listen to the loud voices of the world, as you listen to the radio and read the headlines of a newspaper. If you are afraid of the stillness, then you must necessarily miss hearing them altogether.

And that's why, too, he never loved public miracles, and that's why the five brothers, the representatives of mankind, are not granted, even today, the miraculous spectacle of a messenger from the dead. This would never cause them to meet him heart to heart; it would only stimulate their nerves and conceal from them the love which alone can heal and save them.

Accordingly, there remains to us, the five brothers, nothing but "Moses and the prophets" and all that they have to say about this Jesus. He who does not hear *these* and is not saved *here* cannot be helped by messengers from the dead.

So the fact is that a high and awful gravity hovers over this story, which at first one may read as only a colorful tale. Here the question is the ultimate limits of our life and the ultimate limit of the patience of God. No one can ever get past this story without a ringing in his ears that says, "This night your soul is required of you. Who are you and where do you stand?"

But at the same time this story is filled with a comfort and a joy that covers us like a protecting mantle; for through him who tells this story we five brothers are now actually being called. At the crossroads where we find ourselves today, where we must decide where and to whom we want to belong for time and eternity, he hangs like a beacon on his Cross—a sign, a stirring sign that for him my right decision was so important that he died for me. On the crossroads between heaven and hell hangs Jesus Christ. There he died for you and for me. There he hangs as a sign that the way to life is still open, that *he* has opened it, that the acceptable time is still here, that the hour of visitation is not yet over, that the Father is still waiting for us.

"This night your soul is required of you." But the awful eternity that speaks with majestic gravity in that summons has lost its terrors, because he has prepared a place for us and made us see that the Judge is our Father. Through his love I have become a Lazarus and the mercy of God upon Lazarus remains mine in this world and the next. If I live, I live in *him*. If I die, I die in *him*, and nothing can snatch me out of his hand.

This night will God require of you your life. Who are you? Where do you stand? Tonight, tonight!

IV

The Parable of the Seed and the Soils

And when a great crowd came together and people from town after town came to him, he said in a parable: "A sower went out to sow his seed; and as he sowed, some fell along the path, and was trodden under foot, and the birds of the air devoured it. And some fell on the rock; and as it grew up, it withered away, because it had no moisture. And some fell among thorns; and the thorns grew with it and choked it. And some fell into soil and grew, and yielded a hundredfold." As he said this, he called out, "He who has ears to hear, let him hear."

And when his disciples asked him what this parable meant, he said, "To you it has been given to know the secrets of the kingdom of God; but for others they are in parables, so that seeing they may not see, and hearing they may not understand. Now the parable is this: The seed is the word of God. The ones along the path are those who have heard; then the devil comes and takes away the word from their hearts, that they may not believe and be saved. And the ones on the rock are those who, when they hear the word, receive it with joy; but these have no root, they believe for a while and in time of temptation fall away. And as for what fell among the thorns, they are those who hear, but as they go on their way they are choked by the cares and riches and pleasures of life, and their fruit does not mature. And as for that in the good soil, they are those who, hearing the word, hold it fast in an honest and good heart, and bring forth fruit with patience."

—LUKE 8:4–15

I wonder whether we have caught the sadness that hangs over this story. Jesus spoke this parable at a high point in his life and activity. The people were flocking to him in great numbers. The Gospel of Matthew reports that Jesus was finally compelled to step into a boat and speak from there. When people come in crowds, when they travel for days and endure hunger and thirst to do so, when they do this without ulterior purpose and not merely as thrill seekers, when they do this simply because here a man is speaking about salvation, one would surely think that the crowd's eager desire for salvation and the fervid current of their receptive hearts would be contagious and carry over to the speaker.

Had Jesus been a man like others he would have pointed to the crowds and said to his companions, "We have gotten past dead center, the dikes are bursting in these hearts. I came to kindle a fire on earth; and look how it is burning already!"

But nothing like this happens. The person who would like to find edification in the idyllic picture of the sower and to see in it a symbol of the creative fruitfulness of nature will in the very next moment find himself disturbed by frightening and enigmatic hints concerning the hardening effect of Jesus' parables. The peaceful pictures he paints in his parables are not simply illustrations of the eternal world, which bring that world close to us and make it possible for us to grasp it with our imagination. The very parable which seems to make eternity visible and near is for many others an iron curtain which actually cuts them off from the decisive contact and leaves them groping blindly and helplessly at the gate of the eternal secret.

Because all this is *also* in our parable and because the parable is really pointing out how frequently the divine seed is destroyed—destroyed in stony hearts, by the heat of the sun, by choking thorns and predatory birds—this is why there is in this parable a deep sense of grief and sorrow. And all this is seen and proclaimed while outwardly the people are coming in droves, inspired with festive enthusiasm, and the hucksters are rubbing their hands with delight over this "colossal" attraction and raving about this great new "star" who is able to draw such crowds.

Is it so surprising that the Saviour should be sad when he sees the fate of the Word of God?

"The ones along the path are those who have heard; then the devil" —who is represented here by the birds—"comes and takes away the word from their hearts, that they may not believe and be saved."

First let us get the scene itself clearly before us. The path, which is spoken of here, is not intended to receive seed; its function is to enable people to walk upon it. It is beaten down and quite smooth. There are even asphalted paths and there are asphalted hearts too. They are smooth and often they look quite presentable. In human intercourse they play their part. Paths and streets also have names; you must know them if you want to get somewhere. And there are a great many people whom you must know—just as you must know these streets—if you want to get somewhere. They hold key positions, they are influential, and only through them will you get somewhere. This is good and quite in order. Nobody will blame a person for being influential. And nobody will blame a path for not being a field or for being hard. On the contrary! But that which is an advantage in one way can be a hindrance in another. The fact is that seed cannot very well take root on a much-traveled and smooth-beaten path.

A person who is only a path through which the daily traffic passes, who is no more than a busy street where people go rushing by hour after hour and where there is never a moment of rest, will hardly provide the soil in which the eternal seed can grow. People who are always on the go are the most in danger.

A person who can no longer be receptive "soil" for at least fifteen minutes each day, who never allows himself to be "plowed" and opened up, and never waits for what God drops into his furrow, that person has actually already lost the game at the crucial point. The rich and the great people of this world, whose names everybody knows, because they are always out where the traffic is thick, are often very poor people. It is so dangerously easy for them to think they are something great when the rushing, heavy traffic keeps constantly passing over them. And yet they are infinitely poorer than a poor, nameless furrow where fruit is springing up.

Traffic and bustle are not fruit, but only lost motion. Poor busy people! Where will they be when the great Reaper and King comes with his sickle and crown and gathers his wheat into his barn? The great asphalt street, the "Forty-second Street and Broadway," which is their heart, lies empty and deserted; only a few patches of weeds sprout from the cracks in the gutter. This is all that the Eternal finds when the traffic of men is finally stilled. Which of us does not recognize his own heart in this picture of the empty asphalt street?

But we ought not to think only of the great people with well-known names. We smaller folks are in this picture too. This we see in the image of the birds, which, after all, haunt not only the great highways but also the humble field paths. If we are really to understand what this picture of the birds means to say to us we must first get it straight that when the Word of God fails to take root in us this is not merely because of our lack of religious aptitude or simply our want of understanding, but rather because there are other forces in the field that destroy the divine seed and prevent it from germinating.

What those forces are can only be determined by each one of us for himself, if we are prepared to subject ourselves to relentless self-examination under the eyes of Jesus.

There is one thing, however, that can be said in general. In our hearts there are still many other thoughts and desires which keep pulling us into their wake and prevent us from pausing to hear God's call. In every one of us there are definite thought forces which are seeking to dominate us and making a tremendously vigorous totalitarian claim upon our hearts. I am thinking, for example, of our ambition, of everything connected with the word "sex," our urge to power, our desire for recognition and prestige.

The devout of all times have been aware of these sources of domineering appeal and have therefore mobilized *other* forces against them. Above all, they meditated upon the Scriptures and prayed. But how the great ones in the kingdom of God did that! For them every reading of the Bible was a battle and every prayer a sword stroke. Why is it that so often our prayers do not help us? Why is it that they scarcely rise to the ceiling of our room and fall back with broken wings? Why is it that the Word of God becomes a mere jingle of words that simply bore us? Because we read it and because we pray as if we were skimming through a picture magazine or chatting with a neighbor. We simply do not fight in deadly earnest. When a person is reading his Bible in the morning or just beginning to pray and the thought of bingo or numbers, the next business letter, or the coming meeting enters his mind, he has already blown an inaudible supersonic whistle and summoned whole flocks of birds which one-two-three snap up the poor little seeds.

In other words, the Word of God is demanding. It demands a stretch of time in our day—even though it be a very modest one—in which it is our *only* companion. We can't bite off even a simple "text for the day" and swallow it in one lump while we have our hand on the doorknob. Such things are not digested; they are not assimilated into one's organism. God simply will not put up with being fobbed off with prayers in telegram style and cut short like a troublesome visitor for whom we open the door just a crack to get rid of him as quickly as possible.

Earlier generations and many servants of God today speak, not without reason, of meditation upon the Scriptures. To meditate means to ponder the Word of God in our hearts, contemplate it, think about it, and constantly apply it to ourselves. Then and *only* then can these words become a power of thought which is able to do battle with the other forces. Then there comes into being a divine "pull" which draws into its wake our imagination, our feelings, and also our thoughts.

Who today knows anything about this kind of "pull" or power? Oh, modern man meditates and contemplates all right. But it is depressing to observe that his meditation is confined almost exclusively to a single area: the realm of the sexual. Here he rivets his fantasy upon specific images, contrives vivid situations in his imagination, revels in secret ecstasies, and thus creates within himself an undertow which must eventually suck him into its vortex.

The spirit of care and worry also is a kind of meditation. We visualize dreadful pictures of what is going to happen and here too we allow to form in our minds eddies and suctions which, like "fire, water, dagger, and poison," rob us of our peace.

This, precisely this, is what the birds are that fly in and keep pecking away. This is the devil who creates this false whirlpool within us. Is it any wonder then that all of a sudden the seed of the divine Word should disappear? And then we ourselves are likely to say, "The seed is sterile. Christianity no longer has any attraction. God stopped speaking long ago." Naturally, when the storm is roaring within us we shall never hear a pin drop; but God, when he comes, comes only on the feet of doves, and we must be still.

So we must be mindful of the thought forces and the suctions and pulls in our hearts. We must be careful of the birds, sitting expectantly and ready to swoop from the telephone wires all around us—even around this church while the seed of God's Word is being scattered. Luther once said: "We can't stop the birds from flying over our heads, but we must take heed lest they build their nests in our hair." Once they feel at home and get a foothold in our heads or even in our hearts the seed is done for.

"The ones on the rock are those who, when they hear the word, receive it with joy; but these have no root, they believe for a while and in time of temptation fall away."

At first it would appear that things were a bit better in the case of this second type of person. At first when they receive the Word they are enthusiastic. They are not just bare rocks; there is at least a thin layer of soil in which the Word germinates. It actually begins to take root. These people have been touched; perhaps they even talk about being "converted," or, if they prefer the man of the world's style of conversation, they may say they were "thrilled" or deeply impressed or that it got "under their skin." Others around them say, "Well, it took effect on him. Ever since Pastor X has been preaching here he goes to church regularly and all week talks about nothing else." But one day it's all over. The heart that was a glowing coal becomes a cold, black lump. What has happened?

In most such cases it was a kind of emotional Christianity. Whenever a person says that he was inspired by a sermon, we may usually consider this with some suspicion. For when the Word of God really takes root a man must die; it means going down deep, it means being born again. And if birth itself is a painful thing, then the new birth is at least equally so. There is many a pang and throe until the new life has struggled free. There not only *one* cord but many cords must be cut. When a person is merely "inspired" or "thrilled," this is most often merely rhetoric or spiritual foam and froth. The Word of God, however, is not a feast for the ears but a hammer. A man who comes from it unbruised need not think it has taken root in him. Enthusiasm is in most cases a straw fire.

The rock does not receive the seed. We men can also prevent the seed from striking roots. This happens when our interest is not in Christ himself but in a particular preacher; or when what moves us is the ghostly thrill of an organ-toned liturgy, or the soothing feeling that our

life, despite all appearances to the contrary, is *not* a meaningless
journey, but that a constructive providence is ruling over us; or when
our basic concern is for Western Christian civilization, colored by political considerations, or the preservation of religious traditions, or perhaps
for antitoxins against Eastern ideologies.

All this is fine and good, but it is not Christ himself. None of this
compels us to die, none of it demands repentance. All we have to do
is to practice a few so-called Christian principles—perhaps, indeed, we
don't even have to "practice" them but simply "have" them in the
form of a point of view. This costs very little and never turns us inside
out. None of this inflicts any wounds. And because we have no wounds
we do not cry out to the Divine Physician; and because we are not in
the depths we do not cry out of the depths for the Saviour. But because
we no longer cry out to him, he is no longer there; and because he is
not there, our relationship to our neighbor, our marriage, our anxiety,
our cupidity are not changed. It all remains the way it was before.
Everything that does not become an action, that does not go through us
like a transforming storm, remains dead. And what is dead is nothing,
or rather it stores up destructive, decaying ferments in our life, which
in time poison us. Then it would be much better if we had heard
nothing at all and remained blind. A salty pagan, full of the juices of
life, is a hundred times dearer to God, and also far more attractive to
men, than a scribe who knows his Bible, who can discuss religion
gravely, who runs to church every Sunday, but in whom none of this
results in repentance, action, and above all, death of the self. He is
simply accumulating corruption and his knowledgeable Christianity
and his religious sentiment are nothing but phosphorescent putrefaction, which only a poor layman could consider to be divine light. A
terrible curse hangs over the know-it-all who does nothing—and also
over the theologian who is only a theologian.

There is nothing more cheering than transformed Christian people
and there is nothing more disintegrating than people who have been
merely "brushed" by Christianity, people who have been sown with a
thousand seeds but in whose lives there is no depth and no rootage.
Therefore, they fall when the first whirlwind comes along. It is the
half-Christians who always flop in the face of the first catastrophe that
happens, because their dry intellectuality and their superficial emo-
tionalism do not stand the test. So even that which they *think* they
have is taken away from them.

This is the wood from which the anti-christians too are cut. They are
almost always former half-Christians. A person who lets Jesus only half
way into his heart is far poorer than a one hundred per cent worldling.
He does not get the peace that passes all understanding and he also
loses the world's peace, because his naïveté has been taken from him.

Therefore a constant bickering goes on in his heart and it is quite apparent that one day in a fit of rage he will slam the door on that quiet Figure, who even then has continued to knock and seek entrance. The anti-Christian is always a half-Christian gone mad. This you can depend upon.

Must I say much more about the thorns among which the seed may fall and be "choked by the cares and riches and pleasures of life"? These "thorn" people are obviously people in whose soil something besides the seed of the Word of God springs up. And this is so with all of us.

In any case there is one thing that must be very clearly understood, and this is that, if we cannot believe and if the seed will not grow, the reason lies only in the rarest cases in the fact that we have intellectual doubts, that, for example, the relation of miracle and causality remains a problem to us, or that a person cannot understand from a medical point of view how a dead man can rise again. Rather, when we cannot believe, there is something in the background of our life which is not in order. And it is to this background that Jesus points when he speaks of "the cares and riches and pleasures of life." All three indicate that I am not prepared to part with some very definite things and that these dependencies then obscure my vision. God can have everything, but this *one* thing he *cannot* have! He can have everything, but I am not going to forfeit my standard of living or my private life to an excessive demand of neighborly love. That's where I draw the line!

The chain of doubt and faithlessness to which we are shackled consists of many links. But these links are not intellectual reasons, but sins, dependencies, and secret bondages. *These* are what prevent us from finding peace and block full surrender. These are the thorns that prevent the seed from producing fruit.

Everyone has a hidden axis around which his life revolves; every man has his price for which he is prepared or almost prepared to sell himself and his salvation. Where is this axis in *my* life, and what is this awful price for *my* heart?

Now, everything we have said has already indicated as in a photographic negative what the good soil which yields a hundredfold is like. These are the people who not only "hear" but also "hold fast" to the Word. Hearing is easy. But to hold on to the Word and budget one's life upon it, this is the great test. And this means to count on it and reckon with it, simply to take seriously the fact that Jesus can break our chains and that therefore we do not need to go on staring with horrible fascination at these chains. To take the Word seriously means to face an anxious care (whether my sick child will get well, whether I shall pass my examination, whether another war will come and the great flood pour down upon us all) and to say:

> Thou everywhere hast sway,
> And all things serve thy might.

To take the Word seriously means really to see in my neighbor the brother of the Saviour. It means confidently to cast to the winds all my doubts as to whether my acts and sacrifices are worth while, as to whether I am not really crazy to be troubling myself over some poor wretch. It means simply to believe this Word and to believe that it does commit me to this poor wretch, and that the Word itself accepts the responsibility for everything that I now dare to do in his name.

Never will I get into the clear with God and never will I have peace, if I only hear and go on hearing, if I reflect and do nothing but go on reflecting upon it. God must be obeyed if he is to be understood. I must reckon with God—reckon with him and his promises in utter realism—if you want to bring him into your life.

God is known only when the chips are down. You can think, you can "cerebrate," about God only on your knees. Anybody who shies away from repentance, from bowing down, from dying, is slamming the door upon God. For him the "last station" may be yearning or despair or stubborn defiance, but it can never be peace.

There are two things which must be stated before we close.

The first is this: No one dare draw false conclusions from this parable and say: Now we see how it is, everybody is predestinated. Everything depends upon what type a man is. That is, one person has a superficial "inherited structure"; he is constitutionally a shallow person. Another has within him an overly strong pull of vital energies. A third is unstable and changeable (the term today is "discontinuity") and a fourth is simply "religious" by his inherited structure. There is nothing one can do about these types, they are simply given to us. And therefore we are never primarily to blame; we are exonerated. At most we are only fellow travelers of the devil.

Nobody should draw these snap conclusions of a falsely understood doctrine of predestination. For this has nothing whatsoever to do with definite types and classes of people. On the contrary, the fact is that every individual has all four kinds of soil within him. There are certain times in our life and there are also certain levels in the self in which we are hard ground, rocky ground, thorny ground, and fertile soil all in one.

We dare not leave this rather grim hour of admonition without resolving to enter into judgment with ourselves and sternly asking ourselves: to what birds, what thorns, what superficiality am I exposing the Word of God in *my* life; what are the threatening forces and the roots of peacelessness in *my* life?

The second point is this: Jesus is not telling us this story in order to give us the agricultural statistics of the kingdom of God. We should be misunderstanding him disastrously if we thought that this was simply an enumeration of the forces which obstruct and choke our faith for our information or even for self-examination. This is more than "analysis." Jesus is never interested in counting and statistics; he always puts us to work. He says: Weed out the thorns; see to it that the seed does not fall on the path; be careful lest you be people so shallow that the Word cannot take root. Jesus says: Be good soil. And that means: Hold on to the Word in stillness, get rid of the hardness and callousness; don't squeeze God into a few cracks and crevices of your day's business, but give him a space of daily quiet *and*—don't duck death and repentance. "Work out your own salvation with fear and trembling." For God cannot be had cheaply. You come to God only if you allow yourself to be mobilized and if you march. This is not easy and it means saying good-by to many things. But this is the only way to find his peace. No battle, no cross, no crown. He who does not toil and sweat and does not daily fall in line for service to God is exposing his inner man to decay.

God's grace is no cheap grace; you must pay for it with all you are and all you have. You can loaf your way into hell, but the kingdom of heaven can only be seized by force. It is an exciting thing to be a Christian. It always goes the limit. And in the quiet fields far more is happening than at the great crossroads where the red and green traffic lights flash their busy signals.

V

The Parable of the Mustard Seed

Another parable he put before them, saying, "The kingdom of heaven is like a grain of mustard seed which a man took and sowed in his field; it is the smallest of all seeds, but when it has grown it is the greatest of shrubs and becomes a tree, so that the birds of the air come and make nests in its branches."

He told them another parable. "The kingdom of heaven is like leaven which a woman took and hid in three measures of meal, till it was all leavened."

—MATTHEW 13:31–33

If we are to understand this parable properly we must first understand the mood of these people who have gathered around Jesus. They are partly discouraged and partly expectant and excited. It makes an ultimate difference whether a man looks at the strange enterprise of this Nazarene with the reserve of a sympathetic spectator—this costs nothing, and if the affair gets too hot he can always bail out in time— or whether he throws in his whole existence with this Jesus of Nazareth, whether, for example, he has given up his job and staked everything on this one card. This is actually what these men around him had done. And now, quite understandably, they are asking: What's going to come of it? What will be the outcome?

The answer seems to be: Nothing. Almost nothing is happening. Sure, a few poor people, a few sick people have been helped. But this is a mere hole-and-corner affair and it has, so to speak, fizzled out. The upper classes, intellectual and political, reject him or, what is worse, simply ignore him. The capital city acts as if he did not exist. The Greek and Roman centers of culture pay no attention to this storm in a Galilean teacup—just as the classics of the later, so-called modern, age will take only the most modest notice of him.

Jesus had asserted that the kingdom of God had begun. But when a man asked quite realistically and soberly, "Where?"—the results looked pretty meager. The few dirty children who run after him, the beggars, and the few hangers-on from the outskirts of society, with whom a fleeting contact has been established—these cannot very well be the kingdom of God. And this is the kind of thing one has staked his whole existence on!

The world therefore takes no notice of him. But isn't this a repudiation of the whole Christian enterprise, including its directorate, which will later be called the "church"?

When I became a pastor and conducted my first Bible-study hour I went into it with the determination to trust in Jesus' saying: "All power is given unto me in heaven and in earth." I said these words to myself in order to assure myself that even Hitler, who was then in the saddle, and his dreadful power machine were merely puppets hanging by strings in the hands of this mighty Lord. And in this Bible-study hour I was faced by two very old ladies and a still older organist. He was a very worthy man, but his fingers were palsied and this was embarrassingly apparent in his playing.

So this was the extent of the accomplishment of this Lord, to whom all power in heaven and earth had been given, *supposedly* given. And outside marched the battalions of youth who were subject to altogether different lords. This was all he had to set before me on that evening. What *did* he have to offer anyway? And if it really were nothing more than this—then isn't he refuted by this utterly miserable response?

Something like this was the mood of the disciples as it is reflected in this parable, and I believe that we too have need of some encouragement, just as the disciples did.

"Yes," says the Lord, and he proceeds to give his people this encouragement. "You are right; with me everything begins in a very small way. Seen from the outside, my work and I myself look minuscule." And then he paints a picture of a man who reaches into a seed packet with two fingertips and takes out one seed—a real minimal minimum, God knows! Actually, it is quite a trick to get hold of a single seed because they are so tiny. It takes hundreds of them to make a gram. And if a man's eyes were not very good he would have to put glasses on even to see it.

But, strangely enough, when it is put into the earth it grows up into a great shrub, and a fat sparrow, who has picked hundreds of these tiny seeds for his breakfast, can teeter on its branches.

Here the question arises: Did Jesus mean by this that Christianity would conquer the whole world? Quite definitely he did not. When Jesus speaks of the mysteries of growth he is not thinking so much of the quantitative process by which his church grows ever larger and finally, in a mighty Christian invasion, conquers the continents and islands, but rather of the fact that in his church there is an indwelling dynamic which must lay hold upon everything around it.

In other words, in order to understand this we must think for a moment of the other images in which the church is portrayed as a dynamic force, a kind of vitamin in the world.

This is the point of the "leaven," which leavens the whole mass of meal and changes its quality. This is the point of the "salt," even the smallest quantity of which changes a whole plate of soup. And this is the point of those sayings which speak of the church as a "light" in the world. How exceedingly small is the source of light in an auto headlight, and how tremendously great is the cone of light it cuts out of the gigantic darkness of a nocturnal landscape!

So it is with the Christians, says our Lord. As far as numbers are concerned they remain a small group, a hopeless minority; and Luther knew what he was saying when he called the Christian a solitary bird, sitting somewhere on a rooftop and warbling his little song. We have all experienced, haven't we, what it means to have no one in our job or our office or our class in school who is at one with us in the ultimate things of life? Often we fear the surprised glance which otherwise very nice and reasonable people cast at us when we happen to drop a remark about matters of faith in a conversation or even when we bow our heads for grace at table. Then we often feel as if we were surrounded by an invisible insulating wall which, despite all the cordiality of our relationship and despite all the good companionship, leaves one a bit estranged, estranged at the crucial point. Well, so it is; we are in the minority. Except that now Jesus is indicating to us that this quantitative way of counting is completely false. How ridiculous it is to say: Here are a few ounces of yeast and there are two pounds of meal. According to the democratic point of view, the meal would then be the one to call the tune, because the yeast is outrated. But Jesus tells us just the opposite: It all depends on which has the real dynamic, and this is what the yeast has and not the meal. This the salt has and not the soup. This the light has and not the vast expanse of darkness.

Of course, as long as the grains of salt remain in the saltcellar, as long as the light is under a bushel, others cannot see the power that dwells within us. And if light could think and dream it would probably contract an anxiety complex when suddenly it realized: Outside everything is pitch-dark night and I am only a little light. What can I do against that?

This is precisely the anxiety image of many Christians, perhaps the secret incubus of us all when we get caught in the spell of this cursed habit of thinking in terms of numbers and land in the inferiority complex of the minority. When we realize that so many prominent and influential people will simply have nothing to do with this thing which has gripped our life, and when we then proceed to withdraw into the salt cellar and under the bushel of our Christian communities where we all share the same presuppositions, where a few Christian seeds and a few Christian candle stumps huddle timidly together and moan the blues.

What we need instead is to let God give us the godly nerve and the stouthearted audacity to venture out into the soup and the darkness of the world. Wherever we are, we should dare to say who we are and what we believe. Then we shall have the surprise of our life. We will find that the Lord is right when he speaks of the power of leaven and light. If we do not leaven others, if we do not leaven our environment, in other words, if we do not allow our Christian gift to *work*, we ourselves grow sour. And the many sour Christians and the many "stunted" lives we have in the church are simply products of the saltcellar, who do not scatter themselves about, and the result is that they themselves are infected by processes of chemical and mental decay. We must see very realistically that the people around us who do not know Christ are actually very poor, insipid meal, even wormy meal at that, even though on the surface they may be "big shots" and smartly turned out, far from seedy-looking seeds. We must simply remember that they badly need us as salt and leaven. Then quite spontaneously the fear of being in the minority will roll off and we shall become aware that we have a mission and a task and that it pays—yes, quite literally *pays!*—to trust the promises of Jesus and count on them realistically.

This is precisely what the parable of the mustard seed means. Here too the emphasis is not upon external growth and bigness. How stupid, therefore, are many interpretations of this parable, which read out of it something like the total Christianization of our planet, and how soundly and massively is this interpretation refuted by the facts themselves! (We have only to look at the religious statistics.) No, this has nothing to do with increasing denominational membership statistics. This is rather a matter of the growth of a Christian's functioning, a matter of his maturing in his mission and his effectiveness.

At first there is only a tiny seed, which cannot move of its own power, which anyone can take in his hand or let lie where it is, or which may be picked up by a sparrow. It is completely passive. But this ceases as soon as it gets into the earth. Then it becomes a great tree which casts its shade and shelters the birds.

And so it is with Christians. Sometimes only a single seed of God's Word falls into a human heart. And often how minute and insignificant were the words which Jesus Christ sowed and which then became the very destiny of men!

"Follow me," he said, and when Matthew the tax collector heard it, it was all up with him and he became a messenger for the whole world.

"Behold, the Lamb of God." And when John the fisherman heard it, everything he had ever thought and said before was hushed within him and he became a witness who feeds our faith to this day.

"Go your way, your faith has made you well." And when the sick and sorrowing heard this, there began to burn in their hearts a fire that still makes them shining witnesses of the Saviour in our world. These little seeds of words became words of destiny, shining like stars in our skies too, words that will blaze up in the world's night when the last throes of history descend upon us.

So that which concerns the whole world, that which abides for eternity, when tinsel and tawdry and seeming greatness shall be scattered to the void, had its beginning in microscopic smallness, in utter privacy, with a few hardly audible syllables. Then this quiet Word began to stir in someone's heart—and we must immediately add, not in the heart of some genius, but in the hearts of poor fishermen, insignificant individuals who play only the role of supers on the stage of history —and something began to *grow,* something was let loose in the world. Have you ever observed what happens when a seed falls into a crack in a wall, how the roots of the tree which grows from it burst the stone? So it is with these little seeds of words which God has buried in our hearts. They refuse to remain in the cracks and crevices of our inner life; they burst open the inner man and go seeking light.

Of course it is true that faith begins in stillness of the heart, and it must constantly be returning to quiet communion with God. But when it remains *only* on the inside it decomposes and becomes a musty, unventilated piety. On the other hand, when it seeks only the outside it withers and becomes sterile in a Christian busyness that is cut off from the eternal springs. Even a growing tree enlarges its invisible roots in the same proportion as it increases its visible form.

And we people of today, who usually have so terribly much to do, always on the go, sitting in the midst of clanging telephones, and whirled about on the daily merry-go-round of business, we, of all people, should realize that we can permit ourselves to be visible and public only in proportion as we sink deeper roots into the earth and through ever-increasing rootlets absorb the strength of eternity and the peace of God.

The man who lets his day grow recklessly and blindly, that is, the man who does not begin his day by talking with God before he goes on to the thousands of words, written and oral, which he must speak to men, that man grows rotten, both physically and nervously. And what has been called "executive's disease," the symptoms of which are ulcers and heart attacks, is often only a symptom of these deeper disorders in the soil of our life.

All too often the seat of this disease is not in the branches of our nerves at all but rather in our roots, which are stunted and starved. Luther prayed four hours each day, not despite his busy life but because only so could he accomplish his gigantic labors. To work without praying and without listening means only to grow and spread oneself upward, without striking roots and without creating an equivalent in the earth. A person who works this way is living "unnaturally." This is what the parable of the tree teaches.

But this is only one side of the story. For just as the growing tree strikes down into the ground so the roots also push out and burst the crust of our inwardness. The Word of God which has fallen like seed into our heart contains within it a tremendous explosive power; it wants to get out, it yearns to become a tree and bear fruit. In the botanical gardens in Tübingen there grows a palm tree which has outgrown its glasshouse. The house has already been extended by another story of glass; but soon this will no longer be sufficient. This, it seems to me, is the case with many Christians. They live in their pious circles, edifying themselves and thinking themselves wonderfully good. They build more and more glass walls around their piety so that no breath of cold air may touch the palm tree of their faith. But they cannot get around it; they must decide whether to break through the glasshouse or truncate and destroy the tree. For the kingdom of God demands free growth and it grows irresistibly, once the seed has fallen into a heart. Then its will is to grow out of these hearts and spread its branches over our marriage and our family. And there its purpose is to form something new. Our children too are to grow up in this ozone and breathe the good air provided by this tree. And then it would go on and grow out into our vocation, and our friends and associates should sense that a creative power is at work.

Thus the seed of the Word creates a hidden revaluation in the world. First a few people are changed, then the conditions in which they live are changed, and finally this growing thing pushes on to the outermost shell and even the state begins to take notice.

Over and over again do we not see in our countryside a parable of the opposite process? Isn't it true that wherever the seed has been uprooted and the trees cut down this stripping has brought about a change of climate and every storm produces floods, erosion, and landslides? Shall I name nations which live more or less systematically without God and now have become centers of unrest, the very ferments of decay in ancient Europe? And is not this fate, this poison of decay, already reaching out toward us?

But I must stop here, for this metaphor of the slashing of forests threatens to lead us astray.

For is it actually true that faith in Jesus Christ is exterminated by the ax of others? Was that the case even in Bolshevist Russia? Was it not, and is it not still, true that wherever the Antichrist rules or wherever the vacuum of existentialism and nihilism prevails it is because, first, Christianity became sterile and dead, that it was because it did not let the tree grow, that it did not possess that explosive power that bursts every shell, every glasshouse, every bushel and saltcellar? There have always been pious people, even among the heathen. They should not imagine that piety is a guarantee that the kingdom of God will be set in motion. How many turn that phrase about the "quiet in the land" into a pillow of pious rest. Of course a Christian without quietness is a tree without roots. But a Christian who is only quiet, a Christian who keeps his mouth shut about what has been bestowed upon him, a Christian whose nature and acts, whose laughter and comradeship do not show it, is—I beg pardon for using the expression, but it expresses the thing so precisely that I dare not allow mere pulpit politeness to forbid me to use it—nothing but a dud. He is dynamite that fails to go off.

If the world has not yet changed and if the worldlings are spiteful enough to harass us with the question of what actually has changed in two thousand years of Christianity, then the fault lies not with the wicked heathen who have sabotaged the kingdom of God but rather with the large number of Christian duds who have burrowed themselves into the ground and think they have done their duty.

We ought to check sometime and find out whether even the slightest discernible impact has been made upon our immediate neighborhood which would indicate that we have been entrusted with a dynamic, explosive power. We ought sometime to look at our family or the place where we work—and here I return to the far more pleasant and comforting metaphor of the parable—and see whether there are even one or two persons who are privileged to dwell under the boughs of that tree which was planted in your heart and mine, and whether they are being refreshed and strengthened in its shadow. Then perhaps we may realize whom we have denied, despite all our piety; then perhaps we may turn back and repent before the cock crows the third time.

And now there is one last point in the text of our parable which we must explore, for it contains a hidden but very important clue to its meaning.

It does not say that we as *Christians* or that we as the *church* are like a seed or leaven. What it says is that the *kingdom of God* is both of these. The distinction is important. We have not been commanded to mobilize the moral and spiritual forces of Christendom and infiltrate the modern world, including its social order, its culture, and its technology—perhaps even with the express intent of giving this old and rather weary Europe a shot of moral vitamins and pep it up religiously. What is involved is something incomparably more simple than any such expansion of the Christian mind and spirit. This emerges, if at all, only incidentally, as a pure by-product of the real thing. And this real and simple thing consists in our doing nothing whatsoever except to let the Word of the Lord germinate, grow, and flourish within us. Or, to put it the other way round, simply that we grow into ever-deeper fellowship with Christ (I Cor. 1:5; Eph. 4:13, 15). But if Jesus is to grow large, I must grow smaller and ever less important. Jesus can win the world only with people who want him and therefore want nothing for themselves. If Christendom wants to gain its own life—if it wants to be a factor which the world will regard, which will set the masses going, and show up in the newspaper columns—then it will lose its life. And only the one who at the outset does not look outward at all, but is simply and solely intent on magnifying Jesus day by day in his *own* life, quite automatically becomes a herald and a conqueror of the world. He will possess the earth.

I think that in this message of our parable there is also a hint with regard to the sinister problem of East and West which haunts us all.

When we consider today what we really have to oppose to the soulless, depersonalized, and mechanized world of the East, what we really want to defend, the answer we get, and the answer we like to give ourselves, is this: We want our free world, we don't want to be afraid of being pulled out of bed at night, we want every man to have his rights, we want a "human" world which is warm and homey; we don't want a cold, sinister world of robots and termites. And perhaps it will be added: We want a world in which Christianity forms dependable values and orders, in which it has molded an ideal of man in whom the primitive bestial instincts have been tamed and the human values of conscience and personality have become basic, sustaining ideas. How many say this and how many really mean it honestly and seriously! And yet when we say this we do nothing but embalm the corpse of old Europe instead of remembering what should really animate and vivify us. May I illustrate what I mean by another parable of Jesus?

When the prodigal son left his father and went to the far country he did this not just to be perverse but in order to grow. He said to himself (I referred to this in a previous chapter): "I can't develop under the thumb and authority of my father. I have to be free, for once I need to be myself. Therefore I'll go out where I can realize my ideas, where nobody can turn me away from the road that I have to travel according to the law of *my* life." He says to himself, "After all, I have a good 'inherited structure,' I come from the best of homes, and materially I am well equipped. With this endowment I'll make my way all right."

But then it turned out that all this was used up in no time and that instead of growing with all this good inheritance he went to the dogs. You cannot have the Father's gifts if you will not have the Father; for then they only trickle through your fingers. The fear that this might also happen to us always comes over me when I read so much in the newspapers about the "Christian West," Christian political principles, and Christian social charity and hardly ever read an anniversary speech in which this pathetic refrain of the prodigal son is not chanted.

Why am I so afraid of these phrases which sound so solid and dependable? Because people want the gifts of the Lord Christ but they do not want him. He once walked among our people and trod our soil. His apostles and missionaries and reformers were the messengers who brought his Word to us and invited us to let him be our Saviour. And because our forefathers grasped this Hand of God, because they entered into his peace and found deliverance from fear and guilt in the atonement of the Cross, there grew in them a whole new concept of humanity. What we today call "conscience," "freedom," "humanity," all this we got from him. All this accrued to us when we gained the eternal heart. It was the image of the Saviour that formed our image of man. Our ideal of freedom was patterned on the freedom of a man whose sins are forgiven, whose chains are broken, who is "the free lord of all." Our ideals of life and death are stamped with the image of him who overcame the world.

And now we want to hold on to all these good ideas and principles, for they have proved their worth, but we want them without him. We have learned enough from Jesus of Nazareth, we have said good-by to him, and we carry in our hearts the legacy of his good ideas about life and death, humanity, and neighborliness. But he himself has become a myth, and we propose to get along without him. So, without being aware of it, we go wandering into the far country. The intellectual and cultural machinery of the West, the Christian West, keeps on running for a few centuries afterward but the motor has been shut off. The inherited capital lasts for a time, but the Father's house is behind us. We go stumbling along on this presumptive Christian heritage, thinking that it is still something worth living for, that it is still a decent, real world of values, capable of putting down the specters of the East. And all the while we are living on capital that is being consumed at a furious pace because there are no replacements, because contact with the Father has been broken.

And while we naïvely prattle about the Christian West, those whose ears are sharp to hear have long since heard the howling of the wolves pushing up from the cellar (Nietzsche was one of the "clairaudient" admonishers of Christendom) and already the clear-seeing ones see the pigsty in the distance and descry the bestialization that ensues after these humanist dreams are done and reality returns. And then may not the movement once begun by Jesus of Nazareth also be brought to a final standstill?

Do we understand, then, what the parable means when it says that it is not Christendom that grows, not the church, not the Christian West that grows? If the Body of Christ seems to be growing bigger, if Christian phrases appear in the press and radio, if it has become almost a fashion to listen to the counsel of the church, and if even those who will have nothing to do with Jesus of Nazareth personally nevertheless "affirm" the ideas of Christian parties and similar movements—if the Body of Christ is growing in this way, may this not be (and here I pose a dreadful, depressing question) a cancerous swelling and therefore a pathological proliferation of cells? May it not be just sound and fury and therefore have more to do with nerves or even tactical prudence than with hearts that have found peace beneath the Cross and regained a home in the Father's house?

How can we distinguish between these pathological, cancerlike proliferations and a real growth of the organism itself? And the answer of Jesus' parable is: We can do this only as we grow into *him,* as his Word is formed in us, as we allow everything we are and think and do to be permeated by him, as we wake with him in the morning and let him be our first thought, as we see in our fellow men and fellow workers the men for whom he died, as we allow our work to be hallowed by him, as we give thanks to him for the joys and fulfillments of our life and accept the pains and disciplines as from his hand, and finally, when death comes, as we "let him put his hand beneath our head to lift us up and hold us" (Matthias Claudius).

Only as we let him into our lives in *this* way will his Word grow in us and not some Christian cancerous growth. Only so will we stop living on the heritage of the fathers and be joined directly to the living current from the Father's house. Then we shall know why this life is worth living, because the true life has been made manifest to us. Then, and *only* then, shall we bring the Lord Christ into politics, into the social order, and perhaps even into desolated and thirsting Russia, into blindly searching China, and into Africa which Christian Europe has so dreadfully wronged. But the promise that the tree will thus grow over the whole world is given to us only if we allow the seed to grow in ourselves, in complete solitude, in complete stillness, and in communion with Jesus Christ.

To you and to me has been entrusted the seed from which one day are to grow branches which are to spread over the earth and give shelter to the birds of the air. Don't seek these branches, but rather nurse the seed. Seek first the kingdom of God, seek first to receive and keep this smallest thing in your heart, and all these other things— including the Christian West and the Christian mission to the world— shall be yours as well.

We have a Saviour to whom the world belongs and before whom every knee shall bow. And because we are marching on to his day with power we are not short-winded and shortsighted. And therefore even the smallest need not be too small for us. But the great things are hidden in him, and he gives them with his left hand.

VI

The Parable of the Tares among the Wheat

Another parable he put before them, saying, "The kingdom of heaven may be compared to a man who sowed good seed in his field; but while men were sleeping, his enemy came and sowed weeds among the wheat, and went away. So when the plants came up and bore grain, then the weeds appeared also. And the servants of the householder came and said to him, 'Sir, did you now sow good seed in your field? How then has it weeds?' He said to them, 'An enemy has done this.' The servants said to him, 'Then do you want us to go and gather them?' But he said, 'No; lest in gathering the weeds you root up the wheat along with them. Let both grow together until the harvest; and at harvest time I will tell the reapers, Gather the weeds first and bind them in bundles to be burned, but gather the wheat into my barn.' "

Then he left the crowds and went into the house. And his disciples came to him, saying, "Explain to us the parable of the weeds of the field." He answered, "He who sows the good seed is the Son of man; the field is the world, and the good seed means the sons of the kingdom; the weeds are the sons of the evil one, and the enemy who sowed them is the devil; the harvest is the close of the age, and the reapers are angels. Just as the weeds are gathered and burned with fire, so will it be at the close of the age. The Son of man will send his angels, and they will gather out of his kingdom all causes of sin and all evildoers, and throw them into the furnace of fire; there men will weep and gnash their teeth. Then the righteous will shine like the sun in the kingdom of their Father. He who has ears, let him hear."

—MATTHEW 13:24–30, 36–43

When in the preceding chapter we considered the parable of the mustard seed, it may have appeared at first glance—but surely only at the very first glance—that here we were going to be presented with an optimistic prognosis of the development of Christianity, a very reassuring and comforting preview, in which the church of Jesus would develop from very insignificant beginnings into a world-wide organization.

After we read *this* parable we can hardly slip into the misconception of a "happy ending" for church history. For this parable speaks of a dark menace, a mysterious power that is everywhere at work—and not only out there among the dubious excrescences of civilization, the politicians and the executives, the mummers and the Mardi Gras, and the movies, but also in the innermost sanctuary itself. In this very moment in which the Word of God sounds from the pulpit that sinister power is also sowing its toxic seed among the furrows. Even in the assemblies of bishops and synods that power mingles the seeds of ambition, the praise of men, and clericalism with this desire to be obedient to God and to act spiritually. Where theologians sit poring over the Scriptures that dark power sows between the lines the seeds of man's own thinking, causing the wisdom of the Greeks to triumph over the foolishness of the Cross and spreading the graveclothes of human, all too human thoughts upon the open Easter grave and turning the mighty acts of God into the humbug of idle self-assertion.

Now, depressing as these intimations of Jesus may be, they may also reassure us, for at least they accord with our own experience. And at least they do not expect us to see bright progress where we see darkness and where we are troubled by humanity's merely marking time—and also by the sterility of the church!

For we have only to look at life with open eyes to see this strange ambiguity: There are no fields or gardens in this world where *only* grain or flowers grow; the weeds are always there too. And when we declare somewhat resignedly, "There is nothing perfect in this world," this is only a somewhat trite expression of this experience.

We have this experience even outside the church of Jesus. We need only think of technical science to demonstrate this. To be sure, technology is a gift of creation which helps us to "subdue the earth." And yet we human beings are in much the same position as Goethe's sorcerer's apprentice. He learned the art of invention and how to exercise his power, but then all this got beyond his control and there he stood trembling before the spirits he had conjured up. How much God-given intelligence is being expended today on the problems of nuclear physics! But all this intelligence has not been sufficient to contrive methods which will protect us from the *effects* of these atomic energies which we have released. We have evoked them with the magic word of knowledge and now they turn against us and banish us to the zones of fear. It is as if an evil power had conjured substances of corruption and decay into the very gifts of creation which God *himself* has committed to our hands.

True, there is such a thing as progress in technical science. We have penetrated deeper into the mysteries of nature and are able to coax from it energies undreamed of by former generations. But since, with all this progress, man has remained the same, has *not* changed, his increasing power over creation is paralleled by the increasingly cruel and murderous power which he uses against himself and his fellows. And it is like a dreadful *mene, mene, tekel* pronounced upon our world that our technological mastery of the world has *not* led to the humanization of the world and the fulfillment of the Creator's command, but rather that the *first* product of this progress was two world wars with their murderous, wholesale slaughter, and the fact that we have excellent prospects of blowing up the whole earth in a third world war, instead of "subduing" it to the glory of God. Who is it that is mixed up in this thing? Who has been sowing something else during the night?

And now this parable shows us that this same mysterious twilight hangs over the church of Christ and that here too another figure, spectral and shadowy, a demonic double, follows the divine Sower, scattering seeds of negation and destruction.

For example, there is that Word of God, formulated by Paul, which says that where sin abounds grace abounds all the more (Rom. 5:20), that God wants us, wants to be our Father as we are, and that despite our guilt and wretchedness and filth he takes us to his heart. But strangely enough, "overnight" even this greatest of the gifts of God is poisoned. We turn it into a "pretext for evil" (I Pet. 5:20). That is, we say to ourselves: Well, if we are always in right with God anyhow, a little more or less dirt on our conscience doesn't matter. The Catholics have to toe the mark, of course, because otherwise they will have to suffer the hardships of purgatory. But we Protestants are radiantly and joyfully liberal, we rejoice in grace. A few side trips more or less into the far country don't matter to us, for, after all, God is not really angry and nothing really bad can happen to us in the end anyhow. The catechism says—doesn't it?—that grace is insurance against sin and accident and that we already have a ticket to heaven in our pocket or we will be able to get one at the last minute. Seats in heaven are reserved. In fact, heaven even feels flattered when we latecomers finally decide to come in after all.

So we turn this costly grace, for which Jesus shed his blood, into cheap, marked-down merchandise, as Dietrich Bonhoeffer expressed it. When we remember what it cost our Lord, what pains he had to suffer and what a death he had to die in order to reopen the Father's house for us, surely this must lay a tremendous obligation upon our life. Then there is no alternative except to live this life under the stern light of eternity, under the eyes of God. But instead of this we use this gift of freedom to break out of the radius of this light; instead we go following a will-o'-the-wisp and escape into that night where all cats are gray and where a little bit more or less of looseness and "nonchalance" doesn't matter. If there is more joy in heaven over *one* sinner than over ninety-nine righteous persons, all right, then we'll treat ourselves with pleasure to being this one sinner. The cue is: Carry on as usual!

But then in the distance rumbles the melancholy question whether when we do this we are not missing the meaning and purpose of our life, whether we may not have switched ourselves onto the wrong track.

Yes, it is very strange how everything—even the greatest thing that Jesus gives us—mysteriously spoils, decays, and is delivered over to ambiguity when that dark power gets its fingers on it. Beneath these fingers it is not only the wheatfield that is sown with weeds; the grace of God itself becomes a cadaver and our Father's royal declaration of emancipation is turned into wastepaper.

Thus the weeds are always mixed with the divine seed. On the one hand, God is concerned that his gospel should give a man some inner support. For when a person gets into the clear with God his life, too, changes and he becomes a more stable person. But no sooner is God there than others too are approaching him. Overnight somebody comes to him and whispers something, plants something in his ears—telling him: "If we're going to rule and carry out our program, we need people who have some inner stability. Religion must be maintained among the people or we must furnish them with a religion." What kind of religion is a purely secondary question. And so they turn Christianity into a political ideology, something to hold the body politic together, opium for the people. So they use faith as a means to political ends, though Jesus' death and resurrection are a matter of complete indifference to them. Just because all this shallow blather about their Christian point of view costs them absolutely nothing, they twaddle about Christian principles in culture.

Always during the night that dark figure has gone through God's fields, and the next morning something altogether different comes up. Alongside of the Word of God something else grows up high. From a distance it looks very much like the Word, just as the weeds look like real grain from afar. But when one looks a bit closer one finds that what is left of the divine words is nothing but empty Christian words in which there is no fruit. There is the word "grace," and it is only a religious term for "nonchalance." There is the word "Christianity," but instead of containing the seed of eternity it represents nothing more than sterile hypocrisy. People think the purpose of the gospel is only to make people better, more serious, more respectable, when its real concern is rather that death may be conquered, that we may be delivered from fear and find a new security.

And what is true about the *content* of the message is true also of the *people* who have gathered around it. There is Judas in the midst of the apostles, here are real disciples alongside of merely nominal church members, here are martyrs and apostates, orthodoxists and heretics, people with haloes and sham saints, Pharisees and harlots, all mixed together. How in the world can we ever distinguish between them? How can we refrain from crying out: Get rid of the weeds! or even: This Christianity is a dreadful mess!

What really happened during that mysterious night the parable speaks of?

The man who sowed the good seed went home and laid himself down to sleep. Having done his work, he could do so with good conscience. He had done his duty and now he must let the rest take its course. What happens next—the outcome of his sowing, the effect of the Word—this is no longer under his control. He may perhaps be thinking of Matthias Claudius' hymn:

> We plow the fields and scatter
> The good seed on the land,
> But it is fed and watered
> By God's almighty hand.

But is there not another hand at work here besides the Hand of God?

At first nothing happens that can be seen. But one morning he is bewildered to discover that overnight and altogether unnoticed something terrible has happened and there ensues a lively argument with his servants which is replete with expressions of amazement and dismay.

How many a father, how many a mother has had the same experience. They have reared their child carefully, surrounded him with a good clean atmosphere, cherished him with love, and prayed with him and for him at his cradle at night. And, despite all this, something else begins to grow. Strange things happen in him. They see stirrings and impulses in him that they do not want to see at all. Another influence comes beaming in from an altogether different quarter and they can do nothing about it.

And what happened to the seed which Jesus Christ himself sowed? He sowed love and along with it the martyrs' stakes sprang up from the ground, and in Christendom men (including the theologians) bombarded each other with hard objects and poisoned words just as much as they did elsewhere. He sowed peace, but the field of the world is littered with the dead and disabled.

What should be done?

We understand the angry reaction of the servants, who want to go out immediately and rip out the weeds, even though, from a farmer's point of view, this is almost impossible. Nor does the Lord permit this. Rather, he says, "Let both grow together until the harvest. You can't change things. Leave the decision, leave the separation of the weeds from the wheat to the judgment day of God. This is not your affair. God will take this thing in hand in his good time."

What is it that causes our Lord, so strangely, it seems, to stifle the holy zeal of his people and to say to them, "Hands off! You cannot change the field of the world as it is anyhow"?

If I am not mistaken, he had three reasons for this.

First, he is saying: Please do not think that you can exterminate the evil in the world by your activity and your own personal exertions. After all, that evil is within you yourselves. This is not some human resistance that you must break down; rather it is the power of the great adversary which is at work in what is happening and intervening here. You are not fighting against "flesh and blood," but against the secret ruler of this world.

This is the tragedy of all social reformers and moralists; they want to root out vice, drinking, smoking, free love. And as they set out in grim earnest on their virtuous crusades these good people are quite oblivious of the fact that (to speak with Goethe's Faust) the devil has hung himself about their necks. Why is it that as a rule we find it so hard to endure these do-gooders and reformers? Why do they make us feel so uncomfortable? Because we sense something Pharisaic and superior in them, because the very vice upon which they are making a frontal attack is at the same time in their own hearts, like a partisan army fighting in their rear. The fanatical reformers do precisely what the servants in our parable wanted to do. They want to exterminate the tares with force and will power, failing to remember that their own wills are filled with weeds. Not to see this is their Pharisaical error; and to see this is the royal realism of Jesus Christ.

Werner Heisenberg, in his book *Modern Physics and Its View of Nature,* made this profound and deeply Christian statement: "Man can do what he wills, but he cannot will what he wants to will." And by this he means precisely what we learned from our text: Man cannot change himself. He may want to free himself of a lot of things that bind and fetter him (and every one of us knows what that is for him in particular—a sexual bondage or a consuming ambition, a hot temper, or whatever it may be). We want to be rid of all this; but the disquieting discovery we make is not that we cannot bring it off but that we cannot even seriously want to do it. In other words, we discover that our will really is sown with weeds, that the evil enemy and his poisonous brood have already entered the house of our own ego, that he himself has occupied the cellar of our unconscious and is influencing the direction of our will.

Therefore at this point human power is of no use whatsoever. "If your own power were of any use," Jesus is saying to us, "then I would not have had to die for you, then a moral appeal would have been enough. Therefore, judge not, but rather think of your own vulnerability! As for the rest, wait for the surprises of the Last Judgment. Until then let God's sun shine on the just and the unjust. Let God's clouds drop their rain on the good and the evil!"

Second, the householder in the parable rejects any forcible intervention on the part of the servants for the same reason that Jesus forbade his disciples to call down fire from heaven to consume the hostile Samaritans (Luke 9:52 ff.). On that occasion he cried out in anger to his people, "You do not know what manner of spirit you are of: for the Son of man came not to destroy men's lives but to save them." We would therefore be spoiling God's plan of salvation if we were to organize a great "Operation Throw-them-out," if we were to cast out of the temple the hangers-on, the hypocrites, the "borderliners," and all the other wobblers in Christendom, in order to keep a small elite of saints.

For this would mean that we would rob these people of the chance at least to hear the Word and take it to heart. This would be to slam the door of the Father's house in their faces—and we would become a sect. But the very reason why Jesus died was to open the Father's house to everybody, including the superficial, the indifferent, the mockers and revilers. The bells of invitation which sound over market place, fields, and alleys would be silenced, and the comforting promise, "Everybody can come, just as you are," would be turned into a questionnaire in which everybody would have to list his accomplishments and merits. And finally somebody else would add them up and evaluate them and give the verdict: "You passed" or "You failed."

Then how bleak and dreary would be our outlook, and how cruelly futile would Jesus' death have been, with all its expenditure of love and dearly purchased grace! And how dreadfully we would corrupt and pharisaically poison our own souls if we took on the job of calling down fire from heaven, if we became such inquisitors and bigoted snoopers! "You do not know what manner of spirit you are of."

When I reflect upon all this I am reminded of two situations.

First, the one in which not long ago somebody said, "All this fuss that's going on about the preaching in St. Michael's* has nothing whatsoever to do with spiritual fruit; it's pure sensation seeking, almost a fad. The people come to get a thrill or see what's going on, but certainly not to attend divine worship." The man who said this to me did not, it is true, identify himself with the servants in the parable and draw the conclusion that we should exterminate this weed patch, stop the whole business, and require the people to submit to a test of their spiritual sincerity before we let them in. Nevertheless, he did intimate that what was flourishing here was some kind of weed anyhow.

What would Jesus' attitude have been toward such a phenomenon? This surely is the one legitimate question we should ask at this point. Perhaps he would say: "It may be that many come because of very different and probably very complex motives. Many come, perhaps,

* The church in which this series of sermons was preached. (Trans.)

because others come, because they like the music and the mighty singing of the hymns, many because they love the place itself." Of course, there are many motives at work, possibly even that of curiosity. But I can conceive of Jesus' continuing, in line with our parable, and saying, "Why do you decry the people for this? Can you separate the false wheat, the curious and the sensation seekers from the other completely different plants that stand right beside them? Can you distinguish all this from the real hunger and thirst that tugs at many a heart and drives many a person to seek the Word? Can you distinguish it from the yearning, the anxiety to get away from oneself and find security? Do you know the sickness and weariness, the boredom, and the stings of conscience that dwell in these hearts, and how they yearn for something to hold on to, for real freedom, how they are really crying out for redemption? And now you disparage them just because all these seed grains of eternity happen to be in such strange pockets, perhaps even wrapped up in a bit of curiosity and sensation seeking?" Perhaps for many a person who actually came here for these questionable reasons and this afternoon may again be doing something altogether different, having forgotten everything that was said, it may happen that in his last hour, or in some hour of great loneliness or terrible despair, there will come back to him one single word which he heard this morning, perhaps a word of the Lord's Prayer, possibly even a word of this sermon. And then this despised and forgotten word may comfort and accompany him as he goes through the dark and pathless forest. How much more merciful and understanding is God compared with us men, how patient he is and how long are the seasons of grace he grants to his seeds!

And the second situation is this. Not long ago I was in the huge palace of the United Nations in New York in which the representatives of the nations assemble when crises come in order to search out ways to escape new wars. I asked an attendant to show me the chapel which was said to be located there. "Oh," he replied, "you probably mean the meditation room." As he accompanied me to it, I thought about this rather strange name "meditation room." Apparently one was not to pray there, but simply to meditate. I could not help asking myself whether this was sufficient when leaders of the nations came together to patch up a world that has come apart at the seams. Would they not do better to call upon the Lord of the nations, rather than just sit there alone with their own feckless thoughts?

The meditation room turned out to be what its name implied. In a completely empty, blank white room, without any decoration or symbols whatsoever, stood a few chairs. "Does anybody ever sit on them?" I asked the attendant. Somewhat embarrassed, he shook his head.

The front wall—that part of a room where the altar is usually located in churches—was glaringly lighted with spotlights. And on it, being spotlighted, was—nothing. The spotlights were ignorant of what they were illuminating and the responsible men who were invited to come to this room were not shown to whom they should direct their thoughts. It was a temple of utterly weird desolation, an empty, ruined field of a faith long since fled.

Involuntarily, I was seized with a terrible anger, which, unfortunately, I expressed somewhat rashly.

Here all the conference rooms were furnished with the utmost in comfort. Here were elaborate translation devices, the ultimate in technical perfection, a kind of attempt by modern man to overcome the Babylonian confusion of tongues by technical means. Everything had been thought of, nothing was missing. Only here, where the ultimate was at stake, only here was emptiness and desolation. Would it not have been more honest to strike this whole pseudo temple out of the budget and use the space for a cloakroom or a bar?

Afterward I was ashamed of my anger, which was not unlike that of the servants in our parable. Was this room nothing more than the baneful flower of nihilism? Was it not a small, very forlorn, very timid, even pathetic sign that somebody knew that the fate of nations not only is a matter of political debate, strategy, and diplomacy, but that one must reflect upon the ultimate mysteries of man? That one must include in one's deliberations the fact that man is created by God, that he has the Fall behind him, and that the Babylonian confusion of tongues really exists? That this dubious planet of ours and its still more dubious inhabitants live only by the grace of God and therefore go on existing only because he does not deliver them over to their own madness, that he is still giving them reprieve? Who is capable of separating the nihilistic, mendacious element in this worship room from the seed of a true knowledge which may yet spring up here, from the spiritual poverty which here awaits its promise?

Thirdly, the householder in the parable explicitly points out that the servants are completely incapable of carrying out any proper separation of grain and weeds because they look so much alike and therefore in their zeal for weeding out the tares they would also root out the wheat. Here we come up against a point which is by no means a simple one for the interpreter. The problem is this: All of them, the householder as well as the servants, see that tares have actually been sown. So the fact is that they *can* distinguish between them. And yet the householder says, "Do not rip out the weeds too soon; otherwise you will destroy the real fruit along with them." And this means that they *cannot* distinguish, after all.

How are we going to resolve this apparent contradiction? Certainly not from any merely agricultural or botanical point of view. For this parable is an allegory which cannot be understood by itself, but only as we see what is intended. But when we take this into account it all becomes clear: taken by and large it is actually possible to distinguish between tares and wheat. We can say, for example, that in Luther's sermons or in Kierkegaard's Christian discourses the divine seed has grown into rich and blessed fruit. And, conversely, we can say with equal certainty that nihilism or the myth of the twentieth century or dialectical materialism with its atheism each certainly has in it something of the poisonweed.

But when the Lord in the parable nevertheless counsels caution and restraint, he certainly does not intend that we should be vague, timid, and indifferent in our judgment about these things, that we should cultivate a characterless, hazy tolerance. Of course we should "distinguish between spirits." Of course we must call what is godly godly and what is satanic satanic. The Lord Christ himself did this.

But then when we examine the weed patch more closely and try, on the basis of what we know about sin, blasphemy, and nihilism, to determine clearly just who is a sinner, a blasphemer, a nihilist, we encounter a strange difficulty. We find that nobody is *merely* a blasphemer or *merely* a nihilist, but always at the same time an unhappy, misguided child of God. The soldiers who drove the nails into Jesus' hands and then mocked him were not *only* blasphemers and functionaries of Satan. On the contrary, the Father in heaven grieved over them, because they really belonged to him and, tragically, they seemed to be completely unaware of this and went on heeding the prompting of another, dark, power.

I venture to ask this question: Have we ever in our life met a person, no matter how depraved, unbelieving, or vicious he may have been, even some malicious, quarreling, clacking neighbor or a slippery, scheming fellow worker—I ask you, have we ever met a person of whom we dared to say, "This person is really a weed and nothing but a weed"?

Or were we not at the same time brought up short and challenged to see that Jesus died for him too, and that none of us can know whether God may not still have something in mind for him, whether some altogether different seed may yet spring up in him? Would not our hand wither if we were to root him out as a weed? Must not this hand draw back and perhaps open in a gesture of blessing and prayer that God may yet bestow his mercy upon this seemingly lost and condemned failure?

Just recently I had this experience. I was deeply impressed by a great writer (Gottfried Benn), who delivers a nihilistic message to our generation with demonic power and a tremendous mastery of language. I asked myself, Are not these poems weeds, seductive, iridescent flowers of evil, and are they not the more perilous simply because they are so splendidly colorful, so polished in form, and so fascinating in their imagery? And then suddenly I came upon something totally different that he said, a remarkable and moving confession. He says to a young friend: "When your back is to the wall, in the grief of weariness, in the gray of the void, read Job and Jeremiah, and stick it out!" May not this be the opposite of what happened in the parable? May it not be that the dark power sowed poisonous plants and then, overnight, God cast *his* seeds in the soil? (It could, of course, still be his seed even if Benn's admonition to his friend were not to be interpreted in the sense of Christian devotion and pious Bible reading.) Who dares to separate wheat and tares here? Ought we not rather wait for God's great day and pray that God may mercifully prosper these two little seeds which have fallen from Job and Jeremiah into one man's heart? Again, who dares to separate and root out here? Must we not rather *love*, in order that in this very venture of love we may learn to realize that wheat is sown even in the most weed-ridden lives and that God is waiting and yearning for it to grow? Dostoevski once spoke this profound and unspeakably helpful word: "To love a person means to see him as God intended him to be." Mind you, we should see him not as he *is* but as he was *intended* to be.

Or, I think of all the pious fuss in the church about the catchword "demythologization." I think of how eager the servants of the Lord are in this connection to institute disciplinary proceedings, to erect the stake, and pass out heretics' hats. Let us grant for the moment that this may really be the sowing of some very dubious seed and that it could possibly contaminate the field of pure doctrine. But who would dare to exclude and expel persons here and in the nervous anxiety of unbelief and the spirit of carefulness anticipate the last judgment? If he did this, would he not also be nullifying the tormenting and very serious questions with which these people are wrestling? Would he not be simply rooting these questions out of his own heart, instead of facing them? And would he not then be making faith too easy and grace too cheap? And would he not—and this would be the worst of all—be overlooking the fact that these, possibly questionable, sowers (note that we are only supposing!) who operate during the night are nevertheless spending their days poring over the Holy Scriptures and studying them with tremendous effort and care? Who would dare to ignore this and strike them down with these same Holy Scriptures? And would not the patience of the saints be more in place here—above all, the prayer that God may make this his Word too strong for them, that the current of truth and mercy may flow through the contact which they still have with the message and also penetrate their possibly erring hearts?

Who is not reminded here of Jesus' saying: "Judge not, that you be not judged"? We ought rather to pray for imperiled souls—and also for our own souls, which are so beset by the spirit of care and judgment and self-righteousness. We ought to let God give us the long patience that serenely and confidently awaits the last day and its surprises.

Still the season of grace runs its course and in it not only the sinister nightwalker but also the divine Sower are scattering their seeds. Still we have the royal right of sonship to make intercession, and we need not give up hope for any man—no, not one. In folded hands all pious and fleshly zeal is quelled. Still runs the season in which there creeps upon us the dread question, "Lord, is it I?" Have not I on many a night sowed poisonous seed in many a heart and become a stumbling block to many? Let him who stands take heed lest he fall; and above all let him not judge when he sees others fall, but reach out for his brother with compassionate hands.

The last judgment is full of surprises. The separation of sheep and goats, of wheat and weeds will be made in a way completely different from that which we permit ourselves to imagine. For God is more merciful than we, more strict than we, and more knowing than we. And, in every case, God is greater than our hearts. But one thing is certain and that is that Jesus the King will come with his sickle and crown. Then our sickles will fall and all the false and illegal crowns will drop from men's heads. Then all will be changed and everything will be different, utterly different. But one thing will remain: love, the love in which we have believed and hoped and endured, the love which never let us forget that God can find and bring home and set at his table even the blasphemers, the erring, the deceivers, and the deceived.

May he give us the grace of the long view and the calmness to live confidently in the name of his victory—until one day he shall say to us and to those for whom we have interceded: "Well done, good and faithful servant; enter into the joy of your master."

VII

The Parable of the Seed Growing Secretly

And he said, "The kingdom of God is as if a man should scatter seed upon the ground, and should sleep and rise night and day, and the seed should sprout and grow, and he knows not how. The earth produces of itself, first the blade, then the ear, then the full grain in the ear. But when the grain is ripe, at once he puts in the sickle, because the harvest has come."

And he said, "With what can we compare the kingdom of God, or what parable shall we use for it? It is like a grain of mustard seed, ,which, when sown upon the ground, is the smallest of all the seeds on earth; yet when it is sown it grows up and becomes the greatest of all shrubs, and puts forth large branches, so that the birds of the air can make nests in its shade."

With many such parables he spoke the word to them, as they were able to hear it; he did not speak to them without a parable, but privately to his own disciples he explained everything.

—MARK 4:26–34

In his widely read book, *The Future Has Already Begun,* Robert Jungk tells of a lecture given by an American specialist in aeronautical medicine. In this lecture the statement was made that measured by the tasks which he faces in aeronautics—that is, breaking through the sound barrier and later in space travel—man is from a biological point of view a misconstruction. What the blunt frankness of this statement really means is that the body given to us by the Creator, with its sensitive circulatory system and its even more sensitive nervous system, is no longer equal to the possibilities opened up by the technical ingenuity of man. We can express this even more pointedly: the contribution which God has made to our existence (by putting a body at our disposal) has now been outstripped by the contribution of man and his technical intelligence. Now, man has invested the larger share of capital in the firm of "creation." He has acquired the majority of shares. The divine partner in the firm has been pushed to the wall and the directorate of creation will undoubtedly work out in such a way that from now on the human voice will be given more weight.

Now, what will this human voice say? It will say: Man must be biologically re-bred. The obsolete apparatus of the created human organism must be modernized. "Biometrics" (as this new method is called) will take these long-since outworn designs of the Creator, this hoary and somewhat antiquated old dodderer, and breed the new man, the space man.

Why do I mention this little story? Because it expresses a feeling about life which is shared more or less by all of us, even though it may not be stated as drastically as it is here. We can describe this feeling by reference to an idea which has already become almost a commonplace: we are convinced that we can make anything. Good heavens, what have we not made with our technology! We can see things that happen a thousand miles away, we can even produce rain artificially, we can make stockings out of coal, we can change the course of rivers, transform landscapes, produce test-tube babies—why shouldn't we be able also to change the biological construction of the *author* of all these things, man himself? After all, this is what the Marxists have always wanted to do. All you need to do—this is their formula—is to change the social conditions and man will change. Then you can turn him from a human person with an unpredictable will and an unmanageable conscience into a compliant marionette, indeed, into an insect which will conform without friction to the termite state. The possibilities are endless. No rules are laid down for us, nothing is prescribed as far as creation is concerned; we are not limited by any alleged Lord of the world.

"Everything is created," you say. Nonsense! *Everything can be made!* You haven't seen anything yet. And Adam and Eve, the human beings of the first morning of creation, will still marvel at what we shall make of this world supposedly made by God, at how we shall turn it upside down.

What place do these statements have in a sermon?

They have their very proper place in it because all this concerns our soul. For anybody who holds that everything can be made must also *want* to make everything. And anybody who has taken everything in hand must then keep on moving that hand. He can no longer be still. Our overactivity, which constantly keeps us on the merry-go-round and yet, no matter how fast we go, gets us nowhere, but only makes us dizzy, is not caused by the fact that we were so nervous or that we had no time. It is just the opposite. We are nervous and we have no time because we think everything will stop without us and because we think we are so tremendously important—we parvenus in this old business of creation! And this is why we can never let anything get out of our hands and be entrusted to others. That's why we hold on to everything convulsively and thus wear ourselves out all over again. Undoubtedly, all this is connected with the ultimate decisions of our life and not so much at all with medicine or with the problem of our modern way of life. And because we have thus taken over the management of the bankrupt assets of creation, because now we do everything ourselves and therefore must always be producing something, we never get away from constant care and concern. For anybody who takes everything upon himself finds that everything depends on him.

That's why we go about worrying over how we shall pass tomorrow's examination, what will happen to our children, and what will happen when the market turns. We are literally beset by threatening possibilities. We have forgotten how to rely on the fact that it is God who clothes the lilies and feeds the birds of the air, that he provides our daily ration of bread, and that his kingdom comes no matter what happens. God the partner on whom we used to depend has become insolvent, and now we stand alone, utterly alone, on the commander's bridge as the wild weather blows up, and nobody is there with authority to command the waves and bring us through winds and icebergs to safe harbor. The *Titanic*, our world, is unsinkable and our navigation is perfect. What can be made has been made and we can dispense with this "Christian navigation." Christian! Nonsense! We don't need the Man who walks the waves. "Nearer, my God, to thee"? No, nearer to the statue of liberty! We and our children will win history's blue ribbon—what glorious things we have accomplished!

But why is it then that the captain keeps pacing the bridge so anxiously? After all, it must be a grand thing to have control of this smoothly vibrating, powerful ship and guide it over the ocean—that ocean which is no longer, as Gorch Fock once expressed it, a tiny pool in the hand of the Saviour but an element that challenges the omnipotence of man and offers him chances of undreamed-of triumphs. "Hast thou not accomplished all things, O holy, glowing heart?" Why doesn't this Promethean assurance cheer the captain? Why does he worry? Because now there is nobody there upon whom he can cast his cares. Why is he active and overwatchful? Because he no longer sees the eyes that watch over him. Why can't he sleep? Because he can no longer let himself go. For the world has become a weird place. Whatever happens without him and when he is not there himself he cannot trust. So he has to be everywhere. That's why he can no longer *let* things happen; he must always be on deck. Not for one moment can he live like a lark or a lily. He can never let down or let up. Perhaps when he is drinking he gets away from himself for a moment. To drink or to pray: that is the question. (And drinking need not always mean the consumption of alcohol.)

Yes, the *Titanic* is our world. We and the captain are no longer able to *let* things happen. For this you can do only if you know that somebody is in control and if you know who that somebody is. But we stand alone on the bridge. We have taken charge of the firm and the ship, and now we are dying of our privileges and prerogatives.

Count von Moltke when he was an old man was asked what he was going to do in the quiet closing phase of his life after years of great activity and responsibility. His reply was: "I want to see a tree grow."

Would Moltke, we may ask, have been able to say such a thing in his old age if during the years of greatest responsibility he had not already found time for quietness, time to see that Another and Higher Being was carrying out *his* plans and guiding events to *his* goals quite independent of what Moltke did or left undone? The man who doesn't know how to let go, who is a stranger to this quiet, confident joy in *him* who carries out *his* purposes without us (or also through us and in spite of us), in him who makes the trees grow and the rainbows shine—that man will become nothing but a miserable creature in his old age. For, after all, what is he good for if he can no longer produce what can be produced and his two eyes, on which he staked everything, have grown dim? Can the reason why many aging people are melancholy and fearful of having the door shut upon them be that for decades they have never been able to "let go and let God" and now can no longer see a tree growing, and therefore are nothing but run-down merry-go-rounds?

All this may sound almost as if we were going to discuss today the question of the art of living or talk about mental hygiene. But the art of living and mental hygiene are only the by-products of something altogether different, a by-product of the very thing our parable means when it says that God lets his seeds sprout in this namelessly quiet way, that this miracle occurs without any aid whatsoever from man and apart from any agricultural intervention—in that natural, old-fashioned way in which God carries forward his work despite all human efforts.

Everything we have said so far, which at times may have sounded like an analysis of our culture, has been seen and said in the light of this theme. We have been standing as it were behind the preacher Jesus Christ, trying to follow his eyes and see the world as he saw it.

Here is a man who has sowed his fields. When he has done this he leaves them, feeds the cattle, makes some repairs on his house, drives to town on errands, goes to bed at night, and rises up early. And while he is doing all this the seed grows, without his moving a hand; first the blade from the seed and from the blade the ear and then the kernels in the ear. What an unspeakable comfort it is to know that in the midst of man's mischief, in the midst of his scheming and bad speculations, his shaping and misshaping, his activism and his failures, there is still another stream of events flowing silently on, that God is letting his seeds grow and achieving his ends.

When the Flood subsided and the rainbow sign of reconciliation appeared against the skies still dark with clouds God pronounced a very strange word of consolation upon this poor, guilt-laden earth whose wounds were now to be closed: "While the earth remains, seedtime and harvest, cold and heat, summer and winter, day and night, shall not cease." We should certainly miss the comfort in this assurance if we saw in it nothing more than an invitation to man to find respite from all the busyness of his daily grind and also from all the folly and confusion of human life by contemplating the constancy of nature, observing the orderly rhythm of the seasons in their coming and going, pondering the perfect mathematical harmony of the stars in their courses, by simply letting God's sun shine upon him and enjoying the lyrical beauty of moonlight shining upon the sea. Certainly this can be a very good thing. But we dare not expect too much from these exercises in spiritual nature-cure. If nature is our sole physician, it may be that we shall only become more miserable. For then we may suddenly feel that we are excluded from its peace and its measured orderliness. Then we may shake our heads and go back to our store, our office, our classroom, and say: "Wherever man is absent, in a quiet forest clearing, in the orbits of the planets, all is well. But wherever this 'beast' appears there is confusion and restlessness. He spoils the loveliest landscapes with his picnic invasions, he desecrates the sublimest of mountain scenes with his heel marks; and where he is all by himself, with his asphalt streets and his neon lights, it is worst of all." So, if we are honest, nature also has something altogether different from a message of comfort to speak to us.

But this is not at all the intention of God's message of comfort after the Flood. Summer and winter, day and night, seedtime and harvest—here these are not to be understood as manifestations of natural law at all, but rather as signs that point to the *Lord,* who is at work here. What this passage says to us is this: The one fixed pole in all the bewildering confusion is the faithfulness and dependability of God. Insane as we men are with our idea that everything can be made, however madly we try, we shall never destroy God's creation. And we shall not be able to smash it, not because it is indestructible (for one day it will be destroyed, and the sea will be no more; the sun and moon will cease to give their light, and the stars will fall from heaven), but simply because God's love, God's faithfulness can never falter. All the confusions of men in their personal lives and the politics of the world, all the many dodges and futilities which only take us farther from the goal, still do not divert God from *his* purposes. In the end, despite all the chaos, all the stupidity, all the sin, it will not turn out to be a hopelessly tangled skein; but rather straight through all the labyrinths of history, even through the conflict between East and West, and also through all the confusions of our personal lives there runs the red thread of God's purpose. He knows what he wants, and he does what he knows.

One day, perhaps, when we look back from God's throne on the last day we shall say with amazement and surprise, "If I had ever dreamed when I stood at the graves of my loved ones and everything seemed to be ended; if I had ever dreamed when I saw the specter of atomic war creeping upon us; if I had ever dreamed when I faced the meaningless fate of an endless imprisonment or a malignant disease; if I had ever dreamed that God was only carrying out his design and plan through all these woes, that in the midst of my cares and troubles and despair *his* harvest was ripening, and that everything was pressing on toward his last kingly day—if I had known this I would have been more calm and confident; yes, then I would have been more cheerful and far more tranquil and composed."

If we want an illustration of how this certainty works out in a human life, we have only to look at the Lord himself. What tremendous pressures there must have been within him to drive him to hectic, nervous, explosive activity! He sees—Manfred Hausmann has given this magnificent literary expression in his essay "One Must Keep Watch"—he sees, as no one else ever sees, with an infinite and awful nearness, the agony of the dying man, the prisoner's torment, the anguish of the wounded conscience, injustice, terror, dread, and beastliness. He sees and hears and feels all this with the heart of a Saviour. And this means that distress and misery are not merely noted and registered as with a tabulating machine but actually suffered in compassionate love, as if all this were happening in his own body and his own soul. Must not this fill every waking hour and rob him of sleep at night? Must he not begin immediately to set the fire burning, to win people, to work out strategic plans to evangelize the world, to work, work, furiously work, unceasingly, unrestingly, before the night comes when no man can work? That's what we would imagine the earthly life of the Son of God would be like, if we were to think of him in human terms.

But how utterly different was the actual life of Jesus! Though the burden of the whole world lay heavy upon his shoulders, though Corinth and Ephesus and Athens, whole continents, with all their desperate need, were dreadfully near to his heart, though suffering and sinning were going on in chamber, street corner, castle, and slums, seen only by the Son of God—though this immeasurable misery and wretchedness cried aloud for a physician, he has time to stop and talk to the individual. He associates with publicans, lonely widows, and despised prostitutes; he moves among the outcasts of society, wrestling for the soul of individuals. He appears not to be bothered at all by the fact that these are not strategically important people, that they have no prominence, that they are not key figures, but *only* the unfortunate, lost children of the Father in heaven. He seems to ignore with a sovereign indifference the great so-called "world-historical perspectives" of his mission when it comes to one insignificant, blind, and smelly beggar, this Mr. Nobody, who is nevertheless so dear to the heart of God and must be saved.

Because Jesus knows that he must serve his neighbor (literally, those nearest here and now) he can confidently leave to his Father the things farthest away, the great perspectives. By being obedient in his little corner of the highly provincial precincts of Nazareth and Bethlehem he allows himself to be fitted into a great mosaic whose master is God. And that's why he has time for persons; for all time is in the hands of his Father. And that too is why peace and not unrest goes out from him. For God's faithfulness already spans the world like a rainbow: he does not need to build it; he needs only to walk beneath it.

So, because Jesus knows which way the switches are set, because he knows what the outcome of growth and harvest will be, the words he speaks are not prepared, tactical propaganda speeches. The propaganda of men, even when it masquerades as a kind of evangelism and becomes an enterprise of the church, is always based on the accursed notion that success and failure, fruit and harvest are dependent upon our human activity, upon our imagination, energy, and intelligence. Therefore the church too must guard against becoming merely a busy enterprise and pastors must beware of becoming religious administrators devoid of power and dried up as far as spiritual substance is concerned.

Jesus is not a propagandist. And there is one fact which shows that he is not, and that is that for him speaking to his Father in prayer is more important than speaking to men, no matter how great the crowds that gather around him. Just when you think that now he must seize the opportunity, now surely he must strike while the masses are hot and mold them to his purpose, he "passes through the midst of them" and withdraws into the silence of communion with the Father.

Why was it that he spoke with authority, as the scribes and Pharisees did not? Because he was rhetorically gifted, because he was dynamic? No; he spoke with such power because he had first spoken with the Father, because always he came out of silence. He rested in eternity and therefore broke into time with such power. That's why he is so disturbing to time. He lived in communion with God; that's why his speech to men becomes an event of judgment and grace which none can escape.

Jesus' powerful speech derives from the power of his prayer life, and the very reason why he can afford to pray so diligently and give the best hours of the day to this communion with the Father is that he knows that while he rests in eternity it is not that nothing is happening but that in doing this he is rather giving place to God's Spirit, that then God is working and the seed is growing. Woe to the nervous activity of those of little faith! Woe to the anxiousness and busyness of those who do not pray!

Luther once said, "While I drink my little glass of Wittenberg beer the gospel runs its course." That is truly the finest and most comforting thing I have ever heard said about beer. The conversion of a man is not something that can be "produced." The new life comes into being only by letting God work. Therefore, Luther can cheerfully and trustfully step down from the pulpit; he doesn't need to go on incessantly crying, shouting, and roaring around the country. He can quietly drink his little glass of Wittenberg beer and trust in God. The Lord "gives to his beloved in sleep." In most cases today we do not sin by being undutiful and doing too little work. On the contrary, we ought to ask ourselves whether we are still capable of being idle in God's name. Take my word for it, you can really serve and worship God simply by lying flat on your back for once and getting away from this everlasting pushing and producing.

Now, some of you may say, "All this may be so, but how do I go about achieving this detachment in which I stop allowing myself to be carried away by busyness and simply let God work?" This is the problem, after all. How can we attain this stillness?

There are some things which cannot be appreciated merely by understanding them, they must be practiced. For example, I may have listened to a piano concert of Mozart music and had a clear insight into its musical structure, I may even have plumbed its spiritual depths intuitively or intellectually; but I am still miles away from being able to play this piano concert, for I have not practiced it. In *exactly* the same way it is possible for me to have understood the mystery of the seed growing secretly and still not be able to let God's seed really grow in *my* life. I know very well that I should drink my little glass of Wittenberg beer now, that I should be trusting enough to disconnect the gears and let myself relax. But I cannot do it; I cannot find the switch by which I can turn off my own activity and my own compulsive desire to do everything myself.

I should like to close therefore by suggesting a little prescription, even though prescriptions in a sermon always have something shady about them, since they may give the impression that there are certain tricks, certain forms of self-training by which one can learn the art of faith. As if faith were an "art" at all! Faith is nothing but being quiet and receptive when God speaks, being still when God acts. What I have to say, then, applies only to this quiet receptiveness. Or, to express it in a different way, it is suggested only in order to help us stop putting ourselves in the limelight and asserting ourselves when God wants to turn on his light and enlighten us.

When we are sitting in a train or bus or the back seat of our car, when the telephone is silent for a moment and secretaries and appointment books are gone for a time, we should try for once not to reach for the newspaper or the next file folder or for some kind of button, be it a radio knob or a bell push. Then we should try taking a deep breath and saying, "Glory be to the Father, and to the Son, and to the Holy Ghost; as it was in the beginning, is now, and ever shall be, world without end." This will give a sense of distance and peace.

We may then go on and ponder these words meditatively. Glory be to "the Father." This means: Glory be to him who has brought me to this moment in my day's work, who has entrusted to me my fellow workers, and in the last analysis makes the final decision with regard to every decision I am now obliged to make.

Glory be to "the Son." The Son is none other than Jesus Christ, who died for me. Dare I—for whom he suffered such pains, for whom he opened the gates of heaven—dare I go on frittering myself away on trifles and futilities? Must not the *one* thing needful be constantly present in my mind, and must it not show up the merely relative importance of these *many* things which I do? For whom, or for what, did Christ die; for my cash register, for the roving eye of the boss whom I must please, for my television set, or for any other such trivialities? Or did he not rather die for the fellow beside me who is struggling with some burden in his life or for my children whom I hardly ever see? And as far as the children are concerned, did he die for their food and clothing or for their souls, which I do not know at all, because the "many things" are always getting between me and their souls?

Glory be to "the Holy Ghost." Oh, I'm full of spirit, I am not unenlightened. I also have feeling, heart, sentiment, and imagination. But do I ever hold still in order that the wholly Other may fill me with his Spirit and give me a sense of the true priorities in life?

"As it was in the beginning, is now, and ever shall be, world without end." Here we are encompassed by the everlasting arms, overarched by the rainbow of a faithfulness we can trust, founded upon a foundation which the shifting sands of daily routine can never provide.

If we perform this little exercise repeatedly we shall soon find that it is not merely a mystical rigmarole and much less an inward flight by which we escape from daily duties. Oh, no; we shall go back to our job renewed, we shall become realists in a new way, for then we shall know how to distinguish what is great from what is small, the real from the false. The fanatics who believe that man can "make" everything are really fools at bottom. They are not realistic at all, even though they have the cold, sober eyes of hardheaded men of fact. But the man who has grasped the mystery of the seed growing secretly and, like the farmer in the parable, goes out and does his part of the job and then commits the fields to God and lies down to sleep in his name—that man is doing not only the most godly thing but the wisest thing. For godliness and wisdom are far more closely related than our philosophy and the wisdom of the "managers" ever dream.

VIII

The Parable of the Dishonest Steward

He also said to the disciples, "There was a rich man who had a steward, and charges were brought to him that this man was wasting his goods. And he called him and said to him, 'What is this that I hear about you? Turn in the account of your stewardship, for you can no longer be steward.' And the steward said to himself, 'What shall I do, since my master is taking the stewardship away from me? I am not strong enough to dig, and I am ashamed to beg. I have decided what to do, so that people may receive me into their houses when I am put out of the stewardship.' So, summoning his master's debtors one by one, he said to the first, 'How much do you owe my master?' He said, 'A hundred measures of oil.' And he said to him, 'Take your bill, and sit down quickly and write fifty.' Then he said to another, 'And how much do you owe?' He said, 'A hundred measures of wheat.' He said to him, 'Take your bill, and write eighty.' The master commended the dishonest steward for his prudence; for the sons of this world are wiser in their own generation than the sons of light. And I tell you, make friends for yourselves by means of unrighteous mammon, so that when it fails they may receive you into the eternal habitations."

—LUKE 16:1–9

If you were to go to the trouble of reading a large number of sermons which have been preached on this text you would make a remarkable discovery. These sermons not infrequently begin with the preacher's lament about how difficult and embarrassing this text is and that here the congregation is presented with a rather nasty case of corruption. The preacher implies that it will be a hard and delicate thing to avoid the difficulty and to edify his hearers on the basis of such a story: but since this "criminal record" has a place in the New Testament, there must be something in it and we must never stop looking for the spiritual light in this rather obscure story.

It is conceivable that a similar impression may have arisen among us as we heard the story read. It is therefore important that we should find the right starting point at the very outset. We must understand that Jesus was accustomed to choosing his metaphors and comparisons with a grand and sovereign freedom. It is a matter of indifference to him that he should use even such a dubious figure as the dishonest steward to point out a truth about the kingdom of God. The person who takes offense at the fact that Jesus never depicts anybody with a halo, but employs as models even sham saints, even the dregs of humanity, in order that their very darkness may permit the divine truth to shine more brightly, that person does not understand him at all.

Jesus even dares to represent his heavenly Father and himself in such daring figures as this one.

Thus, for example, he compares his heavenly Father with a hardhearted judge, to whom justice is a matter of complete indifference and who finally helps a poor widow to obtain justice only because she keeps pestering him day and night and he finally cannot stand it any longer (Luke 18:1 ff.). What he is saying is that God too is not concerned with pure justice. Where would we be if God were to deal with us in purely legal fashion, if he were to reckon up our sins point by point? The *one* thing which God has in common with this hard judge is that both do not act according to law, that both allow themselves to be moved, the *one* because of his eternal fatherly heart and the *other* because of his frayed nerves which simply cannot endure any longer the widow's incessant squalling. If even an unjust judge will finally decide—merely because he can't stand being annoyed—to help a person, *how much more will* God help those who cry out to him and trust him like children!

How wrong it would be, then, to interpret the hard judge merely as an *example,* as if the Lord were saying: You judges and magistrates, you must be like this hard judge. This would be nonsense, would it not? For Jesus is here arguing far more from the contrast rather than the parallel between these two. We must always hear those unspoken words, *"how much more."*

Nor can we say that a thief has something divine in him just because our Lord repeatedly said that he—Christ—would come again as a "thief in the night."

In all the parables of Jesus one must find the salient point, and they must by no means be interpreted as moral example-stories. This would certainly lead one up a blind alley.

Sometimes when we read the parables of Jesus it may appear as if Christ has even concealed the salient point somewhat, as one must first carefully search for it, just as a picture puzzle must be turned this way and that and examined closely in order to find the figure concealed in it. Perhaps the Lord did this intentionally in order to make us really reflect upon the parables carefully and ponder them in our hearts and pray over them before we think we have understood them. They cannot be read as one would read a collection of anecdotes in a magazine, which, of course, can be understood right off the bat.

With the Bible, however, one must first pray one's way into it, literally allow one's thoughts to hover over it and circle around it. Sometimes one may carry an obscure passage around for years when suddenly it begins to shine. The last book of the Bible remained obscure and dark for centuries, and now all of a sudden, amidst the catastrophes of our time, it is as if the dark wraps had been removed from this book and the broad landscape of history is plain and in it the wonderful highways of God, all of which by roundabout ways lead to the distant, blue hills from which cometh our help.

So we shall not linger too long over the portrait of the unjust steward; and above all we shall not see in him a model, but rather ask ourselves what in this story is the "salient point" or the "hidden figure."

For the man himself does not really occupy the center of the story at all. The real theme of the story is *money;* the leading role is played by "unrighteous mammon." What does this thing mean or, better, what does this power mean in the life of a person who wants to be obedient to God? How should he handle it? In a time of prosperity and in a vitally commercial and industrial city like Hamburg we may well be concerned with this question. Besides, it is a very practical and worldly question. But our destiny with God is rarely decided by our reflecting upon dogmas and all kinds of otherworldly problems. Our destiny is rather decided by what we do with the altogether real worldly questions and temporal problems which play a part in our *life,* such as sex, money, and personal relations.

The *first* thing we must note is that we should use money and possessions in order to make friends. What this means we shall see. The main thing at this point is to accept the statement that we should use this mammon. This is by no means altogether self-evident. When our Lord speaks of unrighteous mammon, we might very well expect him to go on and say: Keep your hands off it. Rather go into a monastery, take a vow of poverty, or at least strive for an economic order which will do away with property and decisively eliminate the power of money.

It's true—isn't it?—that we understand all too well *why* Jesus calls mammon "unrighteous," why he calls it "the lord of unrighteousness" (which is its literal meaning), the lord of an unrighteous world. We have only to think of certain stock speculations, armament profits, unearned income, many forms of tax manipulation or of gambling pools and games of chance; and unrighteousness, sweat, tears, and even blood become terribly depressing images, all of which are connected with money. "Money rules the world." Doesn't this bring money terribly close to that sinister figure whom Jesus calls the ruler of this world?

But Jesus, quite amazingly, does not tell us to abstain from the use of money. Perhaps he does not do so because it would be impossible anyhow. We can't all become monks. Besides, monks do not live without money either; the monastic revenue office simply relieves them of the necessity of touching the dirty stuff. Jesus tells us to take this dirty money right into our hand; he tells us to do something with it. Hence we positively should not flee from the world and become unrealistic in the name of our faith. In other words, the rightness of our conduct is determined not by *whether* we deal with unrighteous mammon but the *purpose* for which we use it. And this is precisely what is made clear for us in this parable of the steward. The steward with all his corruptness and cunning is intended to show us by means of a negative image what money is really for.

Well, what happened in the story? What happened in the first place was simply that an accusation was made. Certain people came to a large landowner and accused his steward of having committed defalcations and made certain crooked deals. The parable does not say whether these accusations are just or not; the original text simply leaves this open. It is possible even to find in it a hint that possibly the steward was not guilty of corruption at all. He was only "charged" with being a swindler.

The landowner did not investigate the charges, which in justice he should have done, but simply ordered the immediate dismissal of the steward. All that is left for the steward to do is to present his final balance sheet and hand over his accounts. The master appears not to take any account of the possibility that these records might prove the steward's innocence and that therefore he might justly retain his position. No, his boss discharges him merely on the basis of the accusations; undoubtedly a brutal and unfair procedure. This put the steward into an abominably difficult situation; he is actually thrown into an inner conflict. To him it appears that only two alternatives are left.

The first possibility is to act honestly and hand over a clean accounting. This would mean that he would do everything in his power to help the master obtain his proper financial claims. He would return all his property to him and collect all the outstanding debts for him as soon as possible. And now he considers: Should I really do this? After all, his master seems to be a fairly unscrupulous customer. His procedure in discharging him without a hearing is in itself incorrect and legally untenable. How can a man simply kick into the street a person, from whom he himself demands straight dealing, without at least allowing him to defend himself?

Furthermore, this master seems to have been pretty much of a materialist. For when the steward double-crossed him at the last moment and feathered his nest by a trick, this gentleman landowner did not judge this more than dubious move on the part of his steward by moral or legal standards at all—this quite obviously would not have been good form for him—but he judges it simply as a very shrewd tactical move and therefore as a perfectly permissible business manipulation.

So when the story tells us that the master commended the steward this can only mean that he said something like this: "That sly fellow! He really foxed me on that one!" This kind of thing impresses the master, for obviously he himself knows how to pull a fast one. Not only the dishonest steward but his master too belongs in that category of people whom Jesus calls the "sons of this world," the children who have fewer inhibitions and are therefore more cunning than the children of light. Anyhow the master has enough sense of humor to commend his steward and his shrewd move, even though the maneuver cost him money.

Nevertheless, if the master himself is a dubious figure, the steward faces the question whether he is obligated to help such a fellow get his money, whether, in other words, he should bully the small farmers and tenants just to make them fill the pockets of this "antisocial beast" with their poor pennies. Would it not be better, he reflects, to let this money go instead to those who are less well placed socially? Jesus by no means gave an affirmative answer to this question; otherwise he would have had to speak of the "noble" rather than the "dishonest" steward. Therefore he condemns this. And yet we understand that the steward is raising a very serious consideration.

The other alternative that is left to the steward is either to do physical labor or go begging. He is frank enough to admit that neither suits him. However, he does not say that he doesn't *want* to do physical work but that he *cannot* do it. Perhaps he is not strong enough for it, so that for him it is not a real question. But begging is something he doesn't want to do. He is considering his social prestige. This is really rather appealing. He may also have been arguing this way: This certainly would be a more than unjust social order if a clever man like myself should not only end up a nonproducer but also have to live at the expense of other people, all because a crazy sense of honesty prompted me to fill the pockets of my boss, the rotter. After all, what would he do with the money? He would certainly make worse use of it than I would if I were to help these poor people by a small manipulation of the books and at the same time get myself out of a jam by obligating them to me. In this way out of gratitude they will help me over the first crisis and make it possible for me to get a fresh start. In other words, I'll be doing the most sensible thing with the money entrusted to me by doing what is formally incorrect—that is, by falsifying the documents—but nevertheless using the money judiciously and for the general good.

The steward therefore actually commits a highly incorrect act. He is "dishonest" and "unjust." But what he did is not altogether without sense, and after all one can find in it a certain, though very odd and dangerous, very fantastic, morality. In any case, from the point of view of pure reason his act is not too bad. The point is that he is a worldling, and the idea that he should live his life honestly and uprightly to the end and then be willing to trust that God will not leave him holding the bag, but will grant him marvelous experiences of divine help, this idea is simply beyond him. He is a child of the world.

Now, dare we, as people who want to be disciples of their Lord and be counted among the "children of light," consider ourselves to be above the dishonest steward? Dare we act as if we were far removed from this kind of nastiness?

We ought to be a bit more careful in our judgment. Even if we don't want to be "children of the world," who act only in accord with cold economic motives and will not allow their conscience to trespass upon the realm of business, nevertheless as "children of light" we still live *in* the world and therefore in the world of money *and*—this must be said, even though it may not sound very edifying from a pulpit—in the world of finance and taxes. And are these reflections of the dishonest steward really so dreadfully unfamiliar to the children of light among, for example, the business people who are present this morning, but by no means among them alone?

We perhaps do not say as the dishonest steward did: "I have a brutal master and I'm not going to stuff his greedy pockets with unrighteous mammon." We express ourselves in terms that are more modern, more refined, less shady in morality: "We have some very problematical tax laws and it's hardly possible to maintain formal honesty unless you are willing to let your business go to the dogs." "We work only for the revenue office" is a favorite crack today. A man may say: Isn't the purpose of the government finance and tax measures to keep business moving and the social structure in balance? But if taxes are screwed up too tightly, if the state thus puts sand rather than oil in the economic machinery, if despite the upswing it prevents a man from making investments or creating an urgently necessary cushion of capital, doesn't he have to look for ways of reducing taxes on his own account? After all, who will be served if merely for the sake of formal correctness I am prevented from taking advantage of business opportunities because I am chained by taxes, or if I should even go bankrupt because of the tax burden? Will this serve the best interests of the state, which will have to feed me and put me on relief because it has made me an economic invalid? Of course not, many would answer. And it must be admitted that there is at least a modicum of *conscience* expressed in such laments and complaints; for ultimately, the argument continues, if things go badly for me the state will lose even the taxes I am now paying.

Or will this serve my employees who may possibly be thrown out of work? No, nobody is served. Therefore I must use this money in such a way that I can justify it, for the preservation of my own existence, the care of the people entrusted to me, and the rebuilding of business.

Is there anybody in private business or in a private profession who is not aware of this difficulty and this conflict of conscience? Even the "children of light" are by no means exempt from it. This is a matter of guilt and forgiveness, of righteousness and wisdom; this is a question of what is called "dirty hands."

If by chance there should be a profiteer, a conscienceless speculator, or a tax evader among us, he need not see in these words a moral alibi for his dirty gains. We are speaking here only of the conscientious difficulties of those who for objective and perhaps also for humane reasons have fallen into inner conflict with regard to the question of taxes and who are trying to fulfill their tax obligation, if not according to the letter, at least according to the intent and spirit of the law, which means in so far as it can be brought into accord with sound self-preservation. After all, one of the main purposes of all tax legislation is to maintain purchasing power and the power to produce—even though sometimes the practical forms which these laws take, the regulations for carrying them out, may contradict this purpose and intent and thus disturb people's conscience and not infrequently create severe conflicts.

It is certainly unusual—you will allow me this incidental comment—to discuss such things in the pulpit. Perhaps the preacher himself will get his hands dirty if he touches on such questions. It would be much easier to take this text and speak on faithfulness in stewardship or faithfulness in little things. After all, it is easy to take a few words out of the context of this hard and difficult lesson and employ them to edify the congregation. But then the preacher would not be able to shake off the feeling that he was dodging a difficult task and engaging in a pious fraud. The things we have spoken of are a burden on countless consciences; and therefore a pastor must speak about them. In this distress the congregation must look for direction from its Lord. It must allow itself to be told what it means to live as children of light in the midst of the world, to be mixed up with the mammon of unrighteousness and therefore to live with dirty hands—and yet live joyfully under the forgiving goodness of our Lord. If the preacher never dares to touch on certain topics because they are unusual in the pulpit and may perhaps be shocking he simply leaves these troubled consciences behind without giving them any help and makes himself guilty of a false and pusillanimous kind of edification that does no more than create a flutter in the pious flesh. Unless all signs are deceiving, most of the difficulties people today have with God and most of their attempts to escape God are to be found at the point where these ethical and highly secular and worldly problems come into their lives. Observations made here point again and again to the area of economics and the area of sex. Innumerable cases of doubt and indifference, which at first sight must be considered to be "religious," have their deepest root here. And the church's preaching must be clearly aware of the change that has taken place in this deepest human difficulty. Since the Middle Ages these problems actually have changed or, rather, their point of stress has shifted. The church of Jesus Christ must speak about these things; it dare not leave its brothers and sisters without help and comfort.

In any case we see that the conflicts and difficulties of the dishonest steward are not so remote from us after all. "Let him who is without sin among you cast the first stone."

But, even though this steward was acting under tremendous pressure, Jesus never says that he was justified; on the contrary, he calls him dishonest. Isn't this rather harsh?

No; it is marvelous that he does so. Perhaps a worldling may fool himself and say, "I am acting under pressure; the conditions are at fault; I am a victim of 'tragic' circumstances. Therefore my hands are clean and my faults are at most the faults of a gentleman." The result is that in his self-righteousness he more and more loses his sense of sin; he falls into a snare which increasingly robs him of self-control, and gradually in his financial manipulations he becomes an out-and-out grafter, a racketeer and profiteer like the thousands who frequent the dives and night clubs today.

But where Jesus is the air is clean and clear. Here dirty hands are called dirty; here sin is called sin and dishonesty is called dishonesty. Here the wisdom of the world is not equated with godliness. We Christians can be utterly honest with ourselves because we have nothing to fear, because we don't need to be so painfully worried about putting up a good front. For we know about forgiveness. We know that Jesus Christ died for the sake of our dirty hands. We know that "Jesus' blood and righteousness" is our "beauty and glorious dress," and that this is a more dependable garment than all the respectable, easily soiled vestments we may show to the world. We do not need to be afraid of the hard truth, because no matter what happens Jesus Christ is *for* us and he will go with us and stand beside us before the throne of judgment.

But, I ask, *if* we thus stand before the judgment seat with our dirty hands, will we go on dirtying these hands as we please? Doesn't this rather mean that now there is a light shining down upon us and eyes watching us and beneath that light and those eyes it is impossible for us to go on furiously acting only in our own selfish interest, and that now the conscience, our responsibility to our Lord, begins to play its proper part?

The dishonest steward is therefore not our pattern, not by a long shot. Nevertheless, he stands on the same level with us at the place where the children of light get their hands dirty and where Jesus nevertheless reaches out to grasp these dirty hands.

In the middle of this dark picture, however, there is a bright spot; and this is a point at which this remarkable and dubious fellow can serve as an exemplar after all. The point is that this man used money and possessions *for* something, they were not an end in themselves. If a purely materialistic child of the world like the dishonest steward can manage on *his* level to compel money to serve his ends and thus give it its relative importance, how much more—and at the same time, how differently—should the children of light do this on *their* level!

How many people there are who are devoted to their possessions (their clothes, their jewelry, their bank accounts, their homes, and their cars)—devoted to them as to gods! Actually, mammon also means a god. These people no longer own their money; their money owns them. How many children of light, for example, failed to help the refugees, because for them things counted more than people—whether these things were their clothes, which they would not give to the naked, or dwelling space, which they withheld from the homeless.

Strange as this dishonest steward may be, one must still grant that he does not hang on to money; he does something with it. He has only a few days left. Soon he must separate from all the mammon he has in his charge. And we too must very soon separate from it; at latest when we die, but possibly even before then. Who knows whether the great steam roller from the East will not sweep over us all and whether the gleaming show windows will not be shattered by foreign boots? The god Mammon will not defend us then. He will be the first to scram. The worst of all simpletons are those who try to found their lives upon him. The gardens can be swiftly devastated, the fine houses burned, and the fine clothes may hang on others' backs. Who knows? Never yet has anybody taken with him anything more than a shroud.

And in this brief respite—in our parable it is only a few days or hours!—the dishonest steward lets the money fly. It isn't even *his* money. But this is not the important thing here. After all, he could have buried his master's money or stashed it away for future use. No; he lets it fly. He bestows it upon people who need it. But by so doing he performs a work of mercy and makes friends. In any case he is above the money and is not a slave to it. He compels the money to perform a service. The money will one day forsake him, but those whom he has helped with it will remain faithful to him and take him in. And this is precisely what Jesus turns into a parable for our own life. This is what he means by the words: "Make friends for yourselves by means of unrighteous mammon, so that when it fails they may receive you into the eternal habitations."

What does this mean? Here again we must hear the words "how much more" which appear so often in the parables of Jesus: How much more is this so for the children of light! How much more does this use of money for service, which this man in the parable practiced so dubiously, apply to you who should be using your money for service in the sight of God! In other words, it is made perfectly clear to us that one day every one of us will be left destitute. The day will come when we shall stand naked before God, unable to "answer him once in a thousand times." We shall be stripped of all the things in which we put our confidence here below. We shall stand before the throne of God without title, without money, without a home, without reputation —in utter poverty. And in that place where there is neither marrying nor giving in marriage, where money is neither received nor spent, and where all the values have been turned upside down, in that place God will ask: "Who can testify for you?" And then perhaps some one of the company of the redeemed will step forward, perhaps there may even be some who will cry out from the nethermost pit of hell and say: "He once gave me his last penny. He once shared his last cigarette with me in prison. He once put me on my feet again when I was a refugee, even though it was hard on his meager resources."

And then perhaps the devil, in case he should still be there and be allowed to speak his piece, will angrily interrupt and say: "Hear! Hear! It looks as if you can do business with this accursed mammon even in heaven. Here I have been doing everything I can to soak your dirty cash in blood and tears, and now in heaven you summon this evil money, this hellish mammon, that smells of me and my brimstone, as a witness for these people. Do you think you will get by with this before the master of heaven?" So says the devil.

But then God will brush the accuser aside and say: "I have heard what these have said in your behalf. I have heard that they want you to be with them in their eternal habitations. Blessed are you, my faithful child. You have made the unrighteous mammon righteous because you used it to feed the poor and hungry and to clothe the naked. Enter into the joy of your master!"

That's the way it is with this unrighteous mammon. And we ask ourselves, is this really the same money—the money a racketeer takes out of his wallet to pay for a champagne binge and that other money that is dropped into the offering plate in church or into a hat passed around for an unfortunate colleague? I ask you, is it really the same money—the contributions which are dispensed impersonally from a checking account as Christmas bonuses and that other money which I take out of my own pocket, warm from my own body, money that is all budgeted, money which, if I give it to others, means depriving myself? Is this really the same money? Doesn't the money in the offering plate and the hat serve an altogether different master? And doesn't this hallow it and wash away the dirt that may have clung to it as it passed from the mint through all kinds of shady and honest transactions to the offering plate and finally to the eternal habitations? Is there not something like an "alien righteousness" that applies to money just as it does to men?

It has sometimes happened that a person who himself had very little has given me a dollar bill for some need or other. I would sooner have lighted a cigarette with a five-hundred-dollar bill carelessly dropped by a grafter than let anything happen to this poor piece of paper. That poor piece of paper was a living, precious thing because it was hallowed by that "alien righteousness," a righteousness not its own.

Let us therefore hallow the unrighteous mammon by the use we make of it. Let us not make of it a god, an idol, but a servant. In the last analysis there is only one thing in life that matters: the final security, the eternal habitations which the Cross of our Lord has secured for us. For only because of the Cross is there any such thing as an "alien righteousness." Of ourselves we are certainly not precious people; God could never rejoice over us or rate us very high. But we have been "bought with a price." Our admission to the eternal habitation has been paid. Everything else passes away, but that remains. "As you did it to one of the least of these my brethren, you did it to me." And this I have also done for the eternal habitations and for myself. Our pocketbooks can have more to do with heaven, and also with hell, than our hymnbooks. He who has ears to hear, let him hear!

IX

The Parable of the Wicked Vinedressers

"There was a householder who planted a vineyard, and set a hedge around it, and dug a wine press in it, and built a tower, and let it out to tenants, and went into another country. When the season of fruit drew near, he sent his servants to the tenants, to get his fruit; and the tenants took his servants and beat one, killed another, and stoned another. Again he sent other servants, more than the first; and they did the same to them. Afterward he sent his son to them, saying, 'They will respect my son.' But when the tenants saw the son, they said to themselves, 'This is the heir; come, let us kill him and have his inheritance.' And they took him and cast him out of the vineyard, and killed him. When therefore the owner of the vineyard comes, what will he do to those tenants?" They said to him, "He will put those wretches to a miserable death, and let out the vineyard to other tenants who will give him the fruits in their seasons."

Jesus said to them, "Have you never read in the scriptures:
'The very stone which the builders rejected
has become the head of the corner;
this was the Lord's doing,
and it is marvelous in our eyes'?
Therefore I tell you, the kingdom of God will be taken away from you and given to a nation producing the fruits of it."

—MATTHEW 21:33–43

If we were to survey all the parables of Jesus we would note something that is very remarkable. All the parables that deal with nature—the lilies of the field, the birds of the air, the shepherd and his sheep—breathe something of peace and safety and order. But wherever man occupies the center—no matter whether it be the unmerciful servant, the unjust steward, the rich man, or whoever it may be—there is always the element of dramatic tension, conflict, doom, and downfall.

And so it is in this parable of the wicked vinedressers. Here Christ does not appear in the attitude of blessing made familiar by Thorwaldsen's Christ, nor as the kind shepherd, radiating warmth and security. This is the story of a clash between God and man. It is like a drama divided into individual acts. And the main stages in the drama are indicated by a series of woodcut-like pictures.

The historical background to which Jesus is here alluding is easy to recognize. It deals with the sin and the destiny of the most mysterious of all nations, namely, Israel. God allied himself with this "most unpolished and most stubborn of all peoples" (as Lessing once called them) in order to show that he does not seek out the brilliant examples of humanity, that he looks not for man at the point of his greatness but at the point where all this is doubtful, that he wills to meet human destiny at its darkest points. He sends to these people his prophets and men of God. He seeks them and bears with them so intensely and pathetically that the parable is stretched almost to the breaking point and some of its features actually become improbable. For where would you ever find an owner of a vineyard who would allow his tenants to treat his servants so shamefully and, instead of putting his foot down and showing who was boss, kept on making repeated attempts to win them over by sending more messengers?

This very impossibility, this gross distortion in the parable-picture is intentional. For in the strict sense its purpose is to illustrate God's "incomprehensible" concern for man, the lengths God will go to keep on his track and maintain contact with him despite his stubbornness and his blind delusion. We may behave as madly and pigheadedly as we will, and yet God's faithfulness is greater than our folly. We may play dead like a dog and treat God as if he did not exist, we may be blasé and ignore him, but God still sticks to us and will not let us out of his sight.

So God sends his prophets to warn men and stir them up, he allows them to be killed and then goes on throwing fresh reserves into the great divine struggle. His reinforcements seem to be inexhaustible. Finally, he sends his Son. Surely, one would think, men would show some respect for him. When Jesus comes they will surely draw back, as the soldiers did for a moment at his arrest. When Jesus of Nazareth, when the "Saviour," comes they must surely see that God is seeking them and risking his dearest for them. But even the Son found neither home nor welcome in the place which, after all, belongs to *him*. Even as an infant he was not received, but is thrust out of the homes of men into the stable of beasts and banished to the endless, alien road of the refugee's trek. And before they finally killed him, this Son who desperately strove for their souls until it drove him even deeper into dark loneliness, he still cried out: "O Jerusalem, Jerusalem! How often would I have gathered your children together as a hen gathers her brood under her wings, and you would not!" And then the cross was lifted on the hill called Golgotha.

Yes, that's the way it is; every one of God's onslaughts failed. The rebels hold the field. And the field is strewn with victims, with all that God has expended for us. No sentimentality and no symbolical glorification should delude us as to the fact that the Cross is the very sign of God's defeat—a towering sign that cries out to us: Here is where God went down in defeat; for "he who loves the most [says Thomas Mann in *Tonio Kröger*] is always the defeated one and always suffers the most." And here God is the defeated one, because he loved the most. Here God was defeated, here man triumphed. Here man achieved sovereignty over his earth. His philosophers and poets will glorify the men who make history and they will extol the autonomy which is the sign of the dignity of this man who has emancipated himself from God.

If this story really comes close to the nerve of Christianity—and the truth is that it actually does expose this nerve—then how can anybody call Christianity a mere "religion"? Here is scent more the smell of blood than the aroma of incense. There are no liturgies being celebrated here. What is heard here is the yawp, the yackety-yack of derision. Here is no sound of worship, but only the sound of a shriek: God is dead!

It is a good thing, therefore, that we should be perfectly clear about this one thing; under the impression of this story it is not so easy to drift off into pious emotion. We shall never come to terms with this story unless we see ourselves involved in it and accept our role in it. Mere "religion" has to do with Sundays and high days. And that's why it generally means so little to us after the pious moods have evaporated. We are actually very serious, matter-of-fact people. In our business, our office, our place of work everything runs in high gear. There we've got to hold on and keep our wits about us. And when evening comes we have an engagement or collapse in a chair. There is little time for sentimentality and thoughtful contemplation.

To me it is always a comfort that nearly all the incidents in which people become involved with Christ happen on these sober, serious workdays when a man has to stick to the job. The disciples are caught while they are fishing, and therefore at pretty hard work, and the tax collectors are accosted in their offices. And if it is not work, it is some need or distress. When a man has leprous sores, when a man's little daughter has died, as with Jairus, when a man is blind and crippled and is obliged to cadge a few pennies in any crowd that comes along he is not likely to be in a solemn, religious mood. He is more liable to be depressed or indifferent. And this is always the time when Jesus comes. If this Jesus means nothing to us in the area where we spend the largest quota of our time, which means precisely the routine business of everyday life, if he is not the Redeemer *here,* then our Sundays are no good to us either. And even the voices of St. Michael's choir are already drowned out on Monday by noises that come from altogether different quarters.

It does us good, therefore, to be presented with this story of the vinedressers, for it addresses us precisely in the situation where we work and live our everyday lives. God always wants entrance into the elementary domains of our life. The New Testament says nothing about the religious comfort of a pious, spiritually enjoyable life.

Now, what is really wrong with these vinedressers that they should respond in such surly fashion when the owner of the vineyard appropriates the product of their labor? To understand this we must first understand quite simply that in the language of the Bible the vineyard is the accepted figure, a kind of shorthand sign for everything that belongs to the owner. The vinedressers therefore are not independent contractors but rather employees or tenants. They are not working (or in any case not *only*) for their own pocket. But they act as if this were the case. For they claim for themselves that which has only been lent to them. And that which has been assigned to them purely as a function they view as work the product of which they can dispose of as they see fit. Normally, no honest employee would venture to assert such an idea; for naturally he works for his company. And here we are told that these people treated God worse than an employee would treat his firm. What nobody would presume to do with an earthly employer these people took for granted with regard to God.

Now, of course, this is a very drastic assertion. And yet this is what Jesus Christ says. We must therefore try to find out what he meant by this statement. Is it really true that normally we are embezzling from God, that we are taking from God what belongs to him and diverting it to our own pockets? That this is actually so I should like to illustrate with a very ordinary, almost trivial example.

I find myself, say, in the company of a number of automobile owners. Almost inevitably they all begin to brag about their cars. One says, "Mine goes ninety miles an hour easy on the highway." Another is already interrupting him and saying, "Mine goes up Main Street hill in first." And a third butts in, "You ought to see the pickup mine has." The passion with which these people praise their cars undoubtedly comes from the fact that they are identifying themselves with their cars. I'm the one who has the pickup! I'm the one who climbs steep hills! We are always inclined to identify ourselves with everything positive which we happen to possess. Not long ago I said to one of my students, "You are a gifted boy." Whereupon he blushed and hardly knew which way to look. He was embarrassed and self-conscious because he had the feeling that I had praised him and ascribed some great quality to him. But of course I was doing no such thing; on the contrary, I was merely saying that he was "gifted," which means that his gifts were entrusted to him by someone else. But he too identified himself with them.

But examples in the opposite direction can also be found. I walk, let us say, through the cell block of a prison and talk with prisoners condemned to long terms. It is a curious thing that one of them should say to me, "The reason why I am here is the fault of the environment in which I grew up." Another says, "It was my parents' fault." A third says, "It was bad friends that did it." A fourth says, "It was my neurotic constitution." Here we see how people refuse to identify themselves with their faults but rather dissociate themselves from them, doing the opposite of what the car owners and the gifted student did.

If we try to formulate the meaning of this very simple observation which any of us can make we may make this assertion: Everything in our life which is positive, worthy, and honorable we regard as our own. We identify ourselves with anything like this, no matter whether it be our automobile or our talents—even though all this has merely been entrusted and given to us, even though all these things and these gifts in no case constitute "ourselves." But everything that incriminates and compromises us we disclaim and push aside. We dissociate ourselves from all these things and chalk them up to our upbringing, our environment, our fate—and ultimately we blame it on the final court of appeal which is responsible for all this, namely, God himself.

But now, having made this observation, we have discovered the key to our parable. For this is precisely what the vinedressers are doing. They claimed everything as their own: their capacity to work, their output, and finally the whole scene of their work and their life, namely, the vineyard itself. In the end they even take the credit for sunshine, rain, and good climate: "Ah, we are the ones who produced this good wine!" And if one or another of them is quite aware that he is not the immediate author of all this and that God provided good fortune and favorable weather, he still says: It was *my* good fortune exhibiting itself in my success. I am Sunday's child and the stars are smiling at me. Even luck is a virtue which not everybody possesses!

Don't we all do this? Don't we all have this "master-in-the-house" attitude, we people who have had a little success? Isn't this just what the people who built the tower of Babel did? They quickly forgot that God had entrusted the earth to them. Swiftly they built their great this-worldly stronghold; they tried to evacuate God from heaven in order to be able, like Prometheus, to say of all that they created and accomplished: "Hast thou not accomplished all things thyself, O holy glowing heart?" Where is the executive celebrating an anniversary and deluged with eulogies, where is the doctor whose cured patient expresses his gratitude to him, the worker who by dint of faithfulness and thriftiness has succeeded in buying his own little home and is now celebrating the housewarming, the preacher whom people thank at the door for the words he has spoken—where is the man who does not think in his heart, or at least is not tempted to think: What a fine fellow I am; really God must be delighted with me. These people are not so far off after all when they say: By George, what a guy he is! Which of them thinks in terms of Matthias Claudius' words, "It went through our hands"—of course, what was accomplished was done through our hands—"but it came from God"? Who thinks in such terms today?

In the Western world we have great faith in humanity. We have our ideals and we sing our hymns to freedom. Thrills run up and down our backs when we think of the noble traditions we have, the tremendous fund of spiritual energies we possess to be able to produce such great ideals. Have we forgotten where these (already somewhat tarnished, God knows) ideals really came from? Have we forgotten him who was the pure image of man in its divine design and who dwelt among us in our flesh and blood? Have we forgotten him who did *not* love us because we were worth loving or because he expected love in return, but loved you and me precisely in our need and guilt, because he saw in me the lost child of his Father? Are we really going to be like these vinedressers and claim as our own what we call our Western humanitarianism, as if this ideal were the product of our own mind and spirit? If so, then this ideal will decay and degenerate in our hands. Then man will become material, community will become no more than an apparatus, and love for one's neighbor will become merely "human relations." And hasn't all this already happened? Where do we vinedressers stand, really? How many deputies of our Lord, whom he has sent across our path at some time or other in our life, have we not ignored and sent to the devil?

With Jesus all this is totally different. Here we learn to give thanks for everything we have received. When we have healthy children, when we are granted success in our calling, when we have a happy marriage, we do not say, "This is my doing," but rather, "Here we see thy gracious hand in its exceeding abundance." And conversely, when we have sinned, when our conscience accuses us, we say, "Lord, this is *my* doing. Against thee, thee only, have I sinned. Cast me not away from thy presence. It is because of thy merit and thy faithfulness that I may still stand before thee."

We men have forgotten that we can stand before God despite our sin, forgotten that there is such a thing as forgiveness, forgotten that something happened for us on Calvary, and only because we have forgotten this do we assume the warped defensive attitude of these vinedressers; this is why we give ourselves over to all the crazy twistings and turnings by which we try to maneuver everything that is positive and meritorious to our side of the ledger and ascribe everything that is negative to God. What a cramping, laborious, lying business all this is! And what a liberation, what a blessed breakthrough would take place in our life if we were really to give thanks for the great and good things in our life and not look upon them as our own but rather as merely entrusted to us. And if, on the other hand, we accepted responsibility for the bad things because another has accepted responsibility for *us*. The point is that we can afford to be honest and realistic with ourselves; we can afford to shake off our hostile, defensive attitude. For we are free, relaxed children of God. Someone has come into our life and accomplished this. It is impossible to describe what it means to be able to live in his name; but here is where we begin to realize what the word "life" can mean.

The vinedressers, poor wretches that they were, had no comprehension of this. They denied their lord and asserted themselves and thus lived in strain and tension.

At this point it would seem essential to consider briefly *how* the vinedressers rejected the master or, expressed in more immediate terms: In what form do *we* reject the servants and finally the Son himself? Do we do this, say, by quitting the church? Or by staying away from the services? Or by being religious skeptics, by grubbing about in our doubts and sometimes even fondly nursing these doubts and using them to confirm our intelligence?

As a rule these are only symptoms of something happening at a much deeper level. The way we think of God and the way we react to the church depend in most cases on secret judgments which have already been made at an altogether different point in our life, at a level far deeper than all intellectual thought.

Instead of philosophizing about this at great length, I should like to choose an example in which this process can be clearly seen. I should like to make a statement, which at first may sound a bit legalistic, and then demonstrate it with an example.

The statement is this: We reject Christ when we practice justice instead of love. And because we are actually doing this continually in our lives we are also constantly rejecting him. Because this prior decision has already been made in our hearts, often without our being aware of it, we never come to terms with the question of God in our minds, nor in our thinking either.

Now, this must be particularized and can best be done by using an example of the most intimate of all personal relationships. I am thinking of marriage. My young, unmarried readers will now have to transfer the analogy to friendship or to their relationship to comrades in school or at work, to relatives and neighbors. It also applies there.

Here is a marriage or a friendship which is threatened by profound crises. Perhaps the other party has quite clearly broken the marriage. He or she may have acted, possibly over a long period of time, quite intolerably and contrary to the marriage. Then it is right and fair, that is, it is in accord with "justice," for him to get a divorce or at least to withdraw and break off human, perhaps even diplomatic, relations.

Every representative of the law, whether he be a divorce court judge, an attorney, or a member of the family who thinks in legal terms, will bear him out in this and say that this is "just."

Now, there are in fact cases in which there is no other way out. But these are much rarer exceptions than is usually thought. Very frequently what happens is that a person does indeed act "justly" when he draws the consequences and divorces his partner, but that he does so without "love." Then what he is doing is simply abandoning the other person. It may be that he is the other person's last stay, the only brake he has on a steep incline, the one solid foothold in a slippery and perhaps loathsome wilderness in which he is wandering about helpless and alone. And at that point he lets him drop.

No earthly court could blame him, no judge, no lawyer, perhaps not even "Dorothy Dix," though she was a very human, wise, and kindly woman. For the fact is that he is acting "justly." He is "righteous," he is in the right. But the question is: Does God approve of my "righteousness," my "justice," when I abandon a person for whom he grieves and for whom Christ suffered? When Paul stormed against the law and the legalism of men, this was the problem he had in view.

At first all this sounds dreadfully dogmatic. But this is a matter of utterly human and very elemental things. In this context I am even prepared to risk making this hazardously pointed statement: Justice does far more harm in our life than injustice.

This massive thesis which I have ventured to assert does not, of course, apply to general civil and criminal law. But it applies definitely to all personal, intimate, and interhuman relationships. This is the area in which justice is always becoming a catchword and behind the catchword is the desire to insist on one's own rights and cover up the lovelessness to which we abandon the other person. This is also the only thing that explains a curious and otherwise puzzling observation we can make with regard to Jesus, and this is that he always dealt so mildly with the unrighteous, with harlots and publicans, whereas he dealt so harshly with the fanatics for righteousness (whether they appear as Pharisees in his own life or as symbolic figures in his parables).

This seems to me to be the great surprise we meet with here. Long before we have posed the religious question in our conscious mind at all, Christ has alrady been rejected by us—simply because we have denied him in our neighbor and abandoned one who is dear to his heart (and done so in the name of justice, in the name of a moral person). Can we proceed to solve the "problem of Christ" intellectually, can we come to terms with the question of God at all, if we have started out from this wrong junction? *Everything about God is decided beforehand in altogether worldly, altogether human areas.* As against this the so-called religious sphere in our life recedes completely into the background. Therefore we should take care what we do with our neighbor in this altogether human and worldly way.

We should not be concerned primarily to be "just" to our neighbor, but rather to love and to support him. And this we can do only if we are ready to forgive. And I can be ready to forgive only if I have learned that Jesus Christ has forgiven *my* sins and given me another chance.

This business of forgiving is by no means a simple thing. It is not so hard because we are opposed to it on principle. Oh, no, we're not all that stubborn. It is hard because we are so just and because in our mania to be just we proceed to divide the burden of forgiveness among both partners and thus again parcel out forgiveness "justly." We say, "Very well, if the other fellow is sorry and begs my pardon, I will forgive him, then I'll give in." We make of forgiveness a law of reciprocity. And this never works. For then both of us say to ourselves, "The other fellow has to make the first move." And then I watch like a hawk to see whether the other person will flash a signal to me with his eyes or whether I can detect some small hint between the lines of his letter which shows that he is sorry. I am always on the point of forgiving (for even as a purely secular person I know that life can't get along without forgiveness; the machine of society would immediately burn out its bearings without this oil) ; but I never forgive. I am far too just.

Forgiveness—and this is the secret of it—is never merely following suit when the other person has led with his regret; forgiveness is always taking the initiative. It is initiative or it is nothing. Life generally follows the law of retaliation. A neighbor turns up his radio too loud. I rap on the wall. He squawks; I roar. He won't speak to me any more. And when I pass him on the street I look right through him. All of life is nothing more than reacting in a good sense and a bad sense. It is almost a law of nature. But forgiving means breaking through this natural law. It means breaking a hole in this entangling net at *one* point at least. And this happens only when somebody takes the initiative, when one person makes a new beginning and does not merely keep on repeating the old muddled beginnings.

What I have done is to describe the secret of the gospel in human terms. For the gospel is nothing else but the message of the divine initiative. The master of the vineyard did not descend like a thunderbolt upon the vinedressers when they maltreated the first and the second deputation of servants. He ventured a new beginning. If God had wanted merely to retaliate and react to what we do, there would have been no rainbow over the Flood and we should never have been able to celebrate Christmas or New Year's or Easter. The gospel means that God has broken the inexorable law of sin and retribution, cut straight through the world's tragic entanglement, and made a new beginning with us. When Paul speaks of the righteousness of God, this no longer means that God reacts to me like a judge, that he gives me what is coming to me. It means rather that God wants to be just to me as his *child*. We live by virtue of this miracle, this initiative of God.

When we do to our neighbor all that God does to us, a new, vivifying, re-creative atmosphere comes into our life. For one thing is sure and that is that every human being wants to love and be loved. If you have a husband or wife, a neighbor, an associate who is filled with resentment against you, who holds a grudge against you, treats you underhandedly, whose eyes glitter with hatred and contempt, you can be sure that he does not feel right underneath, that he is suffering under all this, and that he would be happy if he could love instead of hate; indeed, that he would be grateful to you if you would give him the chance to come out of his dark hole. For loving and being loved is a natural process like inhaling and exhaling. It is simply unnatural when it is otherwise. But the other person cannot find the switch. It needs an initial spark, otherwise he remains crippled and wastes away in his hatred. When a person ceases to love, his inner man ceases to breathe and he suffocates. Therefore, through my loving I must provide the initial spark. Often a single word breaks the dismal spell. A handclasp can burst chains. Do I really wish only to be just and let the other person stew in his own juice?

Vincent van Gogh once wrote to his brother Theo: "Many a man has a great fire in his soul and nobody comes to warm himself at it, and often the passers-by see only a bit of it above the chimney, and they go their way hence."

Don't I see that my neighbor, this enigmatic fellow who is such a stranger to me, also has this fire in him and that he wants someone to be warmed by his love? But his inner man is like a stove whose drafts have been shut tight. The fire grows smaller and smaller and emits nothing but acrid, biting smoke which torments his fellows. He is no longer able to open the drafts by himself. Should I not help him to get a fresh breath of air; am I really determined, as van Gogh says, to go my way hence? Then I would be denying him who died for this unfortunate man with the fire locked up within him. I would be "just," true enough. Nobody could blame me. But could I face the One who then would have died for this man in vain?

If we do not make use of what Christ has done for us, if we do not seize the chance to be bearers of new beginnings, then Christianity becomes a burden and a judgment. And it is upon this note of judgment that the parable closes.

What is this burden which Christianity can become? It shows itself in the questions that trouble me. Can I ever become a Christian at all? Can I muster up the strength to take the initiative? And, furthermore, can I really believe in all this queer dogmatic and supernatural business? How can I simply brush aside my intellectual difficulties? It is as if we were facing a stone wall. But, after all, we must start somewhere, and this means starting at *one* point. We have seen, have we not, that these difficulties are only secondary matters, which have their proper place when the time comes to deal with them; but perhaps for once we should begin with forgiveness, with what we have called the initiative.

The moment before we get to this point is like flying through the sound barrier. Not until the critical point is passed and the great explosion has occurred do we find ourselves in free space, and suddenly the resistances subside. If we never take the risk, never risk it in the name of him who first took the initiative and moved toward us—then being a Christian will only be a burden, because we let grace go to waste. "What is not used becomes a heavy burden," we read in Goethe's *Faust*. Is it any wonder then that people dodge becoming a Christian and avoid the zones where such decisions are made? "Who among us can dwell with the devouring fire? Who among us can dwell with everlasting burnings?" says Isaiah (33:14). "The everlasting burnings"—this is what we face: if they devour a man, he avoids them; if they warm him, he seeks them. The vinedressers made their decision. They simply wanted to be the masters of their own lives. And therefore they had to stamp out the everlasting fire.

Have we not for a long time been a nation of Christians? Luther spoke of the shower of the gospel that quickly passes by; and our parable closes with these words: "The kingdom of God will be taken away from you and given to a nation producing the fruits of it." God does not derive his life from us Occidental, Western vinedressers. But we live by the grace of God. He has no lack of continents to which he may send the gospel showers. Asia is still waiting. Europe has no privileges; it has only grace to lose. But we are not talking about continents. Jesus did not think in terms of world-historical perspective, but in terms of human souls. And even though his hand stretched above the globe—"All authority in heaven and earth has been given to me"—he nevertheless was utterly and intimately concerned with the blind man on the road, the little old woman, and small children. The hand that upholds the globe beckons to the poor and blesses the anxious. The Orient, the Occident, both are God's—of course this is true. But far greater is the fact that God seeks not only the great but the small, that he is there for you and me, and that he is waiting and yearning for us—and also for that one person who gives us so much trouble and whom *we* dare not give up.

X

The Parable of the Laborers in the Vineyard

Then Peter said in reply, "Lo, we have left everything and followed you. What then shall we have?" Jesus said to them, "Truly, I say to you, in the new world, when the Son of man shall sit on his glorious throne, you who have followed me will also sit on twelve thrones, judging the twelve tribes of Israel. And every one who has left houses or brothers or sisters or father or mother or children or lands, for my name's sake, will receive a hundredfold, and inherit eternal life. But many that are first will be last, and the last first.

"For the kingdom of heaven is like a householder who went out early in the morning to hire laborers for his vineyard. After agreeing with the laborers for a denarius a day, he sent them into his vineyard. And going out about the third hour he saw others standing idle in the market place; and to them he said, 'You go into the vineyard too, and whatever is right I will give you.' So they went out. Going out again about the sixth hour and the ninth hour, he did the same. And about the eleventh hour he went out and found others standing; and he said to them, 'Why do you stand here idle all day?' They said to him, 'Because no one has hired us.' He said to them, 'You go into the vineyard too.' And when evening came, the owner of the vineyard said to his steward, 'Call the laborers and pay them their wages, beginning with the last, up to the first.' And when those hired about the eleventh hour came, each of them received a denarius. Now when the first came, they thought they would receive more; but each of them also received a denarius. And on receiving it they grumbled at the householder, saying, 'These last worked only one hour, and you have made them equal to us who have borne the burden of the day and the scorching heat.' But he replied to one of them, 'Friend, I am doing you no wrong; did you not agree with me for a denarius? Take what belongs to you, and go; I choose to give to this last as I give to you. Am I not allowed to do what I choose with what belongs to me? Or do you begrudge my generosity?' So the last will be first, and the first last."

—MATTHEW 19:27–20:16

The people and the things which appear in this parable are familiar and close to all of us. The scene which the parable presents to us is again very worldly, and the settings are taken from our everyday life. It tells us nothing that is religious or beyond this world. It says nothing about incense or miracles. On the contrary, it speaks about a labor market. Here are workers, the unemployed, and an employer, and the talk is of hourly wages, labor contracts, and rates of pay.

So far everything is clear. But highly unclear are the rules of the game in the whole method of compensation. I should like to see the rumpus the newspapers would kick up if an employer attempted to introduce such practices in our day, if he were to give to those who did a little work an hour before closing exactly the same as those who had slaved all day. And very definitely—and certainly quite justifiably —there would be some beating of the drums in the unions too.

And if this peculiar employer, who is even given a certain paternalistic character by the term "householder" that is applied to him, were to continue to be obstinate, he would certainly learn from experience in the following week. For most decidedly no man would be so stupid as to come to work at dawn if he could get a full pay envelope so much easier by coming late. The workers would undoubtedly prefer to work only for a little while at the close of the day. Nobody is going to be so brainless as to do ten times the work for the same money! In short, the man is a fool; he is turning the whole economy upside down.

Even when we see the context in which the parable is incorporated the matter does not become plausible. Peter had addressed this question to the Lord: "Lo, we have left everything and followed you," we have staked our existence upon you, given up our jobs, sacrificed our families and homes; "what then shall we have?" Are we, he goes on in thought, are we going to be on the same level as the people who take it easy and enjoy life until they grow too old and too worn out to amuse themselves as they did before and then suddenly have an attack of religion, a kind of last-minute religious panic, and quickly become converted? You too, Jesus of Nazareth, will be turning the whole economy upside down if that's the way you are going to treat your people! Jesus then replies to this objection by telling this parable, and this is his thesis: The very thing you do *not* want is precisely what I do. Anybody who comes at the last hour, I pay him in full.

And this too we cannot understand at first. The great Norwegian writer Jens Peter Jacobsen, in his novel *Niels Lyhne,* tells the story of a man who rejected God, even though secretly he yearned for the comfort of faith and for peace. But he wanted to be honest with himself, and he would rather endure the desolation of a nihilistic life to the end than become weak-kneed and turn "religious" because of weakness. Fate treated him harshly. Death came crashing into his beloved family, and often he felt the deep need of comfort, something like an agonized yearning for home and security, piercing through his heart. But he clung to his hardness and even in the last hour of his life he refused to see the pastor, though secretly he yearned for his consolations. Then the family physician, who had come to love this patient and was moved by the valor of his desolate heart, uttered these words: "If I were God, I would far sooner save the man who does not repent at the last minute." Such a statement appeals to us. All of us are by nature inclined to have much more regard and liking for this Niels Lyhne, who lived consistently and uncompromisingly and held out to the end against the black wall of nothingness, than for the person who at the last moment tries to snatch up the chance of eternal salvation and grabs the emergency brake of piety. And you mean to say that Jesus Christ our Lord thinks otherwise about this? Is he going to rank this Niels Lyhne *lower* than the thief on the cross, who also tried to squeeze through the gate of heaven at the last moment?

Truly, this parable is a coded telegram. We will not understand it unless we know the code. This is true of all Jesus' parables. We have observed again and again that there is always only *one* point from which they can be unlocked. And this is the point at which the Lord wants us. Where is this point in this parable? We shall try to find it and then listen carefully to what it says.

The whole parable gains meaning on only one condition. And that is that we let it tell us that this is work which takes place in the *vineyard,* and that therefore it should be service for the Lord, and for this very reason cannot be viewed as something earned or merited. On the contrary, it says that this work is itself a gift and carries its reward in itself; for it brings the workers near to their fatherly Lord and his care. We shall understand this parable only if we see that Jesus is here speaking against legalistic religion, against *all* religion of the kind that dwells in our hearts by nature. It is a good thing to realize very clearly how men have toiled, and still toil, in the sphere of religion to earn heaven; they pile high the altars with sacrifices, they tell their beads, they do good works, they even go to such lengths as those strangest of all saints who spent their whole life sitting on high pillars, enduring the wind and the weather, growing old and gray in the process, solely in order to gain merits for heaven. We must realize once and for all that these people are not doing all this as children who live and move about freely and happily in the Father's house, but that they are doing it as slaves, doing it out of fear, that all this comes not so much from the heart but is for them a means of making themselves worthy of heaven. *If* these people were right—*if* fellowship with Jesus were a business transaction with a definite *quid pro quo,* with accounts of earnings which we could present to God and receipts entitling us to entrance into heaven—then it would in fact be shamefully unjust if the person who entered the Lord's service at the evening of life were to receive the same as did all those who had toiled and sweated and come home at evening with all their bones aching.

It is highly important to see that our parable characterizes as absolutely false this whole "religious" view of things, which is by no means confined to the ancient Jews or our Catholic fellow Christians, but runs in the blood of us all. This must be understood first; otherwise the parable becomes a caricature.

When we do something for our Lord, when we really take seriously the matter of honoring him in the poorest of our brethren, when we pray to him, when we surrender to him our life with its joys and sorrows, its passions and despondencies, this is not a means to an end—to the end, namely, of securing a claim on eternal salvation, or even to the earthly end of securing an ideology for the Western world, since, after all, men need some kind of religion—but rather this is an end in itself, it is itself "salvation."

Why is this so? The person who knows that he has been given the grace to love God—and anybody who knows anything at all about it will confirm this—for that person this is in itself a joy, an undreamed-of fulfillment of life. For him, everything he does for God is in itself a happy service and therefore the very opposite of a hard drudgery that must then be rewarded with salvation. Does not all the torment of our life, the ambition that keeps gnawing at us, the worry that robs us of our sleep, the bad conscience that keeps accusing us, the anxiety of life that makes everything seem hopeless, empty, and dismal, does not all of this arise precisely from the fact that we have ceased to be coworkers with God and are now stumbling about on our own, that we have lost our Father and therefore life becomes ever more dismal, derelict, and thus more meaningless?

On the other hand, the person who is a fellow worker for God and has learned to love him suddenly finds that his whole attitude toward life is different. He sees his small life and all the little everyday things in it, all the duties he has to fulfill, and all the people he meets, fitting into a great planned, sovereign program in which there are no accidents, no hitches, and no blank numbers. He can dare quite simply to believe—even if he cannot see it—that he has been put in exactly the place in the vineyard where he is needed and that everything that God sends to him is more punctual and planned than a railroad timetable.

It is true that often while we are being thus taught and trained by God we do not understand why he does things in just this way and not some other way, why we have to go through what we do. (No raw apprentice, no pupil, nor even a student understands from the beginning the curriculum by which he is being trained and educated. On the contrary, apprentices, pupils, and students often rebel and say, "Why do we have to spend our time on all this senseless stuff? Why do they go on boring us with this or that?") Not until we know him who has taken us into his service, not until we know his heart, his wisdom, and his compassion does it become a happy service to be employed by him.

Then our life begins to acquire something like direction and order. Then it has a meaning. And it has meaning simply because we are loved, because he will make it come out right, and because he always has something in mind in everything he sends to us.

Then even "the burden and heat of the day" suddenly look altogether different. Anybody who has ever gone through something hard with Jesus holding his hand, anybody who has had him as the companion of his anguish when he went through the bitterness of a prison camp, when he was driven from house and home, when he was dragged from the smoking ruins of a bombed cellar—that person would not for all the world have missed these experiences. He does not say—in any case I have never yet heard anyone say—"Because of all the hardships I have had to undergo, God must surely give me a higher place in heaven." What he does say is this: "Not until I went down into the depths of hunger, fear, and loneliness did I experience the nearness of the Lord. There is where I first learned who Jesus is and how he can save and comfort and sustain a man. For the rest of my life I shall live by the blessings of those hours of 'burden and heat.' I *had* to be sent down those rough roads in order that I might see that he really does know the way. I *had* to go through the valley of the shadow to learn to know the shepherd. Otherwise I would never have experienced all this."

Perhaps now we understand why the workers in the parable are on the wrong track and why they are miserable dilettantes in faith when they insist upon additional and higher wages for their work in the vineyard. When Peter asked, "Now that we have left all for you, what do we get?" he missed the point altogether.

Is there any fuller life than that of a disciple, a coworker with God? The more decidedly a man is a disciple and the more he leaves behind the greater becomes the One upon whose heart he casts himself. For God is no piker. The fact that Peter and the laborers in the vineyard still did not understand this shows that they still had not found the secret and the glory of Jesus, that they still thought that he, whose will it is to bring riches and joy into their lives and to honor them by making them his coworkers, was a slave driver and a tyrant.

But now what about those who came to work last, when the evening sun was sinking, when the twilight began to fall upon their life? What about these latecomers, these last-minute Christians? We must also direct our attention to this second group of people who play a part in our parable.

Are these latecomers to faith really so contemptible compared with Niels Lyhne just because their life does *not* run in a straight line, just because it has a break in it or describes a curve?

Is it not true that this Niels Lyhne, who lived so consistently and refused to capitulate to the highest court of appeal, was after all a very poor and miserable man? Did not his stubborn, inflexible insistence upon consistency cheat him out of the point, the very meaning of his life? Can we really say, "Blessed are the consistent, the logical"? Or must we not rather say, "Blessed are those who remain open to the call of the Father, and open also to a revision of their course; blessed are those who do not refuse when God wants to meet us, engage us, and lead us"?

A much-discussed play by Dürrenmatt, *The Visit*, presents us with another very consistent life which may illustrate the problem of our parable.

Here is an old, filthy-rich woman who has come back to her home town to revenge herself upon the lover of her youth. Decades earlier he had thrown her over, betrayed her, and finally brought her into a brothel. And now her whole life is possessed by this hate-love of hers. She is, as it were, nailed fast, fixated upon this one point in her unresolved past, and she lives consistently with this one motive of hate. Her life is nothing more than this single, fanatical attempt to carry out this theme of hate consistently. And because of this her life degenerates into the fixed rigidity of an arithmetical problem. She no longer has a "history," so to speak, but takes on the timeless mask of one of the Furies. She has been divorced and married again and again. But it is always the same thing over again, and even the changing husbands are always played by the same actor. Nothing happens any more. Her hatred makes her too consistent. Time stands still. But her former lover, the shameless fellow with the huckster's soul, repents. The call to repentance and atonement reaches him, and his miserable, guilt-laden life is made new at the last moment. He still has a "history" or, rather, he regains it. For him there is a future, even though he must die.

Isn't this the greatness of the householder, the greatness of God, that he does not compel us simply to go on unwinding our life, like thread from a spool, as this old lady did, simply letting this life go on as it did before on the track that has been laid out for it once and for all, and paying consistently for all the wrong and the guilt in our lives? Isn't this the greatness of God, that he gives us another chance, that he keeps calling to us not to go on loafing in the market place of life, but to enter into his service and set our life on an altogether new level, to have a "history" with *him?*

If the people who come last in our parable, if the latecomers to faith really understand who he is that has called them into his service, the idea will never even occur to them to laugh at the others because they have worked from early morning through the heat of the day while they have got off so "easy." They most certainly will not flaunt their cheaply earned denarius before the others. No, on the contrary, they will regret every hour they spent in idleness, every hour before they found their way through to the meaning of their life, to the great home-coming.

At evening they will suddenly realize that all this time they squandered away in futile freedom outside the vineyard was not a good time after all, and they were not happy in it either, but that fear of the void was their constant companion. They will regret, perhaps even weep over, every hour in which they did not know this Lord, every hour they missed their happiness, every hour they considered as slavery the very service which would have made their lives rich. They will not say, "Thank God we got our denarius so cheaply; thank goodness that a last-minute repentance is enough." No, they will rather say with Johannes Scheffler:

> Alas, that I so lately knew thee,
>   Thee, so worthy of the best;
> Nor had sooner turned to view thee,
>   Truest good and only rest!
> The more I love, I mourn the more
> That I did not love before!

Our parable contains many more implications and would lead us into many a labyrinthine way of thought. These ways cannot be traversed in a single sermon. We must not close, however, without at least addressing ourselves to one more thought which, if we have grasped it, can touch us deeply and also help us to cope with some things in our life with which we could *not* cope without this thought.

I am referring to that remarkable question addressed by the householder to the grumbling critics of the wage scale: "Is your eye evil because I am good?" or "Do you begrudge my generosity?" Translated into modern terms this means: Do you who have worked the whole day cherish complexes and feelings of envy because I allow myself to show your fellow men a measure of kindness and generosity which they have no claim upon? Look here, I am not giving *you* who have borne the heat and burden of the day any *less* than is coming to you. After all, I am not making you suffer in any way whatsoever by being generous to these part-time workers. The wage scale remains. Are you denying *me* the freedom to give another *more* than is coming to him?

Naturally, this is an ironical question. It is close to being a shrewd catch question. For obviously the only answer that can be given to it is: Of course, we wouldn't forbid you to do this. Far be it from us to say that your kindness is unethical because it is too generous. Oh, no, on the contrary, a man can never be too generous. It's a fine thing to know that there is at least one person who is capable of being so exceedingly good and generous as you are.

But now the curious thing is that when the householder actually puts into practice this unlimited kindness, which we are so ready to accept theoretically and religiously, there is something wrong about it, and we strike. Why? If we really find the right reason for this we shall understand an essential part of our life.

The long-term workers in the parable would certainly have had no quarrel with the householder's generosity if they themselves had enjoyed the benefit of it, say in the form of a voluntary contribution to the welfare fund or an increase in hourly wage or some other kind of bonus. Then, presumably, they would have been grateful and happy. And who wouldn't react in this way? Fundamentally, every man is likely to have a spontaneous feeling of gratitude. All of us every now and then send up our thanks to heaven when we feel that a hand of blessing has touched our lives, when we get a promotion in our job or when a child comes into our life. Everybody says "Thank God" when some success or other is granted to him. Oh, no, we are not ungrateful. We all have a real feeling for the goodness of God and sometimes, perhaps on a birthday or on Christmas Eve, we can be quite overcome by it.

But as soon as I look at my "dear" neighbor and realize that he *too* is included in God's generosity I feel some slight pangs in the region of the heart. I say to myself: Yes, all due deference to God's goodness; I can use all of it there is. If this goodness should make me a millionaire or a famous man or an idolized fullback—O.K., come across with it! I've got broad shoulders, a whole load of blessings is not too much for me.

But when I see God giving something out of the ordinary to my competitor, my colleague, perhaps even to my friend, I get sore and begin to check up on the way the various quotas of blessings are handed out and distributed.

When God in his goodness hands out bonuses to *others* and I grow jealous, I do not normally reproach myself and call myself a miserable grudger. (No, we don't say anything like that to ourselves. After all, one has to be a little bit nice to oneself; a man mustn't lose his self-regard.) Nor do I say: O the generosity, the boundless goodness of God! (For this I say only when the Care Package is delivered at my door.) What I say is that this goodness of God is unjust. Did this other fellow deserve more goodness, more attention than I? Look at me, I saved all my life long and the inflation and revaluation took it all away from me. But this other fellow around the corner always lands on his feet and today he's driving a big car and smoking fat cigars. Or I say something like this: I've worked hard as a student and done everything I could to make myself a little less of a blockhead. And here is this other fellow, my roommate; God gave him a "brain" and he just walks through all his examinations, though he never misses a dance and goes off to Bermuda in his vacations, while I, with my lower IQ, go working my way through college. He's more "gifted"—he received more gifts than I did. Is this fair?

We all know this. We know it all too well. We embitter many hours of our life with thoughts like these; they can make a neurotic of you. And this dismal song always has the same refrain and it goes like this: God's goodness comes to the wrong person because it doesn't come to *me*.

The laborers were well satisfied with the householder as long as they were dealing with him *alone* and as long as they were agreed with him on the wage stipulations in the early morning. Not until the *others* arrived did the haggling over the wages break loose. Then the jealousy commenced and the complexes thickened.

It must be admitted, of course, that this question of justice and the right proportioning of wages is altogether justified in human relations. Naturally work and wages must be brought into proper relationship. It is clear that a part-time worker cannot be paid as much as the executive of a great company. But it is equally clear that two men who do the same job in the same factory and have the same training should receive at least approximately the same wage. It is obvious that one cannot give to the man who works only four hours the same remuneration that is given to one who works eight or ten hours on an assembly line or at his desk. These are clear and obvious proportions.

But now we must not forget that here we are dealing with a *parable*. And if we take this into account, immediately the question arises whether these things are just as obvious and nicely ascertainable in our relationship to God and whether we can calculate the proper proportions with equal ease in that relationship. If we think about this it very soon becomes clear to us that this is precisely what we *cannot* do. For when we are dealing with God it is not merely a matter of measurable units of work but rather of all the areas of our life, including the area of our most intimate and personal life which we cannot observe and assess either in ourselves or in our neighbor.

This can be found out by means of a simple experiment. I recommend this experiment to anybody who is tormented by jealousy. You may think that the other fellow—your talented roommate, for example, or your former colleague who has had such a tremendously successful career, or the girl who shared the third-floor back with you and later married her rich boss, while you go on pounding the typewriter—you may think that all these people are the darlings of God's goodness, that they have simply been showered with good fortune. Do you really know that this is so? Would you—this is the little experimental question I suggest to you—would you exchange places with them, that is, would you exchange in *every* respect? Not only your bicycle for his Cadillac, but perhaps also his deeply hidden marital troubles for your independence? Not only your third-floor room for her mansion, but also her boredom, her anxiety, her emptiness, for your simple but untroubled life? That rich man whom you envy may have a gaping wound in his life because he has no heir or because his dearest is suffering from an incurable illness. Or perhaps you, a harassed, distracted, ulcerated executive, envy the simple, cheerful temperament of your young colleague when all the time he is wrestling with some difficulty at home of which you have no knowledge at all. Would you really exchange—in every respect? Are you really ready to fling down the net product of your life at God's feet and say, "You have divided up these things unfairly; you have done me wrong; you have given me nothing and poured out all your goodness on these other people." Can you see your fellow man's whole life, with all its cellars, its background, its hidden corners, as God does, as he must do every day? After all, you see only the façade. But he sees the nights and the lonelinesses. He sees the other person's heart too, with the same discontent in it as yours. Do you still want a total exchange? Therefore, let this be the final message of our parable (I sum it up in two thoughts):

First, you will never be able to see the goodness of God with a jealous eye. Many doubts of this goodness, many feelings of anxiety, of being deserted and forgotten, do not emerge from our reservoir of intellectual doubts at all, but come from the fact that we have a wrong attitude toward our neighbor. Anybody who looks at God's blessings with one eye and with the other tries to keep track of whether his neighbor receives one mite *more* than he does falls victim to the diseased kind of seeing that makes him incapable of either recognizing what a blessing is or understanding his fellow man. I then become a very poor and unhappy person. Then God becomes for me no more than blind fate and I acquire complexes with regard to my neighbor that rob me of my sleep. And finally I find myself at variance with everything; indeed, I no longer have any use for myself.

Second, this saving certainty—it really does have to do with salvation!—that God is good, that he is good to *me,* enters into my heart only if I trust that he cares for his children beyond all that we ask or think and that I too am safe and secure in this goodness. And therefore when envy seizes hold upon me I must stop this nerve-racking calculation as to whether God is giving more to somebody else than to me. Instead, I should thank him for what he has given to me and pray that he may also support and comfort that other person in those secret trials and troubles of which I have no knowledge at all.

Jesus Christ, when he hung upon the Cross, did not envy the executioners and drunken soldiers standing idle upon Calvary. And yet from any human point of view he had reason enough to do so. For he was writhing in pain and thirst, hanging from the cruel nails, while these rude fellows walked around beneath the Cross free as air. And they were uncomplicated enough not to let it bother them. They were free and full of life and slaked their thirst at will. They were the top dogs. But Jesus did not envy them; rather, he prayed for their souls, "Father, forgive them; for they know not what they do." The Father knew the misery of these top dogs. And as his Son prayed thus for them the Father's countenance shone upon him and he could say, "Father, into thy hands I commit my spirit." Here was one who did not envy, but looked upon his neighbor as his Father looked upon him, sorrowfully, seekingly, yearningly. And that is why he was one with the Father and bowed his head in utter peace.

XI

The Parable of the Pharisee and the Publican

He also told this parable to some who trusted in themselves that they were righteous and despised others: "Two men went up into the temple to pray, one a Pharisee and the other a tax collector. The Pharisee stood and prayed thus with himself, 'God, I thank thee that I am not like other men, extortioners, unjust, adulterers, or even like this tax collector. I fast twice a week, I give tithes of all that I get.' But the tax collector, standing far off, would not even lift up his eyes to heaven, but beat his breast, saying, 'God be merciful to me a sinner!' I tell you, this man went down to his house justified rather than the other; for every one who exalts himself will be humbled, but he who humbles himself will be exalted."

—LUKE 18:9–14

This parable is so simple and seems to have about it so much of the quality of being beautifully self-evident possessed by things with which we have been familiar from our youth that we hesitate to waste another word upon it. Why should we as adults dissect and analyze and mull over what a child understands? Ought we not simply to let the parable stand in its monumental simplicity and merely salute it reverently, as one would an old acquaintance whom we had looked up to even as boys and girls, one of the few things in our life which even now that we have grown older and more skeptical has lost none of its grandeur, its splendor, and the freshness of eternal youth.

But often we miss the inner mysteries of the very things with which we are most familiar simply because we are too familiar with them. And this may well be true of this parable.

The two figures whom our Lord portrays with such quiet simplicity have long since become oversimplified and debased into stereotypes in our imagination and now we can hardly recognize their original features. We are always likely to think that this is rather stark black-and-white portraiture.

Of course, if the Pharisee were actually the vain popinjay who is

126

always exulting in his own splendor with bumptious passion, who never lets a conversation or even a prayer go by without allowing, covertly or openly, all his points of excellence to shine like jewels, and laps up with voluptuous pleasure every bit of admiration that comes his way—if the Pharisee were really a sheer coxcomb, then, of course, the parable would have a point so self-evident as to be downright banal. But this is precisely what the Pharisee is not.

And if the publican were really so touchingly and sentimentally humble as he appears in our imagination, then again the parable would hold no problems. But the publican was not like that at all. On the contrary, he was probably a rather tough fellow who had entered the service of the occupying power and fleeced his own people for the benefit of his own pocket, what we would call a *collaborator*.

On the other hand, the Pharisee is a man who is in dead earnest about his service to God. After all, we can tell at once whether a person's heart is in a thing when it touches his stomach or his pocketbook. Business is business, and for many people this is where sentiment and Christianity, too, stop. But not with the Pharisee! He fasted and sacrificed and thus cut down his standard of living for God. So for him God was at least as real as the jingling coins in his purse.

This really should not be overlooked. And if we do not disregard it, we begin to understand that the Pharisee is a highly respected man. The people sense that he is not merely uttering empty words, that he is not one who would say, "We commend the offering plates in the narthex to your charity," and then collect it for himself, as the publican might do, but that he himself is the first to give. People have a fine instinct for a man's sincerity. And while the publican exerts only a corrupting influence upon the community, the Pharisee works faithfully and sacrificially to preserve its holy traditions and its faith. The community senses that the ultimate foundations of its life are in good hands as long as he stands for what he does.

When we see all this clearly it is no longer quite so self-evident that Jesus should proceed to praise the publican and condemn the Pharisee. We may well suppose that he did not depreciate a respected and in many ways venerable figure without great sadness of heart. Manifestly everything looks quite different in God's eyes from what it does in man's.

But this is easily said and yet is full of difficult and burdensome questions. Is the judgment of men, even of very earnest and morally mature men, of no value at all? Is the opposite of man's judgment always the only right one in God's eyes? Can we never trust our own intellect and are ordinary people never to depend upon their instinct at all? Does God always turn our values upside down, does he always run a red line through our systems of value? Doesn't God, and here his Son, have any appreciation whatsoever of the fact that the publican is a rascal and the Pharisee is a very serious man and therefore a man who should be taken seriously? It is not a matter to be taken lightly that God should always be of a different mind from men, even from very serious-minded and wise men. What kind of strange God is this, who accepts the publican and rejects the Pharisee?

We shall try to understand this God who acts and thinks so strangely and then attempt to look at these two figures as they appear to God's eyes.

We can do this, of course, only with a profound sense of dismay, for both figures are a part of ourselves. How many there are among us who have accomplished something in life, who in their business are mentioned with respect as employers or as employees, who have dealt honestly when it would have been easier to be an opportunist! Will they, too, cut a woeful figure before the Last Judgment and be condemned? And, after all, everything depends on whether they can stand *that* test.

But perhaps there are also among us some who are heavily burdened in conscience. Perhaps they have not been able to control their urges and desires; perhaps they have made another person unhappy; perhaps they have been tricky when everything depended upon being straight; perhaps they are unbearably vain or are consumed with ambition. They are disgusted with themselves but cannot cope with it. Must such a person go away judged and condemned, having had knocked out of him all the self-confidence he had this morning when he left home a respectable and somewhat saturated Christian church member? Or may he be assured that God accepts the sorrow and shame he feels concerning himself, which at times may lead him to the brink of suicide, and that God does not reject him, but, just because he is sorrowful and ashamed, loves him and welcomes him?

But there is one thing that will not do, and that is for him to assume a kind of publican's pride and make a soft cushion of the kindness of God with which he heals and comforts the terrified conscience of a sinner; to make himself out to be utterly vile and tear himself down; to be constantly babbling of his sins and shortcomings—as many pious people do, thinking that this will impress God and thus abate his desire to judge them.

There is such a thing as confessing one's faults and blackening oneself, which is merely a trick. This is always the case when people try to make an accomplishment of their humility. Then the beating of one's breast is nothing less than an elaborate form of coquetry. This is only smacking one's lips with pleasure over the thought of the delight that God must derive from such a smitten conscience and such self-abasement. But when this happens a man does not have a smitten conscience at all; the devil has snared him with publican's pride.

Many of us are less like the Pharisee, with his uplifted head and his solid moral character, than we are like the publican—but a somewhat different publican from the one described in the parable. Perhaps like a publican who says, "I thank thee, God, that I am not so proud as this Pharisee; I am an extortioner, unjust, and an adulterer. That's the way human beings are, and that's what I am, but at least I admit it, and therefore I am a little bit better than the rest of the breed. I commit fornication twice a week, and at most ten per cent of what I own comes from honest work. I am an honest man, O God, because I don't kid myself, I don't have any illusions about myself. Let your angels sing a hallelujah over this one sinner who is as honest as I am, honest enough to admit that he is a dirty dog and not hide it beneath his robes like these lying Philistines the Pharisees."

This publican's pride, in which God has no pleasure at all, is really epidemic among the pious. How many people of the world have timidly begun to ask whether Christ was not the right Man for them and then became disgusted with faith because they became convinced that this coquettish humility was far more indecent than their high-minded and proud striving for ideals.

But I mention this not merely to pronounce a judgment upon ourselves as a Christian church but above all because here is a basic truth of our faith. And that truth is this: Whether one is a publican or a Pharisee, whether one is loved or rejected by God, does not depend on particular qualities, nor does it depend on whether one is outwardly humble or not, whether one has illusions about oneself or whether one is honest. In other words, everything one does and thinks can be used by the devil; he can use even the holiest waters to drive his mills. One can play the deuce even with divine forgiveness and make it a pretext for evil. For example, if one is a theologian—and why should I spare my own "trade" here?—one can be an unjustified, case-hardened Pharisee and champion what may be a correct and legitimate doctrine of justification with an angry, arrogant fanaticism for orthodoxy. One can preach and teach the love of God in such a way as to despise those who do not yet understand it or only half understand it. This disease of publican's pride is particularly rampant among us theologians and ministers. Not infrequently when we speak and write about the love of God we are more dogmatical and disputatious than loving witnesses to justification.

So we must be especially careful of the devout moments in our life. No confession of sin safeguards us against pride. Even humility is not a virtue which is immune to the devil. On the contrary, these are the very nests in which he loves to lay the cuckoo eggs of pride; he is pleased as Punch when the pious hatch them out.

Thus we face the question: Where, then, is the real difference between these two figures, if the publican can be proud and the Pharisee can be humble, if it is obvious that everything is relative, if God can dwell with the rascal and the devil can lodge in the skin of the pious?

Let us therefore take a closer look at the scene presented to us in the parable.

To begin with, there are many parallels between these two men.

Both want to stand before God; they seek his fellowship; they are both in the temple. They are not simply seeking God in nature. The people who do this are mostly seeking only a religious thrill but otherwise they want to remain what they are. In other words, the God of nature does nothing to them. He does not judge them, he gives them no commands; they do not have to die for him, they need only to enjoy him. In his sublimity the nature-god is also above and beyond our private life.

But both of the figures in our parable want more than this and they do more than this: they enter into the holy presence of God. They expose themselves to his will, his claim. They are not trying to escape into cheap non-commitment, but rather take their stand before God. This is in itself no inconsiderable thing.

But their worship of God indicates that they have something even deeper in common: both of them approach God with a prayer of thanks. The *publican,* even though his prayer is expressed in the form of a petition, gives thanks that there is such a thing as the mercy of God, that even someone like himself can approach him, that even an unworthy man can enter the sanctuary and need not go shuffling about outside, sick for home and crying for paradise lost. The *Pharisee* too gives thanks to God. What does he actually thank him for? He gives thanks that God's Spirit has performed a great work in his life, that God's great act of liberation has freed him from the chains of greed and selfishness and made him worthy to approach the kingdom of God with head held high. He does not simply say, "God, look what a fine fellow I am; you must really be gratified with me." To speak of the Pharisee in this way would be a malicious caricature. Even if he did consider himself a fine fellow he nevertheless thanks God for having made him one. So the Pharisee too gives praise to the mercy of God. What could one say against that?

Thus the very fact that both of them approach God with a prayer of thanksgiving shows that they have penetrated deeply into the mysteries of God. Beginners and casual Christians usually confine themselves to petitions, especially when they are in trouble. But in the very next moment they have forgotten God; it was only a passing panic that exploded into prayer. When a person gives thanks to God he always shows that he is not merely concerned with momentary help and using God as a means to an end, but rather with God himself, with fellowship with God and his peace. But why, then, is the publican's prayer of thanksgiving accepted and that of the Pharisee rejected? There must be something wrong with the Pharisee's thanksgiving. We must dig still deeper to find the critical point in the Pharisee and—in ourselves.

Both of these men in the temple are performing an act of self-knowing; both acknowledge and confess something about themselves. The publican confesses that he cannot stand before God with his burdened conscience. And in this he is certainly right. The Pharisee thinks that he *can* stand before God. And the fact is that he actually is made of different stuff from that dubious fellow standing over by the column. Shouldn't he also be able to say so openly? Wouldn't it be hypocrisy, humility carried too far, for him to level all differences abstractly and dogmatically and simply declare: Before God we are both alike? The Pharisee would passionately reject such egalitarianism. Not only because it would go against his honor personally but above all because he would see in it an attack upon the commandments of God.

What he would say to himself would be this: Either the holy commandments of God stand for something, and then it is not a matter of indifference whether a man fulfills them as scrupulously as I do or plays hob with them as does this publican. Or the commandments of God are not meant seriously, and then this rotten publican is O.K. But then all self-discipline, all sacrifice, all moral effort would suddenly be devaluated, then the garbage would be put on top of the heap, then all my endeavors would count for nothing and suddenly I would be put on the same level with every thief and rogue. But this surely cannot be the will of God. This would make mockery of God's holy will and his commandments. Not because of my personal honor and respectability, no, but because of the honor of God there can be no fellowship and no equality with the publican.

Isn't what the Pharisee thinks as he prays to be taken very seriously? Isn't it true that what he is concerned about is God's honor—especially since he does not ascribe to himself the decisive merits at all, but rather ascribes them to the divine grace, which has preserved, saved, and strengthened him, and which he therefore praises?

We see that this story has its depths. It is not at all a simple thing to understand the judgment Jesus makes. So the best thing to do is to ask how these two men arrived at their self-knowledge and their different confessions. And the fact is that this is where we hit upon the salient point.

If you want to know yourself, you must have a standard. And when this standard is applied the differences between the two figures become apparent.

The Pharisee measures himself by looking downward when he tries to determine his rank before God. He chooses the bad publican as a standard. Then, of course, the differences become quite drastically obvious. Sure, the Pharisee knows he has faults, he knows the wolves that howl in the cellar of his soul, the thoughts and desires that frighten him. But he has controlled them. The publican, however, has exercised no inhibitions or discipline and has allowed himself to be driven by these wolves.

True as all this may be—and it is actually true!—this kind of self-measurement by looking downward always produces pride. This can be illustrated by the desire to gossip. Why is it that when we are together we take such pleasure in sinking our teeth into our fellow men, why do men delight in doing this around the lunch table and women when they are at a tea party? Where is the root of this strange delight (which sometimes actually becomes a sensual pleasure) that we take in discussing in whispers and feigned horror the private weaknesses and perhaps the secret amours of prominent people in the world? Quite simply because at such moments we feel so much better about ourselves and because we can say with indescribable moral relish, "Such things don't occur in my life." Or at least, "Such things may occur in my life but they certainly should not happen to a public figure or his wife." Gossip —including the gossip that spills out of the exposé literature in our picture magazines and cheap papers—is always based upon a kind of self-defense mechanism. We want our own superiority to be confirmed and we achieve this by being horrified at others and putting ourselves above them. Anybody who looks downward and measures himself by the weaknesses of his fellow men immediately becomes proud; or, better, what he is concerned about is not primarily to run down others but rather by running down others to make himself look good and feel good.

We encounter here a secret which operates not merely in the private life of the individual but also in public life and politics. There are politicians of such Machiavellian unscrupulousness that they simply say, "Politics is always a dirty business and always has been. Ever since the world began power has always triumphed over justice and subsequently justice has had to legalize the power. Since the world is full of wolves, let us run with the wolf pack. Anybody who acts otherwise as a politician will soon be looked upon as a visionary idealist and in no time at all he will be plowed under." It was not so long ago that such thoughts were openly proclaimed as a party platform in Germany. Today they are cherished more privately. And the world which thus measures and orients itself downward, which takes as its standard the law of the wolf and makes politics "amoral"—the nice scientific term for it—this world then plunges into the anxiety and the megalomania which it itself has spawned.

For this false attitude, for this measuring of oneself by looking downward, the Pharisee is an example. He makes the publican his standard. And this makes everything he says—despite its truth in detail—false and untrue. And then this standard also corrupts the honesty of his prayer of thanksgiving. True, he thanks *God* for having made him what he is now. He knows very well that this is no merit of *his,* and he says so. But once he has slipped into this wrong way of looking at himself and the publican and allowed the evil passion for making comparisons to get hold of him he suddenly begins to look upon himself with satisfaction and complacency: Sure, this is what God has made of me, but after all this is what *I* am too.

I cannot help thinking of many of the stories of conversion which pious people and also many moral movements love to tell in these days. First they paint a picture of what they were before in the blackest possible colors. They work themselves up to an almost masochistic pitch of self-accusation. Then they tell how they came into contact with the Spirit of God when they met up with a particular group or sect, and now their eyes are enlightened, now they can rejoice all the day, they are liberated children of God.

The fact is that this does actually happen; one *can* have this experience with God. And anybody who has had it will always be grateful to God for it. But the more one talks about it, the more one trumpets abroad these stories of one's experience with God, the more one's attention becomes focused upon oneself, and suddenly the devil has turned the whole thing into a pious and vain autobiography. After all, I must have been pretty good raw material for him to have picked me out the way he did. God must have found something rather special in me; otherwise he wouldn't have entered into my life and given me this privilege above so many others.

Thus the devil again succeeds in laying his cuckoo eggs in a pious nest. When a man has had an experience of God let him beware of telling it to men and making comparisons. The sulphurous stench of hell is as nothing compared with the evil odor emitted by divine grace gone putrid. The grace of God actually can be corrupted by spiritual vanity. And the so-called children of the world are quick to note this and are repelled by it. How many a non-Christian, for whom Christ died just as he died for you and for me, has learned to know the grace of God only in this fetid form that reeks of pride and has turned away in disgust, preferring to stick with his honest nihilism?

In the figure of the Pharisee we are confronted with a shocking exposure of the sin of Christianity, your sin and my sin, the sin of us who have subtly made of our Christianity a sign of virtue and given it the unpleasant smack of privilege. Pharisaic pride is one of the most dreadful and also one of the most infectious diseases of Christianity.

And right here and only at this point is the prayer of the publican different. When a man really turns to God with a burdened conscience he doesn't think of other people at all. There he is utterly alone with God. It would never have occurred to the publican to say, "Sure, this Pharisee is a man of a different stripe from me, but he too has plenty of blots on his scutcheon; he's a sinner too." This would have been true,

of course. But when a man is utterly alone with God and dealing solely
with him, then many things that are true are completely immaterial to
him. He has something else to think about. And that's why the publican's attitude is completely genuine and radically honest. He measures
himself "upward." God *himself* is his standard. And measuring himself
by that standard he is suddenly aware of how far removed he is. But
then this is just the time when God is very near to him. He does not
dare to say, "Dear God," because for him in his sordidness this would
be an impermissible familiarity. But then God speaks to him and says,
"My beloved child."

We Germans had some conception of our guilt after the collapse at
the end of the last war and many of us uttered the prayer of the publican: "God be merciful to me a sinner! Remove not thy grace from our
sunken people." But then came one of the most dreadful moments in
the spiritual history of our nation when suddenly we began to say,
"Others are just as bad as we." Then suddenly our aloneness with God
vanished, then repentance and spiritual renewal were gone, then began
that fateful measuring of ourselves by looking downward and compar-
ing ourselves with the hypocritical democratic Pharisees among the
victors.

There are two points to be considered in closing.

First, we know that even the Apostle Paul occasionally boasted
against his opponents (I Cor. 15:10; II Cor. 11:16 ff.). But obviously
this was quite different in intention from that of the Pharisee. Paul
still remained the great teacher of divine mercy; he boasted of his
weakness. The very fact that he calls this boasting foolishness shows
clearly that he is not expressing any ultimate value judgments before
God and that therefore he immediately indicates that his boast is
merely a relative thing and brushes it aside, that this boasting is not
something ultimate but merely penultimate and valid only among men.
And here Paul gives us an important clue to the understanding of our
parable.

That is to say that we would completely misunderstand this story if
we were to conclude from it that there should be no distinctions at all
between men. It would be grotesque if an employer could not even ask
an applicant for a position whether he had experience and could do the
job or not, or if in the name of God I were to put a faithful, respected
workman on a par with a man with seventeen previous convictions.
There must be distinctions of rank on the human level and on this level
there must necessarily be distinctions between good and bad. But we
must beware of acting as if these human and social distinctions of rank
also had validity before that final court where all of us are sinners. No
man who goes to the Lord's Table dare be shocked when suddenly he
finds the publican with seventeen convictions standing beside him and

drinking from the same cup. On the contrary, he can only praise God for the gracious work he has done for this poor man as well as for himself and he will hear the angels rejoicing over this one sinner in whose heart the joy of forgiveness is beginning to stir.

I once visited a family and when I entered the room the son, the "black sheep" or "prodigal son" of the family, was sitting at the piano playing chorales. He had broken his mother's heart by committing many shameful acts. His playing was deeply moving because he played with so much feeling. It was, I believe, the hymn, "Commit thou all thy griefs and ways into his hands." His sister cast a look of hatred at him and hissed with scorn, "That hypocrite!" This girl who had been the faithful Martha in the home, working while her brother dissipated, might also have said, "God, I thank thee that I am not like this fellow." But was not what she said an evil thing—quite as bad as what the pious Pharisee said? How would *God* look upon this brother? Did God see in him a man who wallowed in evil and selfish pleasures and was now going so far as to exploit a chorale for whatever religious, aesthetic, epicurean kick he could get out of it? Or did God see in him a man whose hours of yearning and of disgust with shame drove him into the temple and who down in his heart was playing the prayer, "God, be merciful to me a sinner"? Who was this man, really? Which was the real man? May he not have been precisely the man who was playing the chorale with such feeling? Was not *this* perhaps the real man coming out; was not *this* the divine original suddenly breaking through the overlay of smut and nastiness—or was the chorale only a piece of sentimental religiosity he used to cover up his black soul? Who of us could ever tell? But to God it was plain.

What do we people really know of each other? What do we know about how you and I will look at the last judgment? What did the Pharisee really know about the publican? We live between the false judgments we make now and the surprises which the Last Judgment will bring.

We should therefore stand in reverence before another person's ultimate secret, the secret he shares only with God, which only his heavenly Father knows. We are all known by these sovereign eyes; but we ourselves know no one. And the miracle that happened to the publican was that he was known and seen through and through by those eyes and yet they did not close in rejection of the darkness in his life but opened and beckoned in compassionate welcome and acceptance. But the point is that the publican looked only into *those* eyes and did not allow himself to be misled into looking at the Pharisee and measuring himself by him.

This brings us to the second and last point.

What was the publican thinking when he went away? Did he perhaps say to himself, "Now I can go on as before; now I can go on grafting and smuggling, now that I have found out that God doesn't cut a fellow off, that he justifies a man even if he is a rascal"? Or would he not rather have gone away filled with radiant gratitude for this immeasurable goodness and found it simply impossible to give pain to this Father and disappoint him by committing sin?

Perhaps he too became one who a year later could say what the Pharisee was suggesting concerning himself on this day in the temple: "Behold, Lord, I have not committed adultery any more, nor have I gone on enriching myself. I could not have found it in my heart to hurt thee. I thank thee that through thy forgiveness and thy mercy thou hast given me courage and a new chance. I thank thee for thy manifest guidance." Have we caught the very fine differences, the almost imperceptible nuances that distinguish the way the Pharisee prayed from the way in which it is to be hoped that the publican will pray a year hence? An eternal destiny lies in these very small differences. A false, proud look at our neighbor can spoil everything for us and turn the grace of our God into putrefaction.

Perhaps some of you may now ask the question which the disciples once put to their Lord at the close of an hour of earnest teaching: "Who then can be saved if grace can go bad in our hands? Which of us does not repeatedly catch himself casting this prideful look at others?" And in answer to that I can only reply with the answer that Jesus himself gave: "With men this is impossible, but with God all things are possible."

If we could only learn to come to the end of our pretensions as the publican had come to his. Then God could make a new beginning with us. If only we could learn not to keep pushing ourselves forward and showing off before God. Then he could finally become our Father. And we—well, we could then be new, free persons.

XII

The Parable of the Pounds

As they heard these things, he proceeded to tell a parable, because he was near to Jerusalem, and because they supposed that the kingdom of God was to appear immediately. He said therefore, "A nobleman went into a far country to receive kingly power and then return. Calling ten of his servants, he gave them ten pounds, and said to them, 'Trade with these till I come.' But his citizens hated him and sent an embassy after him, saying, 'We do not want this man to reign over us.' When he returned, having received the kingly power, he commanded these servants, to whom he had given the money, to be called to him, that he might know what they had gained by trading. The first came before him, saying, 'Lord, your pound has made ten pounds more.' And he said to him, 'Well done, good servant! Because you have been faithful in a very little, you shall have authority over ten cities.' And the second came, saying, 'Lord, your pound has made five pounds.' And he said to him, 'And you are to be over five cities.' Then another came, saying, 'Lord, here is your pound, which I kept laid away in a napkin; for I was afraid of you, because you are a severe man; you take up what you did not lay down, and reap what you did not sow.' He said to him, 'I will condemn you out of your own mouth, you wicked servant! You knew that I was a severe man, taking up what I did not lay down and reaping what I did not sow: Why then did you not put my money into the bank, and at my coming I should have collected it with interest? And he said to those who stood by, 'Take the pound from him, and give it to him who has the ten pounds.' (And they said to him, 'Lord, he has ten pounds!') 'I tell you, that to every one who has will more be given; but from him who has not, even what he has will be taken away.' "

—LUKE 19:11–26

The disciples were saying to themselves: Now the time has come. Now the kingdom of God will come. They had traveled up and down and across the country with this amazing Man from Nazareth; they had experienced unheard-of things, things undreamed of in their

137

philosophy. It had been like a great campaign, a general attack upon the misery of the world, upon the hostile front of sin and death. Wherever this Nazarene appeared demon-possession yielded and the spell of sin was broken. They could not forget the grateful eyes of those whose fetters this Master had broken, of those from whose poor blind eyes he had banished the night, of those upon whom he had bestowed new life.

So the disciples had gained the definite impression that wherever this Man appeared he made deep inroads upon the front of the realm of death and that now he was about to roll up this whole front. In a mighty crescendo his redemptive powers would overrun the old aeon and then within a short time the new world of God would be erected upon the ruins of the old: mothers would again hold their missing sons in their arms; there would be no more widows and orphans, because death itself would be interned; and where before there had surged the sea of blood and tears the golden fields of corn would grow.

The signal for this overthrow of all things was the departure for Jerusalem. So thought the disciples.

Deep sorrow must have pierced the heart of Jesus as he watched his disciples cherishing their dreams and pious utopias. He knew that his departure for Jerusalem was not the beginning of a dream-kingdom of peace, but rather the signal of a new night, the deep darkness on Calvary about the sixth hour. He knew that he must suffer many things before he entered into glory and that all would forsake him. In agonizing loneliness Jesus knew that this present world would not simply collapse, as the disciples thought, but would, humanly speaking, triumph over him and spew him out as it would a poisonous, malignant substance, and that then death, suffering, and sin would continue to mar the face of this unhappy earth until the last day. He heard the complaining voices of those who two thousand years later would still be asking: "What has been changed after all by this Nazarene who said he would kindle a fire on earth and bring forth a new world from the blaze of its downfall? People still go on dying, people still are being massacred and terrorized; the rascals and the beasts have a relatively good time of it, 'some in the dark, some in public,' as *The Threepenny Opera* says. What, then, has changed?"

Jesus knew all this. There would be something like the end of a world in Jerusalem, but not of this present world; it would be the end of that dreamworld in the hearts of the disciples. The disciples would either have to understand the mystery of the Passion or else be shipwrecked upon it.

So Jesus must now prepare them for this kind of an end of the world, for the catastrophe on Calvary. How does he do this? Does he, perhaps, let them down easy by telling them the truth gently, much as a doctor cautiously informs a sick man that he is suffering from cancer or multiple sclerosis and gradually disenchants him of his plans and hopes for the future?

No, Jesus proceeds quite differently. He puts his disciples to work. While he is away and the dreadful silence prevails he gives us clear tasks to perform. "Make use of your opportunities; trade with your pounds," he says.

Why, do you suppose, did he choose this way? Well, when I work for someone, when I share responsibility in his work, then I also *think* about him. This follows almost automatically. When Jesus puts me to the work of faith—and it actually is a piece of work to cope with my temptations day by day and fight my way through—then I also have daily contact with him. When he sets me at the task of loving my neighbor he is actually confronting me with his image every day. For it is none other than himself who meets me in my brother and in my sister.

So in this parable we are summoned before the Lord to receive our assignment of work. We all have our place here, including you, and Luther, and the Apostle Paul. For everybody—the unknown Christian and the man who is prominent in the kingdom of God—receives exactly the same amount when the ultimate orders are given out. Each receives the same operating capital for his Christian life and each receives the same command, to trade with it.

Of course it is true that there are wide differences of gifts and talents among those who are in the church of Jesus Christ. And it certainly is not merely glorification of men to say that Paul and Augustine and Luther were unusual people. They received much and we cannot compare ourselves with them.

But here our parable makes it impossible for us to talk ourselves out of it by simply pointing to our meager powers and saying, as we so often hear it said, "After all, as individuals we are merely helpless atoms in the universe." Or we see how the process of technical development, operating according to its own laws beyond the control of our initiative, is tending more and more to automation and how this is making leisure time *the* problem of coming society. The periods of leisure time that result are in one respect desirable social goals, but in another respect they are sources of anxiety. What can a man do with his time and his leisure if he doesn't know what to do with himself? But what can we do *in order that* he may again learn what to do with himself? We would have to be able to transform man totally and from the inside to prepare him for this coming development and prevent him from ruining himself with boredom, anxiety, noisy escape, music, and the search for amusement. But how *can* we transform him inwardly? Who are we to say such a thing? After all, we ourselves are merely drops of oil in the big machine. It would require the spiritual power of a Luther or an Isaiah to reset the foundations and bring about radical changes. We are too small and untalented for that.

But this is just what we cannot say if we read this parable aright. For here the Lord is telling us that in the last analysis all of us receive the same. Tom, Dick, and Harry receive the same as Paul and Luther did. In other words, when it comes to the things that matter God treats all his children alike. At the very point on which everything depends the great people have no advantage over us. The little girl who says her bedtime prayer and commits her doll to God's protection has just as much as Luther had when he uttered his prayer at Worms or Bodelschwingh when he wrestled with God for the lives of his children sick of diphtheria.

Well, what is this pound which is the same for every servant?

I shall try to illustrate what this is about by means of a literary example. Knut Hamsun once said to his wife in an hour of despair, alluding to a story of the sea, "Man overboard! That's what God says, and then somewhere another man goes down. That's what God says. That's how meaningless everything is. And life is so short. So one must not take it too seriously."

There you have the pound that is committed to us presented in reverse, like a photographic negative. This is precisely what God does *not* say. No, all of us, you and I, not only the great in the kingdom of God, have a name, and God calls us by name. We are known. Because Jesus Christ died and rose for us we are no longer nobodies. When a man sheds his blood for somebody he also knows him, for he is infinitely precious. So we are *not* simply nameless little people; we are children who are known and loved. And this name, the name we bear as children of God, *this* is the pound. And even though I should have no more than an attic room in a poorhouse or languish forsaken in a Siberian mine, not even the venerable patriarchs and noble prophets could have a greater name than mine.

And there is something further connected with this. Anybody who has once learned and experienced the fact that he possesses this noble name and is thus valued by God also knows that his neighbor, his colleague, his washerwoman, the refugee from behind the Iron Curtain, also has this name. It was of all of these who live in loneliness and in the shadow that Jesus was thinking when he cried out, "It is finished!" They too bear a royal name.

Must I not look at my neighbor with completely new eyes when I realize this? Will not the scales suddenly fall from my eyes, and will I not see him in a new light?

This knowledge that there are noble children of God all around me, this is the pound I am to trade with. Here I face task after task laid upon me by my Lord during his absence. And here too is where I fall down. A great multitude of people troop past me in the course of my life, all of them directing questions to me, all of them representing a task for me. There are the people with secret troubles: my sick neighbor, the stock boy in my company, the rowdy in my class who almost brings me to despair; the rock-and-roller with his sideburns and his vapid, pomade-slicked emptiness, the joy-starved butterfly of a girl, beating her wings against the window of her poor, gray prison of a life in search of some small ray of meager, dubious pleasure; all the scapegoats of our satiated, superficial society. They all have chains, hidden or plain to be seen; they are all crying for redemption, and in every one of them—even the most deplorable figures whom it is so easy for me to feel superior to—there suddenly appears the Saviour, hungry, cold, imprisoned, naked. He is not ashamed to be their Brother.

Is not this knowledge I have concerning my fellow man a tremendous endowment, a pound which must still spur me to action today? Now that my eyes are opened, can this secret I know about my neighbor ever give me a moment's rest?

This, then, is the pound the Lord has given us to trade with and invest. This is what we are to take and then go right out into the thick of the world and let this thing that has been entrusted to us do the work. What have we done so far with this pound of ours?

We now take a look at the various kinds of servants and we do this again with the unspoken question: In which of them do we find ourselves portrayed? For, as we have observed repeatedly, we shall read the parables aright only if we read them as a piece of autobiography.

First there are the *good* servants who did their work and made a large profit. It appears to be characteristic of these good people that they were not thinking of rewards or bargains when they went to work as they did. Nor, indeed, had the master promised them any such thing. But even common sense would have prevented them from speculating upon any great reward. After all, a man can't do much splurging on a pound (say about twenty dollars). And even so this small bit of capital did not belong to them, nor would the profits they might gain from it be theirs. They were given to understand that the master would demand of them the proceeds of their work. They were not independent, not autonomous, but simply employed servants. The master was not enlisting the aid of his servants to establish life insurance which they *themselves* would enjoy and of which they would be the beneficiaries. On the contrary, he was building his kingdom; he was, as it were, financing this kingdom through their work.

The foolish servant was therefore quite right; he saw that all the profits would be invested in the master's political schemes. When the servants contributed their work to this enterprise this would mean disinterested, unselfish service. Certainly not much would return to their own pockets. And besides, they would always have the secret fear that this so-called "kingdom of the Lord" was only a pipedream, a chimera, a utopia, and that therefore all their work was for nothing after all.

And yet they *did* go to work. Why? Well, they did so quite simply because they were faithful. We can explain this action on the part of the servants only if we assume that they were counting on their master's faithfulness, that what they said to themselves quite simply and positively was this: "Our master, whom we know, will not leave us in the lurch." Therefore they themselves would be faithful.

I believe that we have every reason to prick up our ears at this point, for this touches our own situation. For surely nobody ever became a Christian to make profits. We could often make far greater profits without Christ, for then we should have a more flexible conscience. Then we could be quite easy in our minds and clothe ourselves in purple and fine linen like the rich man in the parable we have already discussed. We could feast sumptuously every day with never a Lazarus to accuse us and embarrass us with the question as to why we are living in luxury instead of giving him the bare necessities. For then we still would not have seen in the face of Lazarus and the refugee, in the faces of the homeless, neglected children, the pale, wan face of our Saviour, the face that gives us pause. Without this Lord we could let ourselves go.

But these were the very people, the people who acted simply out of loyalty and faith and asked nothing for themselves, to whom the Master responded with princely generosity. For two hundred dollars earned, they were set over ten cities; for one hundred dollars earned, over five cities. All this is, of course, "only" a parable. But it may give us some idea of how this Lord repays his servants. He did not say to his servants, he did not say to us, "You will receive this much or that much." He did not speculate upon the servants' self-interest and say to them, "You will get the top positions in my cities. I will see to it that you get moral and social prestige as Christian personages. You can count on my not being stingy!" No, there is nothing like this at all in the parable. Its one concern is that this Lord's commission be carried out without any ulterior motives and that his business be administered not for our own profit but for this Lord's advancement.

This again must be seen in very practical terms. Applied to our situation, it means that when we get up in the morning we servants will commit the coming day to this Lord. It means that we will serve him by resolving on this day not to hate but to love, not to look upon our fellow workers as merely human material but as our neighbors, not to seek our own prestige but to act unselfishly and impartially.

But it is just when the servants act and live thus in commitment, in service, and therefore in the name of Another, that they begin to experience the generous liberality of their Lord. Then—that is, not until later, almost as an afterthought—they begin to realize that it has been *rewarding* to be in his service. Then they begin to see that there are altogether new forms of happiness which this Lord knows how to bestow: new friendships, beatitudes of the heart, a new climate in their life. They will see that it is simply a good and wonderful thing to be close to this Lord and in his company find totally new perspectives opening up in their lives.

The splendor of the cities committed to them will be far less important than the fact that now they are the viceroys of the Lord and therefore among those closest to him and thus will always have access to him and be able to speak to him and tarry in his presence at all times. Their reward is that in the end the Lord will receive them with honors, that they will be privileged to speak and to live with Jesus forever. For heaven does not consist in what we shall receive, whether this be white robes and heavenly crowns or ambrosia and nectar, but rather in what we shall become—namely, the companions of our King, who then will always be able to see him and be near to him as to a brother, no longer seeing through a glass darkly, no longer living under the shadow of the Cross, but praising God with never a tear in our eyes.

Then, finally, there is still the third servant, the man whose life was a failure, the man who failed the Lord. In a vote we took around our family table everybody, both children and adults, felt that this man in our parable was treated rather badly. One of them said, "For me there has always been something pathetic about this figure. He is the man who is resigned, the melancholy man who says to himself it's no use working for this master anyhow." But still there is something touching about his trustworthiness. The way he carried the coin about with him in his handkerchief, well, there is something in that too. The master dealt all too harshly with him.

The fact is that it is not easy to interpret this figure. Of the three he is certainly the most interesting, but also the most complicated. If I see it aright, there are two features that determine the character of this man.

In the first place, he is the typical observer, a man who sees everything from the outside. He observes and analyzes the way things go in the world and declares: God is hard and unjust; he is only a personification of unpredictable fate. He wants to reap where he did not sow. For example, he wants to reap *faith*. But what does he give me to go on, what does he give me that anything like faith should be able to grow in me? When I look at life (he argues) it's very hard for me to believe that Someone is thinking higher thoughts about us and that there is a God of love. When four small children lose their mother because of a drunken driver, where is there any meaningful guidance in that; where is there even the slightest note of love in that? And how about history as a whole? Don't you find there the reign of brutal self-interest or perhaps nothing more than the cold autonomy of process, like that of technical development, for example? Or look at the *church,* with all its dubious human qualities and its impotent phrasemongering, is that a sign to strengthen a man's faith? How can God expect to reap faith when he sows so little *reason* for faith? "Yes, where are you going to get it without stealing?" says St. Joan of the slaughterhouses in Bert Brecht's drama. "Gentlemen," she says, "there is such a thing as moral purchasing power. Raise the moral purchasing power and you will also have morality."

This is the way the third man in our parable thinks too. And in resignation he says, "Nothing doing. This Lord should first raise the purchasing power of religion; he ought to give us some proofs of the Spirit and his power; then he would get some religion, then he would get our faith."

But this resignation is not his only motive. "He's not a book by logic wrought, but a man with contradictions fraught." For without being very consistent he allows himself to be influenced by another point of view. He *preserves* what he has received. He carefully saves it. Thus in some sense he recognizes the existence and the rights of his lord.

If we apply the parable to real life, this obviously means that there is some kind of God (that is, this Lord). He exists. One must recognize that there is a higher being. The relationship of lord and servant, God and man has its legitimate place in life. We can't get along without religion and faith. There has to be some kind of metaphysical foundation if man is not to be left to the mercy of his bestial instincts. What would we have to oppose to the East, this man would probably say if he were living today, if we did not at least have a Christian philosophy? I personally cannot have anything to do with this Lord, but there is no doubt that the Christian enterprise must continue. The institution of the church is indispensable. We must have a Christian ideology. As for myself, I can't be active in a cause that I don't know what to do with, but I can at least be a conservative. I can preserve the Christian tradition. I can submit to a church wedding and send my children to Sunday school. I can take a Christian point of view. I can wrap my religion in my handkerchief and conserve it.

It is worth noting not only that Jesus radically rejects this position but also the arguments by which he does so. He says, "I will condemn you out of your own mouth, you rascal of a servant." "Out of your own mouth"—this obviously means: I am now assuming your position and meeting you on your own level. You say that you feared the Lord. and therefore you took him seriously. (For, after all, what a man fears he usually takes seriously!) But this is just what you did not do, you conservative Christian. If you took the Lord, if you took *me* seriously, you would have fought against me. My unhappy servant Nietzsche took me seriously when he dared to live his life in the dark and icy desert of a world in which God was dead. Gottfried Benn also took me seriously when he admitted that he was encompassed by the trumpets of nothingness and then persevered in his despair. If you had taken me seriously you would have flung your pound away. You would have cried out, "I protest against the Lord who wants to reap where he has not sown! I protest against the Lord who ignores my religious purchasing power and yet expects me to believe!" But you, you conservative Christian, you wanted both at once: you said no to me and yet you weren't willing to burn your bridges. You weren't willing to give up the ultimate insurance you thought I might provide for you. You went only halfway; you were lukewarm. You see, that's why you did *not* take me seriously at all.

There are really only two ways to take a thing seriously. Either you renounce it or you risk everything for it. Either you fling away the pound or you use it and trade with it. There is no third choice. The kind of Christian who is merely conservative and those who want only the Christian "point of view"—these people want this third choice, which doesn't exist. Throw your Christianity on the trash heap, or else let God be the *Lord* of your life; let him be that in dead earnest; let him be someone from whom you receive each day meaning and comfort, a goal for your life, and marching orders, but don't wrap him up in your handkerchief! You can't wish to conserve something that has to do with the very nobility and downfall of your life. Here you can only curse or fall to your knees.

It is well worth noting that, according to these words of Jesus, it is precisely the conservative Christians who produce this caricature of God which is presented by the third servant. Involuntary caricatures are based on a lack of knowledge.

And this brings us to the last secret concealed in this parable.

If, like this servant, we propose merely to *observe* the world and its events and God's role in these events we shall get nowhere. If there is one thing that is certain it is this: it is impossible to "know" God by saying that first we will observe life and analyze history and then, in case we should happen to find him in this way, we will take him seriously, be active in his cause, and make him the standard of our life. It is just the other way around: only he who takes God seriously ever knows him at all. Nobody else ever knows him.

But how is one to take him seriously if one knows nothing about him?

My answer to that would be this: One should deal with God in exactly the same way that the master dealt with his servant. The master said to him, "I will condemn you out of your own mouth." He is saying, "I am meeting you and discussing this on your own level." In exactly the same way we should say to God, "I will convict you out of your own mouth. I shall take your own words and they will either overcome and convince me or I shall beat you with them and show up your absurdity. These are your words, 'Cast all your cares on me, for I care

about you.' Very well, I'll do it and try it at least once. I have cares
and anxieties; I am anxious about tomorrow and about next week. But
for once I will not read my daily and weekly horoscope and instead I'll
pour out my fears before you. I'll put you to the test, O God. You
ought to be worth an experiment to me. I shall see whether this (real
or imaginary) hand of yours will really bring me through tomorrow
and next week. I'm going to find out for myself whether you really do
smooth out the rough places on the road, whether you really will be
my rod and staff in the dark valleys, whether in those darkest moments
of all, when I can see neither bridge nor road, neither shepherd nor
staff, I shall lose my trust in your guiding hand."

Taking God seriously means taking him at his word and giving him
the chance to act the way he has said he will act. We can never receive
anything with closed fists or drooping hands. We must at least stretch
out our hands and "open our mantle wide" (Luther). Perhaps we
shall even have to pray in this wise: "O God (if there be a God), on
the strength of thy word (if thou didst speak it), I pray thee (if thou
canst hear), forgive my sin, be with me in my fears, comfort me in
loneliness, show me my neighbor, make my heart burn with love; and
in every time, good or bad, the high points and the bitter, empty places
in my life, let me feel thy *hand,* reaching out for me and guiding me,
lifting and carrying my burdens, stroking away the care that marks my
brow, and making death itself easy to die, because my heart can rest
in thee. Tomorrow I shall rise and trade with my pound for thee and
serve my neighbor *as if thou didst exist.* Then shalt thou break the
silence and suddenly be near to me. Then shalt thou say: Well done,
good and faithful servant; enter into the joy of your Lord!"

That's the way it is with God. "When we listen, God speaks; when
we obey, God acts."

So let us give him the chance to speak and prove himself. "Him who
comes to me I will not cast out," says Jesus Christ. That's his word and
he died for it. So seriously did he take us. He deserves to be given a
chance.

XIII

The Parable of the Cost of Building a Tower

Now great multitudes accompanied him; and he turned and said to them, "If any one comes to me and dares not hate his own father and mother and wife and children and brothers and sisters, yes, and even his own life, he cannot be my disciple. Whoever does not bear his own cross and come after me, cannot be my disciple. For which of you, desiring to build a tower, does not first sit down and count the cost, whether he has enough to complete it? Otherwise, when he has laid a foundation, and is not able to finish, all who see it begin to mock him, saying, 'This man began to build, and was not able to finish.' Or what king, going to encounter another king in war, will not sit down first and take counsel whether he is able with ten thousand to meet him who comes against him with twenty thousand? And if not, while the other is yet a great way off, he sends an embassy and asks terms of peace. So therefore, whoever of you does not renounce all that he has cannot be my disciple."

—LUKE 14:25–33

We can hardly listen to this remarkable and in many respects harsh account without running into a certain confusion. How often we have heard the stories: the story of the Saviour of sinners, the good physician, the worker of miracles, the shepherd of souls. How often we think we really know him, and how readily forthcoming are the conclusive catchwords and formulas with which he is described: love, goodness, compassion, infinite patience, and all the rest of the pious phrases. Then suddenly we encounter some saying or scene in his life which is so strange and intractable that it simply cannot be fitted into any of these ordinary formulas and at the same time offends us as if we had never heard of it before. This life of Jesus is like a diamond whose facets glisten with familiar and unfamiliar lights, sending out to our wondering eyes mysterious rays in ever-new refractions.

This parable has something of this strange unfamiliarity.

Ordinarily, Jesus strikes us as being attractive, the man with the shepherd's voice calling out for the lost, the man who never wearies of describing the glory of all that awaits us if we come to him—security, peace, new life, a free life. Ordinarily, he calls "Come unto me!"—and here he says, "If any one comes to me and does not hate his father and mother and everything dear to him, he cannot be my disciple." Whoever puts his trust in me must declare his mistrust of all others. Instead of pleading, he repels, and actually warns us against himself. Instead of saying, "I give you *eternal* life," he says, "Count what it will cost you in *this* life and consider whether you are equal to my discipleship." Instead of inflaming, he pours on cold water. Instead of encouraging a person to give up his former way of life, he instills a fear of making the great leap. How can we reconcile all this?

This constant alternation of intimate nearness and estranging enigma doubtless has a deeper meaning, about which anybody who has been long in the company of Jesus can tell some amazing things.

We men have a tendency to cultivate certain favorite ideas. For example, we are quite agreed that Christianity is a religion of "love" and "humanity." It does us good, living as we do in the midst of the struggle for power, the struggle with our competitors, the dreary round of the daily treadmill, to know that there is one court in the world where tenderness rather than harshness counts, where love and the heart rather than accomplishment and reason prevail. How many people there are who need something like religion as a counterbalance for the dreariness of their everyday life! For many people that quiet, faraway figure of the Saviour is a comforting memory which they would like to rescue from their childhood days and keep in their empty adult lives, a memory that can emerge with an elemental power, say, at Christmastime.

Why do we love a writer like Wilhelm Raabe? Doubtless it is because here in a world which the author sees in a quite modern way as a world of anxiety, boredom, and emptiness, there appear such comforting, motherly, inwardly shining characters as Mother Claudine in *Abu Telfan,* Cousin Schlotterbeck in *Der Hungerpastor,* the old woman in the invalid's home in *Der Schüdderump,* or Phoebe in *Unruhigen Gästen.* To know that there are such characters in this often very depressing world, such points of light in the gray landscape, is a comfort and a source of strength. So for many people this Jesus of Nazareth is a figure which, to be sure, does not really sustain their lives, but nevertheless gives some comfort because of the fact that someone like him ever existed. For *once,* at any rate, there existed a man who loved. Once in the world there was someone in whom our yearnings took human shape.

But this figure which the heart engenders from its wishes and its dreams is not Jesus of Nazareth at all. It is a dream, a bubble that dissolves and vanishes when the chips are down. In how many a bomb shelter did not this dream of Jesus fade away into a vapid sentimentality and give way to the dreadful specter of death. In how many cases did not that gruesomely beautiful memorial in the Ohlsdorfer cemetery in Hamburg, with its figure of Charon, the ferryman of the Styx, and the despairing, vacant stares of those he ferries across the dark stream to Hades, express more clearly and more truly the situation and the attitude of men than does the Cross of the Nazarene.

Now, just because all this is so, Jesus is constantly wrenching us out of this self-made dreamworld. Just because this is so, he repeatedly becomes an enigma to us, in order that we may listen to what he himself says and perhaps be offended at him, but in this listening and in this offense penetrate more deeply into his mystery. We should not go on being dreamers but rather become realists who discover the *real* Jesus. For it is not our dreams that make us free and new but only this real Jesus. Therefore we need repeatedly to be astonished, oftentimes even chilled, by this Figure, who is so completely different from what we make him in our dreams and fantasies. Every enigma of his person that we manage to come to terms with thus brings us a bit farther away from ourselves and a bit closer to him. This is probably also the secret of Jesus' fondness for the enigmatic style of speech. So now we shall consider the enigma that lies behind this parable of the building of a tower, behind these words that warn instead of invite, that separate instead of linking us closer together.

In the first place, it is an astonishing fact that Jesus actually went out of his way to offend and antagonize the mass of people who followed him. After all, he had set out to win the world back to God and bring back to his Father the multitude of the lost and broken, of those who had become unfaithful and therefore unhappy. And, setting out to do this, he had something like success. The people crowded about him in shoals, they hung upon his lips, he impressed them and a gleam of new hope was kindled in the despairing eyes and care-marred faces of thousands. If these masses could be committed to this Man, the blaze that would thus be kindled would spread like a prairie fire among them all and beyond them to many others. Then the old, lost world could be reduced to rubble and the new, redeemed world rise upon its ruins.

But, strangely enough, Jesus renounced every kind of mass influence of the kind that suggests itself so readily to our own time. He refused to use the power of suggestion and the torch of popular enthusiasm. Rather, he challenged men to cast up a balance and make a sober estimate of the cost.

Why did he do this? Or perhaps we should first ask another question: What were the crowds of people looking for in Jesus?

Even people who pay little attention, in either their speech or their life, to the fact that there is a God, have a curious propensity for keeping some kind of connection with the holy, even if it be only by a very thin thread. They may go into a church perhaps to enjoy a bit of organ

music or liturgy, or, if they are in the military services, they are glad
to have a Christian or a chaplain in the company, even though they
make no use of his message. It is as if they would like to feel that they
have touched the horns on the altar with one little finger. They are not
quite willing to be totally submerged in a godless world; they want to
keep open a view to one very, very small star.

But in this crowd that follows Jesus there is, of course, still another
sort. These are the people who travel, so to speak, on a double track.
On Sundays they are glad to attend a service and listen to a sermon.
They may even be stirred by it momentarily. But as soon as they are
back at the shop, the machine, or the office on Monday, it is as if they
had turned a switch. There they look upon the others around them only
as associates or competitors, not as neighbors in whom Christ meets
them. There they strive for proficiency and success, with never a
thought of whether or not God is putting his blessing on their work.
There, after all the rush and work, they go chasing after diversion,
never stopping to think that a man really finds re-creation by compos-
ing himself and facing the question: Where am I, and where is all this
taking me after all?

Jesus sees all these people gathered around him. You and I, we are
among them too. And he sees that these people are unhappy and peaceless. Why are they so? Simply because their hearts are so divided. They
want a little bit of God. And this little bit of God is just enough to
bother their conscience and deprive them of their unconcern. They
want a bit of eternity, but not so much that it may seriously disturb
them or cause them to make a radical about-face. And it is just this bit
of eternity that makes them lose their equanimity. Anybody who wavers
back and forth between God and the world, who wants to carry water
on both shoulders, who wants to be partly devout and partly a worldling, is always sure to be unhappy. On the one hand, he can no longer
hate, love, enjoy himself, or cheat with a whole heart, for in him there
burns the tormenting question: Where do you stand and what does all
this you are doing look like in the eyes of God, what is the meaning of
it after all? But, on the other hand, he cannot pray with a whole heart
either. He can never know the blessedness of being rapt in communion
with God and tasting the peace of eternity because he is clinging much
too tightly to all these other things, because while he is praying he is
already thinking of the work he is about to do, or the worries his business causes him, or the meeting he has in the evening. A little bit of
God and a little bit of eternity are always dangerous, for then something begins to bore and to burn down inside of people and make them
restless.

When we are only half-Christians we often feel a kind of envy of the
thoroughgoing worldlings. They have no inhibitions about brushing
aside an undesired competitor. They do not bother themselves with

such sentimentalities as being concerned about the plight of our brethren in the East and devising ways and means of helping others and contributing time and money for them. They get over a bit of tax chiseling or a little adultery without too many bumps and bruises on their conscience. But we—that is, we half-Christians—have our inhibitions, scruples, and troubles in our conscience with such things. We can no longer be tough, red-blooded sinners like these others, but we also are not saints who have at least exchanged for sin the higher joys of peace with God. We have neither, in the proper sense, and this is our trouble. This is also the reason why we half-Christians feel so uneasy. We are always running with half-steam.

This is why great theological thinkers of the Middle Ages said that half-Christianity always led to dejection (*acedia*). Indeed, they said that depression always had its roots in such a divided heart. Only the simple and the singlehearted are happy. For only the singlehearted man has a clear direction, a clear goal. And only he has a whole, unbroken, unambiguous Saviour. The man who wants only a bit of God always finds God to be only a brake, an impediment, a pain. But he who wants God wholly learns that he is the source of power, that he gives a man freedom and verve, that following him is the most joyful thing in the world because he frees a man from all the things that tempt and torment the halfhearted and tug and toss them to and fro. If a man is having a struggle with the shadows of sadness and depression he must ask himself whether the reason may not be this division in his heart.

Now perhaps we understand what Jesus' intention was in demanding of us such a radical decision.

At first sight this seems harsh and implacable. But it is only the sternness of a physician who tells a man: "Only a radical operation will help you. If I do not cut deeply enough into the flesh now I shall only be doing a superficial and temporary patch job and in a few weeks the disease will break out again in fresh growths." So, by his very radicality, Jesus' intention was to free us from this confounded dividedness. He says to us, "If you want to follow me and if you set any real value on what this discipleship gives to you, then you must also make a radical change in your life. Then you must say good-by to many things to which you cling. If you do not, you will only be a man who has been scratched by Christianity and is constantly chafing his bruises. Then you might better have remained a tough pagan." Jesus wants no halfway Christian. He wants a man hot or cold, but not lukewarm.

Can we really imagine that he died on his cross for a few such scratches and for the flimflam of respectable Christianity? He wants to bring us on to the straight road to the Father in order that we may get back to his heart. In no case does he want people who do nothing but run around in circles, people who want the Father but won't let go of the devil· and therefore get nowhere. When Jesus is as stern as this saying shows him to be, this is really his mercy. When he takes something from us he does so only because he wants to give us more, nay, *everything*.

But if this leaves us discouraged and we say, "Then to follow after this Lord is certainly a drastic cure, an operation so radical as to make a man shudder," we shall perhaps not be far wrong. Can we seriously think that the heavy bombs in our life can be disposed of with a little finger? But despite the pain of this radical operation, we should rejoice all the more over the release and the happiness that come in that moment when the pricking stones are removed from our conscience.

So it does these people no good at all simply to gather around the Lord in crowds. They must decide whether they want to be disciples or merely hangers-on and nominal Christians. The mere hangers-on, the fellow travelers are always the ones who are duped. They would do better to stay away altogether.

Now perhaps we understand why Jesus is so severe. And yet a certain offense may remain as we hear the Lord go so far as to say, "Whoever does not *hate* his own father and mother and wife and children and even his own life cannot be my disciple." How can the man who demands that we love our enemies at the same time require that we hate those closest to us?

But it is this very contrast that challenges our attention and suggests that here Jesus meant to convey something quite specific when he used the word "hate" and therefore intentionally chose a strong, alarming word—as one might turn on a siren, with its unusual, almost shock-producing sound, in order to call attention to a danger.

And this is just what Christ is doing here—ringing the alarm to call our attention to a threatening danger. This is what he is saying:

"Just try examining your whole life and the various relationships in your life from the point of view of what brings you closer to me and what separates you from me. This general review of your life will reveal some astonishing things. You may think that it is only what is generally called 'sin' that is preventing you from becoming a real disciple, the big and the little immoralities in life, the little fibs, the little lazinesses, the little grudges and unkindnesses. Ah, perhaps you are moral people who are on guard against such peccadilloes. Perhaps you are people who believe in the maxim, 'Do right and fear no one.' But don't you see that the devil, instead of making a frontal attack at the point of your morality, has organized a clever maneuver and is attacking your flank or your rear where you least expect it?"

Would it ever occur to me that the devil could use the love I have for my child in order to separate me from God?

Yes, you heard me aright; I mean my love for my child. Of course I am aware of the retorts which are now on the tip of everybody's tongue. Naturally, we are inclined to reply, "After all, God gave me my child. When I love my child, this is naturally the right thing to do; it is impossible that this should separate me from God."

This sounds altogether plausible. But yet it is a bit more complicated than that. How do I really love my child? (Naturally, I could just as well say: How do I really love my wife, my husband, my friend?) I may love my child with a kind of natural, doting fondness, with a basically compulsive egoism which must give vent to maternal and paternal feelings. I may pet and feed and clothe my child well. The child may get everything it wants. But have I ever given a thought to that child's spiritual life? Have I prepared it to meet the powers of sin, suffering, and death? Have I brought it into contact with the Lord who will bring it through these trials? In my prayers and my thoughts do I bring that child each day to him who gave and entrusted it to me?

Once I consider these questions self-critically I quickly discover whether my love for my child brings me closer to God or leads me away from him. Here, for example, is a mother who loves her child with this kind of doting affection—with what might be called an elemental maternal instinct. If that child is taken away from her, say in a traffic accident, in that moment she will only be able to cry out in protest, "How can this so-called God of love permit such a thing?" Anybody who talks that way has loved his child more than he loves God. Naturally, it is understandable from the human point of view. Who would dare to judge and condemn anybody who did this! But the parent who each new day accepts his child as from God and each day commits it unto his keeping, the parent for whom the really important question is whether his child will one day go the right way and live in the peace of its Lord, that parent will be comforted by God in the very moment of grievous loss and God the Father will be very near to him. For he has loved that child not merely with foolish fondness but "in God," under the eyes of God. What is wrong with the kind of parental love that concentrates wholly on providing food and drink and clothes and education, perhaps even making great sacrifices to do so, and never gives even the remotest thought to what is going on in the mind and soul of a teen-age boy or girl apart from these things?

A young man before taking his own life wrote to me: "You are the only one whom I am telling what I intend to do. You can tell my parents. They will be thunderstruck. They never knew me, despite all their care for me. They think I am a real sonny-boy when I fall with gusto into my favorite food which my mother prepares so lovingly. They think they have fed me, but I am starved. They made a home for me, but I was cold and homeless."

And what does the young man say in the film *Rebel Without a Cause* (the words are put in the mouth of that young actor, James Dean, who died all too soon)? Here we are shown parents who provide their young son with every American comfort in life and quite definitely give a lot of thought to the question of what they can do and expend to promote his physical welfare and qualify him to meet life. But they are quite unaware of what is absorbing and engrossing him. And when he bursts out with the dreadful stress in his life and his unanswered questions, his father says to him, "Just wait, in ten years all that will be over. Then you will think differently about it." But the youth cries out, "I want to know now, *now!* And right now, when I need it, you don't have an answer for me. With all your love you simply let me down. And when I need help, when I'm in despair, you furnish me with exactly nothing." With these words he leaps at his father's throat, chokes him, and then disappears in misery.

Do these parents, or any of these solicitous providers really love? Are they not merely abreacting their maternal and paternal feelings? And in doing so, are they not really leaving those entrusted to them to their own solitude? Are they not abandoning them to suicide, to the fate of weaklings, or to inner or actual vagabondage? And when the catastrophe comes (though in many cases it never goes that far) they stand in court completely bewildered: "I denied myself cigars and food and vacations for him. I dressed like a scarecrow in order to see that he was well dressed. But the mind and soul of my child was always a blank spot on the map of my life; I never really knew him at all."

These are only a few examples of how the devil can poison the very greatest gifts of God, of how he can poison our relationship to the most beloved and closest of persons and make a dividing wall of the very thing that should bind us to the heart of God. There is a kind of love, a kind of sacrificiality and care which does not bring us *closer* to God but rather carries us and the one we care for *away* from God.

An indication of this occurs in the story of the ten lepers. Jesus healed all ten of them. And health and healing are *also* a gift of God of the kind of which we have been speaking. But the great majority did not thank him for it. This means, does it not, that they loved their health more than the Saviour who gave it to them? He was just good enough to cure their wounds for them. As long as they were in misery they ran after him, whimpering and begging him to help them.

How many people pray when things go badly! But as soon as things are better all this pious to-do vanishes. Why? Simply because for them God is only a means to an end. The "end" is to get out of a bomb shelter alive, to get through an operation, to pass an examination, to get well again. When a person does not give thanks for a gift of God one can be dead certain that the gift is more important to him than the Giver, that his life, his children, his success are more important to him than God. But when he sees this in himself he ought to stand back and look skeptically and critically at the greatest and most loved thing in his life and re-examine it—in the same way that he should possibly pluck out and throw away his own eye, the gift of God, that causes him to sin.

Now, one would misunderstand all this if one were to think only of the negative side. Jesus is always positive. He is never one who merely takes beloved persons and things away from us and summons us to disavow this or that person and drop this or that thing. On the contrary, when we surrender something to Jesus he always gives it back to us renewed and transformed. And that means that then we can love these persons and these things "in Christ." But then we shall love them in an altogether new and positive way.

What this means can be illustrated by the salutation with which preachers sometimes address their congregations: "Beloved in Christ." When this is not merely an empty phrase or a mere convention it means something like this: Here I stand before you as a preacher. Believe me, it tickles the Old Adam in me to be able to stand before you in this high pulpit and have you all listen to me. And perhaps after the service you may say, "Ah, didn't he preach beautifully today?" And that too makes me feel good. And because I know myself and this Old Adam in me I know that the devil can take even the love I have for my listeners and the people whose needs I know, needs which have been laid upon my conscience, and so pollute and corrupt it as to make of it nothing more than carnal coquetry. Therefore as a preacher I must pray in the sacristy before the service, as Elias Schrenk used to do: "Sprinkle me thoroughly with thy blood that the adversary may not approach me."

Protected by that prayer, the congregation then becomes a different thing to the preacher. It is no longer an "audience" he sees beneath his pulpit; now he sees people, people for whom Jesus Christ suffered bitter death and whom he purchased at great price, even though they themselves are completely unaware of it. Then he must say in his heart: Now you must call to these people, clearly and urgently, so that they will see what is at stake: that they have an eternity to lose and that Jesus may have died in vain.

Then his vain pseudo love disappears. Then Jesus stands, as it were, between him and his congregation. Then he can really say, or at least think, these words, "Beloved in Christ." Then he no longer needs to say or to think: My dear public whom I love in the flesh.

But only the person who has tried to love another person through Jesus Christ and allowed him to purify and filter the love knows the happiness and the flooding, uplifting power that come with this transposition of the heart. Only simpletons who have no conception of what Jesus means for us can think that we Christians are people who are always having to forgo and give up things, always living under prohibitions, whereas others can live life to the full with all the verve and joy of the carefree.

If they only knew! Not until a man meets Jesus does he see what life

can really be. Only then does he see that peace with God is not dull
stagnation but a soaring, stirring, happy thing. For who would not be
stirred and excited to learn that now even the great and beautiful
things in life, the persons he loves, the joyful beauty of the countryside, the thrill of art, no longer need to separate him from God, because
his heart has been won by him who is more fair than meadows and
woodlands, more fair than men in all the charm of youth. There is
perhaps no other hymn that proclaims so radiantly and festively the
gladsome transformation which brings the creative breath of Jesus
into our life as that hymn by an unknown poet, "Fairest Lord Jesus."

There is one more question that must be touched upon in closing.
How shall we go about counting the cost? Are we actually to make
estimates of what Christianity will cost us, as a man who wants to build
a tower must do or as a king must do before he declares a war?

I suspect that it has already become clear that this cannot be
answered with a simple yes or no. In fact, the first thing we must say is
that anybody who is facing the question whether he is to be in earnest
with Jesus, whether to venture his life with Jesus, should for once in his
life put aside all calculation. For at this point he still has no idea of all
that Jesus can bestow upon him and what happiness it is to have peace
with God and therefore peace in one's own heart. After all, to make an
estimate of costs one must know beforehand the important items that
enter into it. But here a man does not know the important items beforehand. After all, Jesus is not a huckster who ballyhoos his wares beforehand. What he has to offer we receive and experience only if we are
willing to take a chance with him. And the longer we are with him the
more deeply do we grow into his riches.

Naturally, we too will not be able to dodge this counting of the cost.
For we all would like to have some kind of peace. Often we too will
wish for a reconciled conscience. How often atheists or so-called non-
religious people say to a Christian, "I envy you your faith. You don't
need to worry, you don't have the problems we do. You have a boss in
heaven who thinks for you. Or at any rate you are lucky to be able to
believe that there is such a boss."

Yes, we should all like to have the *gifts* that Jesus gives.

But we cannot have these gifts and these riches without the Cross.
We must commit many things to death. We must say good-by to many
things, even though we shall get back a hundredfold what we offer up
for him. But at the beginning we must be ready to sacrifice. This note
rings out even in the midst of Christmas joy:

> And he who fain would kiss, embrace
> This little Child with gladness

Must first endure with him in grace
The rack of pain and sadness.

We come to peace with God only by way of the Cross. Only the man who stands fast and endures here will come to see the open grave and the Easter glory.

We must love the Crucified more than the joy he gives. "Seek first the kingdom of God, and all these things—a happy conscience, a kingly carefreeness, a liberation from the anxiety of life, a new appreciation of people and the beauty of the earth—shall be yours as well." Then we shall see with new eyes the birds of the air, the clouds of the sky, and the winds in their courses. And even the people who give us trouble will be ennobled by the dignity that Jesus gave them when he died for them.

Where Christ is king, everything is changed. Eyes see differently and the heart no longer beats the same. And in every hard and difficult place the comforting voice is there and the hand that will not let us go upholds us.

XIV

The Parable of the Good Samaritan

And behold, a lawyer stood up to put him to the test, saying, "Teacher, what shall I do to inherit eternal life?" He said to him, "What is written in the law? How do you read?" And he answered, "You shall love the Lord your God with all your heart, and with all your soul, and with all your strength, and with all your mind; and your neighbor as yourself." And he said to him, "You have answered right; do this, and you will live."

But he, desiring to justify himself, said to Jesus, "And who is my neighbor?" Jesus replied, "A man was going down from Jerusalem to Jericho, and he fell among robbers, who stripped him and beat him, and departed, leaving him half-dead. Now by chance a priest was going down that road; and when he saw him he passed by on the other side. So likewise a Levite, when he came to the place and saw him, passed by on the other side. But a Samaritan, as he journeyed, came to where he was; and when he saw him, he had compassion, and went to him and bound up his wounds, pouring on oil and wine; then he set him on his own beast and brought him to an inn, and took care of him. And the next day he took out two denarii and gave them to the innkeeper, saying, 'Take care of him; and whatever more you spend, I will repay you when I come back.' Which of these three, do you think, proved neighbor to the man who fell among the robbers?" He said, "The one who showed mercy on him." And Jesus said to him, "Go and do likewise."

—LUKE 10:25–37

Here is a man who wants to argue with Jesus. At some time all of us have discussed questions of faith with others. When a companion, an associate learns that we are among those who have been with Jesus of Nazareth the time comes when he will speak to us about it, whether it be somewhat jokingly or with a serious question. He may say to us, "Now take this business of miracles, surely there's something fishy about that." Or he may say, "You can't prove even to me that there is a God and a life after death."

I have observed that the people who speak this way and ask such questions can be divided into two classes.

Those in the first group are prompted by a real interest and perhaps even a real intellectual concern. When they launch an attack upon faith, when they deny and dispute, they often want nothing more earnestly than to be proved wrong and have their obstacles to faith removed.

The others like to engage in endless arguments, because they know that this is the best way to keep the Lord Christ at arm's length. Possibly they may also think that this is a way of putting him to silence and at the same time punishing his church with contempt. But they never quite bring it off. For at some point or other they have already been touched by Jesus. They have been "winged." And now they argue and talk with the witnesses of this Christ in order to prove to them, and above all to themselves, that it is nonsense to believe in him or that the endless procession of pros and cons in itself shows that this gets them nowhere and therefore it is best not to get mixed up with him. Thus they try to gloss over the wound in their conscience and produce a moral alibi for their unbelief.

I believe that it is to this latter group that the lawyer in our text belongs: "What shall I do to inherit eternal life?"

It is not without significance that the text says he wanted to put the Lord "to the test." So he was probably not very much in earnest about it after all. He may have been trying to get Jesus out on slippery ice. Perhaps he was a spy of the Jewish high consistory. Perhaps he was moved by the dangerous urge to sharpen his wits with some flashy debate and prove to all the bystanders that he was brilliant.

Certainly Jesus had made an impression upon him. The man surely must have seen how at the touch of his hands people were healed, physically and spiritually. He had heard or had observed that an ineffable love radiated from him, a love that quite obviously attracted from their usual haunts the very people whom nobody else cared for: people with loathsome, repulsive diseases, sinners who cowered before the contempt of society, the dejected and dismayed who normally concealed their misery from the eyes of others.

All these people flocked about Jesus, and into their muddled, bungled lives there came a breath that revived and re-created them. Then, too, this Jesus of Nazareth spoke of his heavenly Father as if he were in intimate contact with him, as if each day he came afresh from the Father's presence. This man could grip and stir a person with his eyes and with his words. In any case, one could not act as if he were not there.

Then the inner voice, the conscience, played a trick upon this lawyer. If this man *should* be right, said the inner voice, then a man could not remain as he was. Then he could not go on being merely the blasé theologian, who searched the Scriptures but was no longer moved by the misery of the poor. Then he could no longer be the proud intellectual, who practiced his individualism and had no time for the pleb., the masses, the boring boneheads with their thousand and one uninteresting daily needs and silly sentimentalities. Nor could he go on being the "rich young ruler," who lived his cultured, sheltered life and forgot that not two hundred yards from his villa there were dirty, overcrowded huts and tenements. Nor could he be the priest, who had his servant girl polish up the prie-dieu every day for his devotions but did not know her name or that she had a sick mother. He simply could not go on being such a person—*if* this Nazarene was right.

Yes; what can a man do, reflects this lawyer, not without a certain misgiving and nervousness, what can a man do to get this termite which has crept into one's conscience out again as painlessly as possible?

Quite simply, he says to himself: Everything that has to do with the background and the meaning of life, with God and eternal life, with the problem of conscience and love of one's neighbor—none of this can be proved. Actually, the only things in life that can be proved are the trite things, such as two times two equals four. But if it is impossible to prove it, he reasons further, then there is no need to worry about it and vex one's conscience over it.

In short, the best thing to do is to challenge this Jesus to a debate; this will prove soon enough that he cannot prove anything. After all, I am well trained in philosophy and I have a hundred Bible passages which can be turned and twisted and used to good advantage. And if he tries to catch me and finish me off with the strength of his speech and his ideas, I know all the proper dialectical maneuvers. Besides, I know a few rhetorical tricks and I'll be able to parry anything he has. Then when the whole thing has fizzled out—oh, this lawyer is an old hand at debating!—one will at least have regained one's peace of conscience and everything can be as it was before.

So thinks the lawyer, and as the first move in the game he asks the question: "What shall I do to inherit eternal life?"

There can be no doubt that the question is well chosen; for, after all, it deals with the very meaning and goal of our life. From times immemorial philosophers have racked their brains over this question and the wreckage of thousands of philosophies lies strewn along the road of this problem. So this Nazarene will not be the first to think he has something final to say and that he can put an end to this comedy of errors. It would really be absurd if one did not immediately have a counterargument at hand in case the opponent should make the next move with the assertion: "I, Jesus of Nazareth, am the meaning of your life."

Perhaps the lawyer had even thought of the next possible move. If Jesus were to answer, "You inherit eternal life through faith," he would counter by asking, "Why, then, has God commanded the many sacrifices?" And if Jesus were to reply, "Perform your due obedience and bring the sacrifices which are commanded," then he would say, "Oh, no! Now am I supposed to bring sacrifices? How strange! Just a minute ago you were talking about faith!"

So the lawyer perhaps had worked out the whole maneuver at home in the sandbox. This Nazarene would not get him. It would be interesting to see what the next hour would bring forth. Theological fencing is really for epicures. He is itching to slip like an eel from his grasp if this Jesus should reach out for his soul. He has rubbed his inner man, as it were, with soap. Countless people do this. Any pastor can tell you about these slippery souls.

So he stands there before Jesus with his question. What is it like suddenly to be facing Jesus and having him look into your eyes?

The first thing the lawyer learned, to his discomfiture, was that his opponent was not going to be caught in his carefully prepared net. He did not reply to his question at all but asked him another in return: "What is written in the law?"

I believe that the lawyer must have been taken aback to be interrogated like a schoolboy and have Jesus intimate that he was asking a question the answer to which he should have known long ago. After all, anybody who has grown up among the people of God knows the answer to this fundamental question of life, how one gains eternal life! It does make him a bit ridiculous that Jesus should not respond at all to his little challenge, that he makes no move whatsoever that would give him an opening and allow him to enter a race down the broad avenue of the intellect, but rather reminds him of the Sunday-school sessions of his childhood. And with some embarrassment he proceeds to answer like a schoolboy: "It is written: 'You shall love the Lord your God with all your heart, and with all your mind; and your neighbor as yourself.'"

As he was reciting his Bible verse he may well have had a strange experience. He knew this passage backwards and forwards, at least as well as you and I know a few Bible passages or even a wall motto that we see every day. But curiously enough, we may have heard or read or even recited such a passage a hundred times—let us say, "Faith, hope, love," or "The Lord is my shepherd"—until the time comes when, suddenly, these lifeless words take on something like a soul; they begin to move and come straight at us. The wall motto suddenly acquires eyes and gazes at us. It may happen at the deathbed of a beloved person, so that I am compelled to face the question of how we can ever go on living. It may happen, perhaps, when to a refugee, tossed hither and yon among strange people, looked down upon, dependent upon begging and charity, whereas back home people took their hats off when he went by. Perhaps it happened in an air-raid shelter, when the next second might have pitched us into death or bitter poverty. All of a sudden that long-familiar saying, which lay, covered with dust, in the lumber room of life, underwent a strange transformation. It began to speak, to judge, to comfort. Those words, "Take no thought for your life"—"The Lord is my shepherd"—"O thou of little faith," enveloped us like a great, protecting, motherly cloak and led us, as by a higher hand, through fire and foreign places, giving us solid ground to stand on in the midst of a sea of fear.

So it may have been with this lawyer as he stood there before the eyes of Jesus, reciting this ancient, familiar saying about loving God and one's neighbor—no, not reciting it but rather, now that he was in the presence of the Lord, as each word passed by, slowly passed by, stopped, gazed at him—and then the same thing happened with the next word: an uncanny, haunting parade, an encirclement of words, with which hitherto he had more or less played but which now formed a ring about him and took his breath away.

How easy it was before to say, "God is a God of love." How easily we let such a sentence pass over our lips! It even sounds a bit trite. But just let Jesus stand in front of us and look at us when we say the words and at once this pious little saying becomes an accusation. Then all of a sudden we hear it spoken by the beggar we shooed from the door yesterday; the servant girl we dismissed, perhaps because she was going to have a baby; the neighbor, whose name has recently been dragged through the newspapers because of some disgraceful affair, whom we let know that *we* always walk the strait and narrow path. Suddenly we hear them all speaking it, because this saying has something to do with all of them, not only with the God who dwells above the clouds. For in them the eyes of the Lord himself are gazing at us.

And so it was with the lawyer when he had recited his piece about this so-called religion of love and Jesus said to him, "Do this and you will live," thereby indicating that this was the answer to all his questions.

What the lawyer wanted was to engage in a philosophical discussion of love or eternal life. One could traverse the entire history of thought. Then as now, one could pursue some highly interesting ideas and find out what Plato, what the Old Testament, what Thomas Aquinas and Goethe said about the subject. One could then go quietly to bed, having polished off a few intellectual hors d'oeuvres. But Jesus says, "Don't start by thinking about love, but practice it." Many things can be known only by doing and practicing them.

To be sure, this is no easy matter. It is easier to discuss a thing than to practice it. Being a Bible scholar, being pious and going to church on Sunday, listening to and delivering lectures on love—and perhaps even speculating on whether God's love will not ultimately evacuate hell itself and save everybody—this too is very much easier than to sacrifice an hour today for some poor, helpless creature.

The lawyer realizes this and perhaps is painfully reminded that this very morning he hated and envied an associate because the man was a little more successful than he. The lawyer is badly disappointed that his theological discussion, his educational conversation, seems suddenly to be coming to an end. It is really very awkward and annoying that spiritual things should be so simple, that they should have to do with ridiculous everyday life, with neighbors, friends, peddlers, or any insignificant, colorless employee who happens to come along. *He* inquired about the meaning of life; he presented a sublime subject for discussion—and here he is, sent to the servants' quarters! It's enough to make one weep, or laugh. So one might as well leave. One can't talk to this man from Nazareth. He is very unpleasant to deal with. He is what one might call an unintellectual man; he immediately starts talking about practical things. But at the last moment there occurs to the lawyer an idea of how he might still force Jesus to further discussion and keep away from practice. Perhaps he need not let himself be sent to the servants' quarters after all, but can keep his dignity and remain in the cultivated, intellectual part of the house.

And so he begins to pose problems and raise questions. This too we are familiar with. How often it happens in life that when a man's conscience is touched by the Word of God he very quickly executes a withdrawal. "Is there a God at all? Surely I'm not going to let someone frighten me who perhaps doesn't even exist!" This is what the lawyer is doing here. He says quite simply, "And who is my neighbor?" And by this he means to imply: Now, Jesus of Nazareth, it is a very problematical thing, this question of who my neighbor is. Is he the man in the servants' quarter, or the poor old lady I see going to fetch her milk in the morning, or are there not other people (for example, my customers or my suppliers, from whom I get something in a business way) who may be much closer to me? This is something that must first be determined. But as long as this is not clear (and it never will be altogether clear, he concludes with some relief, chuckling to himself), I am still not obliged to practice love. How can I love when I don't know whom I am supposed to love?

So he feels a bit easier again. As long as a man has some pious questions to ask he doesn't need to act. He still has a reprieve. And a very nice reprieve too, because then many people consider him a seeker for God, a man who thinks seriously. Above all, there is no need to abandon the comfortable position of the theorist too soon. A man can linger for a while in this state of noncommitment. A man doesn't have to proceed at once to restore his broken marriage and beg his wife for forgiveness; he doesn't need to start immediately to become "democratic"; he doesn't need to go right out the next minute and frequent the back streets with their awful smell of poverty.

The lawyer looks at Jesus with eager expectation. Will he be caught in this carefully laid network of problems? Now certainly this Nazarene must himself begin to philosophize. Now surely he will have to discuss the meaning and nature of the term "neighbor," and perhaps the social order, or the relationship of duty and affection, that is, if he is to be considered an intelligent person and taken seriously.

And again it is highly embarrassing that this Jesus once more responds completely differently from what had been expected. He always does just the opposite of what one expects. He tells a story (a tale, an anecdote!). The lawyer may well have felt it to be outrageous that Jesus should answer him with a tale when he was asking a fundamental question. He might permit himself to do such a thing in the Ladies' Aid or in an old folks' home. But to *him?* And yet there was something remarkably compelling about this story The lawyer had not a moment of time to direct his thoughts elsewhere.

"A man," said Jesus, "was going down from Jerusalem to Jericho."

Ah, thinks the scribe, here we go again. "A man," he says. This is no doubt the neighbor whom I asked about. A very generalized beginning, a generalization, one might say. Just any person, not a fellow citizen, not a member of my firm, not my wife, not my child—just any person should be my neighbor? Perhaps even the accordion player on the ferry? Now, this is going to be funny, if all men are going to be treated alike and called my neighbors just because they are men and walk on two legs. This time I won't recite my piece like a schoolboy; this time I'll give him tit for tat!

So there a man lies wounded, Jesus goes on with his story. He has been attacked and he lies there in horrible pain and fever, suffering the dreadful anxiety of dereliction, added to the nervous shock caused by the attack itself. He sees someone in clerical dress coming down the road, also from Jerusalem. Mortal fear can make a person very sharp-sighted and sharp-witted, and like a flash the thought goes through the aching head of this poor creature who has been beaten black and blue: Here is a priest who has just come from the temple! He must have heard or even preached a sermon on loving God and one's neighbor. Thank God that it is someone who is still under the impression of the temple who should happen to come by. He surely will help me.

But in the same moment the priest had seen him too. The wounded man knew very well that he had seen him. But the priest had a different opinion about the concept of the neighbor from that of the wounded man. This is always the case. When we are in trouble we think that everybody who has more money than we do is our neighbor and is obligated to help us. When the refugee lands here with nothing but his suitcase in his hand he at first considers every businessman to whom he applies for a job to be his neighbor. For after all, he thinks, this man has struck it rich in the German upsurge of prosperity, whereas he himself has been a victim of the process. After all, he, the refugee, has had to pay the costs of this historic bankruptcy for others.

After all, he is the one who fell among robbers. Therefore he must be helped. And therefore this businessman is his neighbor. But the serious, solid citizen thinks otherwise. He sees all this distress in the East, the contributions for Berlin, the thousands of aged and sick people who are dumped upon us here, and perhaps even reunification as merely a ball and chain that is going to be hung on him and the whole of Western Germany, and therefore a man can't take any chances. This is a clear, logical objection. The refugee was *also* thinking clearly and logically. But both of them arrive at completely opposite answers to the question of who is a neighbor. This is always the way it is in life. And this is also the first thing that we must realize at this point: The person who is appealed to for help and the person who needs help sometimes have quite different ideas about the meaning of the word "neighbor." The neighbor is a magnitude which is at least as problematical and disputed as the existence of God—even though we can see him, as we cannot see God.

Therefore, if we are to find out who our neighbor really is we must be very critical of our own ideas. For one thing, we people above all who are perhaps still fairly well off must stop and consider whether the other person, the refugee, the widow, the hard-pressed neighbor, does not see his neighbor in us. And whether we really can dismiss him as lightly as we do with the thought and the poor comfort that we already have other obligations to other people.

This is precisely what happened here in the parable. The priest thought to himself: "O God, the poor fellow! Lucky it didn't happen to me." Perhaps even thanked God for it, for he is pious, and God has graciously preserved him from robbers and all catastrophes—from loss of his home, from bomb damage, from the fate of the war widow, and so on. But for goodness' sake, thinks the priest, interrupting his pious reflections, this surely doesn't mean that I have to help this poor fellow now! The same robbers may still be lying in wait a hundred yards away, just waiting to knock me on the head too. And yet—his conscience compels him to reflect—it would be cowardly not to help. After all, God has put this poor neighbor in my way. I have just heard it said in the temple that to be fainthearted is to deny God and sabotage his law.

Under the constraint of this consideration he was about to resolve to go the way of sacrifice for God's sake. Already his hand was reaching for his handkerchief to bind up the man's wounds and, without knowing it, he had already taken a few steps toward him.

But at the last moment there occurred to the priest a saving thought, which at one stroke released him from this painful and hazardous obligation and dispersed these self-reproaches of cowardice. And the saving thought was this question: Who is my neighbor? This fellow whom I don't know at all? This fellow who may well be a rascal or even a drunk who probably ran his head into a tree? My family comes first. If it were only myself, I would sacrifice my life for him. But I must maintain my family, my vocation, and therefore my real "neighbor." It surely would not be obedience, but sinful, if I too were to allow these robbers to do me in. Bad enough that one person should be assaulted. Nobody would be served if this gang were to beat and maim not only one but two persons. Besides, I have all the collection money from the temple in Jerusalem in my pocket. It would be foolhardy of me to allow this money, which belongs to God, to fall into the hands of the robbers. He thought of a hundred other reasons why this man could not possibly be his neighbor. Reasons always present themselves when we want to duck something. Even the worst blockhead suddenly becomes as sharp-witted as a mathematics professor when it comes to finding reasons for getting out of doing something. The road to hell is paved not merely with good intentions but with good reasons.

So the priest passed by on the other side. This is a sign that this pacification of his conscience did not work quite smoothly after all. He made a wide detour around the poor man in order not to see him. For the sight of him might accuse him and take away from him all his good reasons. This is why the rich man let poor Lazarus lie at his door. He denied him entrance into his house, not because he was afraid he would catch his lice or his T.B., but because he did not want to see him. None of us really wants to see. For to look at our neighbor's misery is the first step in brotherly love. Love always seizes the eyes first and then the hand. If I close my eyes, my hands too remain unemployed. And finally my conscience too falls asleep, for this disquieting neighbor has disappeared from my sight. Therefore at the Last Judgment it is our eyes that will be judged first. When Jesus says to the people at the Last Judgment, "It was I whom you met in the naked, the hungry, the imprisoned, and you did not help me," it is highly characteristic that the accused should reply, "Lord, when did we *see* thee hungry or thirsty or naked or sick?" (Matt. 25:44).

Do we really get the point? What they are saying is "We did not *see* thee." And one day the priest too will say this. He will point out that his footprints will prove that he took a wide detour around the wounded man and therefore he could not possibly have recognized this individual, could not possibly have recognized the Saviour. Except that here he is confusing cause and effect. He did not fail to see the wounded man because his path led him too far away from him but because he saw him and did not want to see him and therefore made the wide detour. It is so easy to make the detour and see nothing. It is so easy to slide over the statistics of misery in the press and turn off the radio when appeals are made for help. Why is it that back there so few of us heard or knew anything about the concentration camps and the Jewish programs? Perhaps because we did not want to listen, because we were afraid of what would happen to our world view and our peace of mind and certain conclusions which would have to be drawn? Therefore once more: You and I will be judged by our eyes. There are certain things and certain people I do not want to see. It may be my Saviour whom I have failed to see.

The first commandment of brotherly love is—eye control!

The Levite too passed by on the other side. He may well have indulged in similar reflections. Perhaps he had a lecture on brotherly love to deliver that evening in Jericho. He made some very quick and precise calculations: if I get held up with this poor chap, I'll miss my lecture. If I stop here I would be helping only *one* person, whereas my lecture on brotherhood may touch off a movement to establish a whole Good Samaritan Society. Ergo: the arithmetic proves the case. The devil is always a good mathematician; he never makes any boners in logic. And the Levite, as he engaged in this devil's arithmetic, was completely unaware that he was traveling on two different tracks: that for the sake of his lecture on loving one's neighbor he was letting his neighbor stick in his misery; that he was trying to serve God and at the same time dishonoring him in his children; that he was praying and at the same time spitting in his Lord's face.

Therefore the second commandment of brotherly love is—control of the place where we live our lives. Taking stock to see whether in the house of our life the worship corner may not be separated by only the thinnest wall from the devil's chapel. There are many dwellings in the house of our heart—any number of them. And some mighty crazy things are lying right next to each other in it.

Is it really necessary for me to describe the moment when the *Samaritan* came to the wounded man, that moment when the poor fellow was in utter despair and after all these disappointments had given up all hope? Or must I go on and describe the solicitude with which the Samaritan performed his task? Must I go on and praise his fearlessness as far as the robbers were concerned? Must I point out that his was not merely a momentary compassion, an upsurge of emotion, but that he also made provision for the immediate future of the wounded man, that he made arrangements with the innkeeper and was prepared to take further responsibility for him? And all this despite the fact that he was a Samaritan and had not learned such binding words about loving one's neighbor as had the priest and the Levite, despite the fact, therefore, that he possessed a very deficient theory of love!

There is really no need to go into all this; for the point of the parable is that we should identify ourselves with the priest and the Levite and repent. It would have us remove the blinders from our eyes. It would teach us simply to get to work and do something. For the parable closes with the same words as the first part of the conversation: "Go and do likewise!"

It would be wrong to speculate and brood upon the Word of God before ever setting about doing it. We would have a long time of it and, I am afraid, we shall not be finished with it even at the Day of Judgment if we are going to insist that first we must know all about predestination and the freedom of the will, what happens to those who cannot believe or do not hear the message of Christ, why there must be a Cross of Calvary and the whole doctrine of atonement, and—last but not least—who then is my neighbor. We shall never get any light on all this unless this very day we "go and do likewise."

May I again give you a few altogether practical precepts? You will never learn who Jesus Christ is by reflecting upon whether there is such a thing as sonship or virgin birth or miracle. Who Jesus Christ is you learn from your imprisoned, hungry, distressed brothers. For it is in them that he meets us. He is always in the depths. And we shall draw near to these brethren only if we open our eyes to see the misery around us. And we can open our eyes only when we love. But we cannot go and do and love, if we stop and ask first, "Who is my neighbor?" The devil has been waiting for us to ask this question; and he will always whisper into our ears only the most convenient answers. We human beings always fall for the easiest answers. No, we can love only if we have the mind of Jesus and turn the lawyer's question around. Then we shall ask not "Who is my neighbor?" but "To whom am *I* a neighbor? Who is laid at *my* door? Who is expecting help from *me* and who looks upon *me* as his neighbor?" This reversal of the question is precisely the point of the parable.

Anybody who loves must always be prepared to have his plans interrupted. We must be ready to be surprised by tasks which God sets for us *today*. God is always compelling us to improvise. For God's tasks always have about them something surprising and unexpected, and this imprisoned, wounded, distressed brother, in whom the Saviour meets us, is always turning up on our path just at the time when we are about to do something else, just when we are occupied with altogether different duties. God is always a God of surprises, not only in the way in which he helps us—for God's help too always comes from unexpected directions—but also in the manner in which he confronts me with tasks to perform and sends people across my path.

Therefore the third commandment or counsel for the practice of brotherly love is this: Be flexible, adaptable, maneuverable, and ready to improvise!

We cannot close without mentioning the fact (which, of course, should have been behind every word we have spoken) that it is Jesus Christ who is telling the parable. We hear the parable from the lips of him who is the Good Samaritan of us all, who became our neighbor. When we come to die we can sing, "Thence with joy I go to Christ, my Brother." The noises of the world will be hushed, we shall be left in utter loneliness; even our dearest must be left behind. But then, precisely then, is *he* our neighbor, the neighbor who will not forsake us; for he faced the robber, Death, and allowed him to strike him down in order that he might walk with us down this last bitter passage. And when we suffer some distress in which nobody understands us or anxieties that deliver us to terrible loneliness, there is one who is our neighbor, because on the Cross he submitted himself to imprisonment in the dark dungeon of ultimate loneliness. And when we stand all alone, quivering beneath a sense of awful guilt, which nobody else suspects, which would cause our friends to desert us if they knew about it, then here too Jesus is the neighbor who is not shocked by the dark abyss, because he came down from heaven and descended into the deepest pits of misery and guilt. Jesus loves us and therefore he finds us. And therefore he also knows us. He knows us better than we know ourselves and still he does not drop us, still he remains our friend, our nearest friend.

In this happy certainty we can proceed to act. Who would not wish to do something for him, since he himself has become our neighbor; who would refuse to honor him in his poor and miserable brothers!

Therefore let this last thing be said about loving our neighbor. All loving is a thanksgiving for the fact that we ourselves have been loved and healed in loving; we grow into all the mysteries of God when we pass on what we have received and when we learn by experience that a disciple of Jesus becomes not poorer but ever richer and happier in giving and sacrificing and that whatever of his feeble strength he puts at God's disposal comes back to him in twelve great baskets. For God is princely in his giving and incalculable in the abundance of his mercy.

"Therefore, being engaged in this service by the mercy of God, we do not lose heart."

XV

The Parable of the Wise and Foolish Maidens

"Then the kingdom of heaven shall be compared to ten maidens who took their lamps and went to meet the bridegroom. Five of them were foolish, and five were wise. For when the foolish took their lamps, they took no oil with them; but the wise took flasks of oil with their lamps. As the bridegroom was delayed, they all slumbered and slept. But at midnight there was a cry, 'Behold, the bridegroom! Come out to meet him.' Then all those maidens rose and trimmed their lamps. And the foolish said to the wise, 'Give us some of your oil, for our lamps are going out.' But the wise replied, 'Perhaps there will not be enough for us and for you; go rather to the dealers and buy for yourselves.' And while they went to buy, the bridegroom came, and those who were ready went in with him to the marriage feast; and the door was shut. Afterward the other maidens came also, saying, 'Lord, lord, open to us.' But he replied, 'Truly, I say to you, I do not know you.' Watch therefore, for you know neither the day nor the hour."

—MATTHEW 25:1–13

I wonder whether we men really understand ourselves as well at any point in our life as in the realization that all of us together—Christians and pagans, young and old—are waiting for something? And may not this be the reason why the lights of Advent and Christmas have such a magical attraction for us, even though all of us are waiting for something different? Pascal once said that we really never seek for things; what we enjoy is the search for things. And Ortega y Gasset, employing the illustration of the hunt, makes it clear that we actually do not seek the trophies and the game itself, the real object of the hunt, but that we get pleasure from lying in wait at the blind and from the act of hunting itself.

Even as children we were waiting. At first we waited for the great moment when we learned the ABC's. Then we waited for the first long pants and later for the first job and the first money we earned for ourselves. Then for our life partner and our children. We waited for terrible things and beautiful things: for the wars we saw coming and

170

the peace treaties we looked forward to with fear and hope. And finally we grow old, the children leave or have already left home, our life's work lies behind us, and we are hardly wanted any more or we are not wanted at all. Then we ask ourselves perhaps, when time stretches out before us so strangely empty and the things that filled the daily round are gone: What shall we wait for *now?* What meaning is left in life *now?* Does it have any meaning at all?

In earlier days we waited with Jules Verne for a utopian world that would come to fulfillment in the scientific era. The utopian novels of today are full of terrible visions and Nikolai Berdyaev even goes so far as to suggest that earlier man dreamed of the unlimited possibilities of science, whereas today mankind is concentrating all its efforts upon escaping the utopian possibilities which are now capable of being realized, just because they are so depressing. And here too the ultimate question arises: What do we have to expect? Shall we join Orwell and wait for 1984; shall we join Aldous Huxley and wait for the "brave new world," which may turn out to be utterly hideous? We are beginning to turn around a bit and we find ourselves asking the question: What is awaiting *us?*

This is also true of Marxism. It is waiting for the classless society of social justice. But anybody who studies Bolshevist literature will note that increasingly another question is coming to the fore. When this utopian fulfillment is achieved, then what shall we wait for? Will not history then come to a standstill? Then what means shall we have to crank it up and get it moving again? There are some tremblings going on in the ideological systems of the East. And the source of this trembling is to be found in this one question: What shall we have to wait for when all the human fulfillments have been achieved? The world's hope for the future, the secularist Advent spirit, appears to be threatened. This seems to be becoming a world in which there is nothing to wait for. The lights are going out. To what shores are we really drifting?

But if this waiting, and also this fear that waiting and expectation may someday cease, so profoundly affects our life, if this Advent mood is something that can be suddenly choked out of existence, then we prick up our ears when we hear this parable of Jesus about waiting.

But naturally we are suspicious. We have had our experiences and are quick to ask: Is this another one of those utopias? Or, even worse: Isn't this an old utopia warmed over—a dream bubble that has been punctured, deflated, and gone "pop" just as egregiously as the utopian dreams of the scientific age are vanishing for us today?

Now, even at first glance an essential difference is to be noted. That which we men wait for always relates to conditions that "result" in the course of events or through our efforts: either through natural development (for example, that we grow older, that experience and ability increase, and that we must finally die); or we wait for a particularly favorable constellation of events which we call lucky; or we hope to achieve something through our own efforts. Our utopias and hopes always depend upon a future that is achieved through human power or through the course of events.

But in our parable we find an emphasis completely different from that found in these utopian dreams of modern humanity. Here it is not a matter of something that we men can achieve, nor is it concerned with goals envisioned by our faith in progress. Here someone from the other side comes to meet those who are waiting and expecting. The people who appear in this parable can do absolutely nothing to bring about this meeting. And therefore neither do we see them working and running themselves ragged like people who are trying to achieve some goal by force. On the contrary, they are sleeping (the wise as well as the foolish) because they have no control over the coming of the bridegroom anyhow. And this is a good sleep, a perfectly justifiable sleep, for they know that while they sleep there is Another who is on his way, seeking them.

What are we waiting for, what are we really expecting, when we dare to speak of the coming again of the Lord?

Well, the one thing above all that we are saying is that history will surely arrive at its goal. We do not say this because we think that we men are capable of making our way to the ultimate goal of our life or of history. For the fact is that we grope like children in the dark. Even the statesmen and the men who make history do not know how their calculations will turn out and where the trains will go whose switches they set today. And is it any different in our own lives? But here we receive a message that tells us there is Another who determines this goal, because in his time he will be there, because he will appear on the horizon of the world.

This, I am fully aware, is a tremendous assertion. And it is tremendous above all because, if it is true, then suddenly, beginning right now, our whole life is radically changed. This is astonishing; for normally we are not interested in the distant future but only in how we are going to get along today and tomorrow. The next few pages in our date book are the tough ones. We think about what may become of the political situation in the near future and whether the time will come when somewhere sinister hands will go on fidgeting with a perilous switchboard until suddenly a button is pressed which will touch off the signal for the apocalyptic horsemen. In the words of Jesus, we are "anxious about tomorrow" and "in the world we have tribulation."

But how all this is suddenly changed, if this message is true, this message that tells us that One is coming to us from the other side and that the world's history will end at his feet! When we see what will happen on the world's great New Year's Day, then all the pages of the calendar that lie between are relegated to their proper place.

Pascal once said that it is a glorious thing to ride upon a ship that may well be shaken by storms and tossed by the waves but of which we know that, no matter what happens, it will reach the harbor. This dictum of Pascal stands in cryptic, distressing contradiction to another saying about the sea and its storms—a saying used by Bert Brecht in his *Berlin Requiem:* "Only a ship that will sink and a shoal that does not blink; that's what we must resign ourselves to." Both sayings, that of Pascal and that of Bert Brecht, remind us that in one way or another our life is a venture.

What is a venture? It is a situation in which the outcome is unknown. And which of us, whether we live in a hut or a mansion, really knows how our life will end, really knows what derelictions or what fulfillments still await us? Yes, we live at a venture.

In a proper detective story (and these are always adventure stories) one never knows, even at the next to the last page, how it will turn out. This is precisely what makes it so exciting that often we cannot help taking a peek at the last page in order to bring our pulse back to normal again.

But there is still another, quite different kind of adventure, and this second type can also be illustrated by some literary examples. Whereas the author of a crime thriller obscures the outcome of his story by employing an artful technique, in order to surprise us at the last moment, the greatest writers, and precisely those of the classical periods, tell us at the outset, perhaps even in the subtitle, that their book is a tragedy and that therefore the most brilliant and fascinating character of the drama will go down in the end. This is revealed already on the title page. In Homer's great epics one knows right from the first page what to expect. Then the art of telling the story consists in keeping the interest of the reader despite this circumstance. However, now this tension possesses, so to speak, another nature, another climate. In a detective story one asks, "How will it end?" In a tragedy or a great novel one asks, "What will happen *in order that* the sad or happy ending, which I know from the very first page, may ensue?"

Pascal, I think, had been listening to the Bible when he told us in his metaphor of a ship that God has not made our life a detective story with an uncertain ending, but rather that on the first page (the first page of the *Bible* and the first page of our *life,* when the baptismal blessing is pronounced upon us) he has already revealed what the end will be. He has told us that at the close the Victor alone will be left upon the battlefield and that on the horizon of our little lives and also on the horizon of history itself there stands One at whose feet all the zigzag, circuitous roads of existence will end. Even my little life, lived in this Advent certainty, is an adventure—an adventure of a higher order.

I know that my ship will reach the harbor; I know that the next pages of our calendar contain only the prologue to this grand concluding chapter. I know that even the operation I may be facing, the business crisis I feel is coming, the examination I have ahead of me, the trouble I am having with my child, that all these things will be only stages on the way to this one great point.

It is part of the pleasure of the Christian life, if we may use this rather bold expression, to abandon oneself to this eager expectation, this fascinating interest in how God will go on writing the story of our lives, in how he will fashion the fabric of adventures, whose *partial* endings we cannot foresee, in order to reach that ultimate goal of which we know and are certain. From God's point of view it will all be in harmony with the strict, thematic laws of the fugue. But we shall be running from tone to tone, and, even though we still cannot see the continuity of it all, the next note that God will strike tomorrow will nevertheless be an exciting experience, because we know that a master is seated at his instrument.

So first of all we must learn from our parable what kind of writing, what kind of composition our life is, namely, that we are not living out a detective story, an "atonal" adventure, but that everything is moving on to the finale and that we are adventurers only in the penultimate sense, not the ultimate.

On my voyage to America we had a dog on board, both going over and coming back. And during the long passage I observed both of them very carefully and thought about them. On the voyage over it was a big shepherd dog, which had been entrusted to the ship's company by his young owner since he himself was coming over by plane. The poor beast was shaking with misery. I often patted him and spoke to him gently, but it was no use. He was in a strange world and did not know how his adventure would end. For all he knew his whole familiar dog world had come to an end. No fields, no forests; everything smelled strange and unfamiliar and on every side the world ended at a railing. Beyond was only enemy country; for a dog it was the absolute void. Nor did he have any idea whether this strangeness would ever cease and whether he would ever again see fields and other dogs and smell again the familiar odor of his master. It was quite impossible to make him understand that this strange ship-world was subject to the laws of navigation and that this blue-clad, two-legged being with four gold stripes on his arm who often spoke to him knew the course of the ship and the date when all this would come to an end. The poor dog was condemned to a creaturely form of nihilism. He lived and moved in a void and in endless torment.

On the return voyage we had a different dog on board. And though he was a bit degenerated and his stunted legs were always trembling, he was nevertheless far more confident and content. For he had his mistress, a little girl, with him. He too missed the familiar streets and did not know what was wrong with this strange world. But when his small dog's heart would flutter too anxiously he would turn to his mistress with a pathetic look, a look of animal trust, as much as to say, "As long as you are here it can't be too bad; for you, after all, are a higher being. You surely would not have let yourself in for this abstruse world, which is shattering my whole dog's world view, if it were not to come to an end someday when we shall return again to a sensible world with the proper kind of smells."

Not only out of the mouths of babes, but also from the eyes of dogs, can God bring perfect praise.

Neither do we know the laws of navigation that lead us to this particular experience or that particular suffering. But we know Him who stands upon the bridge; we know the One who waits for us in the harbor. All the metaphors break down when we try to express all that Jesus Christ is for us and we are obliged to resort to paradox: he is the helmsman of the ship and at the same time the man who walks upon the water and at the same time the faithful servant who kindles the lights on the lightship and waits for me in the harbor. Yes, we Christians are adventurers of a higher order. Everything is uncertain, nothing is sure, except this One Man, who is with us in the ship and at the same time is our goal. One look away from him—and our ship becomes an uncanny, alien place, drifting in a void. One look at him—and the strange and alien becomes familiar. We do not understand the navigation, true enough; but we know the Navigator.

Now the wise maidens in the parable are people who live on the strength of that one moment when they will arrive, people who live by the faithfulness of this One Man.

We dare not think of this as meaning that the wise maidens were merely rapt, like Johnny Head-in-the-Clouds, in some distant future and had forgotten all about the present. There is one small feature in our parable that shows us that this is not true, and that is the uncertainty of the time when the bridegroom will arrive. He may come today, or in a month, or within ten years. And it is precisely this uncertainty, says Kierkegaard, that heightens our passion and strains our watchfulness to the extreme. I once studied with a professor whose custom it was to pick out any one of us to give a summary of the preceding lecture. Nobody knew whose turn was next. You can be sure we all paid strict attention. Other professors had a different method. Before the hour began they assigned a student to prepare a report. Then we knew that everything was taken care of. Nothing could happen; it all proceeded according to schedule and you could go on carving your initials or a heart on the desk.

With Jesus we do not know when he will come again or when he will summon us to come to him. We do not know the moment when everything that is so madly important to us—our career, our success, our failure, and our dejection—will vanish. We do not know when he will become the only thing that has any importance to us. Therefore we must be on the lookout and be ready for him at any moment. For every single hour of our life is marked with this one, unpredictable moment when we shall stand alone and face Jesus Christ. If we miss him, if we act as if our life would always go on as it has, if we go on sleeping and muddling through like the foolish maidens, we shall have missed the point of our life.

In our parable a very somber, balladlike note is struck: it is possible to be too late. My last hour is much less important than my whole "existence toward death," the span of life I have traversed up to this last hour. And so, too, the real theme of this parable is not so much the last hour of history (good heavens, that may still be a long way off, and I am still in good shape, a healthy, active youngster!). What is far more important is that the present moment, my work, my life, and also the adversities in my life be determined by this *one* fact, that all of this must one day be confronted by Jesus Christ and that this is the point where it will be decided whether my life has been meaningful or meaningless. The hour of the bridegroom is unknown. Therefore we live in hope, and therefore we are always in extreme peril. Even though in practical life we may be wide awake, always on the ball, and not to be "taken in" by anybody, he may come to us when we are in a semi-conscious state. And what if we have fooled and hoodwinked ourselves in this *one* thing on which everything depends? There is such a thing as being "too late." It may be that in the end God will have to write beneath the story of our life: A remarkable performance, lively, interesting, fascinating—but you missed the point! But by that time the story will have ended and cannot be rewritten.

Now let us look at the waiting of the wise maidens—the people who keep their eyes on the goal of their life—and see what it is like and what is their experience.

And here we must surely be struck by one curious feature of the parable.

What it says is that all of them, not only the foolish but also the wise maidens, fell asleep while they were waiting. And we note further that Jesus recounts this without any criticism whatsoever. In his goodness he knows that his people need rest, and there are even times when he says to them, "Rest a while." After all, the disciples cannot be on the stretch all the time. Nor can we pray all day long or do nothing but think of how soon the Lord may be coming again. We must therefore not think of the waiting of the wise maidens as if they never had another thought in their heads except waiting, praying, and hymn singing. The Christian housewife has to keep her mind on her cooking and the worker must keep his mind on the machine, otherwise the food will be burned and the bolts will go in askew. This is not the way to think of waiting and being religious. In his great mercy Jesus understands this, and therefore he does not measure the wakefulness of our piety and our waiting by the yard. There is no such gauge for measuring our spiritual blood pressure. Jesus lets his people have their rest; they are permitted to sit in the springtime sun and be lazy, without constantly thinking spiritual thoughts and consciously "waiting." And they can also lie down at night and go peacefully to sleep, even though this means they will not be able to pray and sing and wait for eight hours. Perhaps it may actually be a sign of trust in God and real discipleship if we do lie down and sleep peacefully as these maidens did. For the wise ones among them lie down to sleep because they know and are sure that they do not have to force the bridegroom, the kingdom of God, to come. He will surely come and the kingdom will come of itself, even against the will of men. This is expressed in the evening hymns of the church when they affirm that, though we sleep, God is watching and doing his work, that he is the Eye and Keeper of Israel while we poor men take our rest. Rest and quiet, confident sleep may in themselves be a song of praise: Thou art waking and thou art at work. Our fretting and worrying, our impatience, and trying to force the situation cannot accomplish it anyhow, and thou givest to thine own in sleep. All our restless care may cease, because we live under thy care.

So the wise maidens lie down to sleep. They put their lamps in order, they have a supply of oil, and their last thought is of the joy of awakening; for the coming day will bring them nearer to the great hour and God's goodness is new every morning.

May not much of the sleeplessness that plagues us be due to the fact that we do not have this joy and this trust in the "Eye and Keeper of Israel," and thus cannot let ourselves go and relax, but rather we become tense and therefore do not avail ourselves of the merciful privilege of being able to sleep while he secretly prepares his advent. Even our sleeplessness may have something to do with unbelief.

But there are two quite different kinds of sleep. The sleep of the foolish maidens cannot be compared with the slumber of the wise maidens. For the foolish maidens simply grew tired of the endless waiting and dropped off to sleep. When a person waits without hope, simply goes on vegetating nihilistically, he very quickly grows weary, discouraged, and sleepy. And actually, the foolish maidens fell asleep because they had given up hope that the bridegroom would ever come at all, and therefore that there could even be someone who would be the end and goal of life. One can see this from the fact that they failed to provide themselves with a supply of oil for their lamps. This surely would not have happened if they had considered that this bit of concern was worth while, that is, if they had really been seriously counting on the advent of their lord.

Naturally, this sleeping must not be taken literally. It is possible for us to fall asleep while waiting in such a way that we turn to other things altogether and throw ourselves into frantic action. A man can put his expectancy, his hope, his faith, his conscience to sleep by plunging into all kinds of activity, by working "like blazes," by rushing about his business like a madman, and taking every free minute to listen to the radio or to look at the pictures in the magazines—as the people before the Flood did in their way. For they too fell asleep and gave no thought to the coming judgment of God. But their sleep was such that they were highly active; "they were eating and drinking, marrying and giving in marriage." And the same is true of us, who dance around the golden calf of our standard of living and forget why we are here and who is waiting for us. And I am sure that when the Lord Christ returns and his cry, "Sleepers, awake!" reverberates like a peal of thunder over the earth, only the fewest of men will rise from their beds; the majority at their benches and their desks, in the trains and in their cars, in the movies or the taverns, and certainly not least in the churches, will rise up in terror, because they have no longer counted upon this voice of thunder and have turned away from the question of eternity to the order of the day. They will remember perhaps, as the thunderous sound of "Sleepers, awake!" rumbles above them, that one day in their baptism they were dedicated to this invincible, unbreaking Lord. They will remember perhaps that they went to church on Good Friday and year after year lighted the Advent wreath and the Christmas tree in his honor (though they were never quite clear as to why they did it). And then in panic fear, as the thunder peals above them, they will seize upon the light of these festivals they once celebrated. But that light will have turned dark and sooty. They will remember that once in their lives that light had gleamed, that once they took some hesitant steps toward it. But now they snatch at emptiness and darkness. The oil has long since been consumed, and what once was a flickering gleam has guttered into gloom.

So that's the second difference between the wise and the foolish maidens: the first have oil and the others do not. Now what is meant by this oil?

The oil obviously points to the fact that there is something in our Christian life that is constantly being used up and therefore needs to be replenished. And it is not very difficult to discover what it is that needs to be renewed.

There are some Christians, for example, who think that once in one's life one must be converted or join the church, be married at the altar, or decide to pay the church dues. Then everything is finished. Such people strike me as being like a woman who, once she has heard her husband say, "I do," at the altar or in the registry office, says to herself, "Now I've got him. After all, the marriage contract is settled. Up to this time I've always made myself pretty for him and shown him my most charming side. After all, I had to get him first and get him tied. But now that I have the final and official word I can let myself go, neglect myself, and be a frump." But the fact is—as all experienced married people know—that marriage is renewed every day and that each must woo the other so that every day remains the first day of marriage, or the marriage goes to pieces—even if there is no divorce. The dead marriages and the extinguished lamps of love, whose dismal soot is only a sad evidence that *once* a light had burned here, these are far worse.

In exactly the same way the lamps of our Christian life can go out, because the oil has been consumed. I shall mention only one kind of oil which needs to be constantly replenished, and that is prayer. Our prayer life can be consumed like oil, and then suddenly life grows dark. For the person who does not pray is always standing in the dark, because the heavens above him are closed. And therefore he is always under the dominion of fear. And the oil supply of our prayer life can soon run out. It runs out, not only when we no longer take time to pray, but also when we come to the point of merely rattling off the Lord's Prayer or some other prayer. It finally becomes tedious and boring, like a handful of burned-out cinders in which the fire has long since ceased to glow. We say it when we get up and already we are thinking of breakfast or the morning's mail. And soon it gives off more smell than light, and this is a sign that the oil is running down and that there is more soot than flame.

But how does one replenish the supply of oil? This is something that requires consideration, just as the wise maidens considered where they would get the oil and how they would have to go after it and sometimes stand in line for it.

Our spiritual life too is quite simply a piece of *work* to be done, and I am always glad that there is such a thing as the "service of God" and that it is not called the "enjoyment of God."

Fresh oil and a living flame are obtained only by constantly relating one's prayers to everything that occupies and actuates the day's doings. Wherever I am, in bed or on the train or in my car, I must tell God about my joys and also about my cares. I must think about my sick neighbor and also about the associate with whom I am at odds. I can even do this with the individual petitions of the Lord's Prayer, not simply by saying it in a general way but by applying it to myself. I say, for example, "Forgive us our trespasses," and then specify very precisely, just as one specifies in a bill of indebtedness: "Forgive me for constantly succumbing to my sexual impulses. Forgive me for letting myself be pushed around by worries and not mustering the confidence to let thee lead me. Forgive my jealousy and my ambition."

Then my prayers will come alive, because I take my whole life itself into them and in this way prayer finds a "seat in life."

The same is true of the Bible. Its purpose is to be a light to our path, but it can grow dim. This always happens whenever I read it without praying, whenever I fail to keep asking the question, "What is God saying to *me* in this passage?" Whenever I devote myself to it merely as reading matter that must be read for duty and decency's sake, it is soon covered over by the stupidest of picture magazines or the day's news in my morning paper, just as a stronger transmitter drowns out a weaker one.

A person who wants to be a Christian is always and immediately put to work by his Lord. And the promise that God desires to give everything out of pure grace is not for lazybones. The grace of God is not cut-rate goods thrown in for a song, and it is anything but cheap. We have to fight honestly for a quiet hour in our day's work and sometimes we have to get up earlier in the morning. We have to make a list of the people for whom we pray, and we must perform many hard and burdensome tasks if this is what God wants us to do. But all this is abundantly rewarded because this is the way the oil in our lamps is replenished; this is what keeps our Christian life fresh and clear.

So this waiting for our Lord, this bridal waiting with lamps alight, is not a passive thing at all. Waiting does not mean that we are to twiddle our thumbs until something happens. That would be a sleepy, boring business. When the lamps go out for a person he very soon falls asleep. And that means that a person who is not a vital "pray-er" soon becomes a hustling, bustling, empty "doer." And then suddenly he is confronted with the anguishing question: Why do I go on running myself ragged? Where's the sense of it, where's the meaning of it all?

But when the lamps are burning we do not fall asleep so easily. For, after all, the light of these lamps is a gleam of the splendor of that Lord who one day will come in glory. Every vital prayer that comes from the heart is like a blinking signal in the great night of the world, a beacon which we set alight in order that the Lord may see where we are and where he can find us. Every prayer is a sign that we are watching and waiting; and not only this, it is at the same time a light that also keeps us awake and alert and lifts up our heads, because our redemption is drawing near.

It is in this sense that we would light the Advent wreaths and candles, and thus banish all the empty sentimentality. Our wreaths and lights should be forerunners of that glory which is even now setting out to rise upon the darkness of this earth. They should be a sign that we are on the way—on the road, like happy, confident travelers whose hearts are unafraid and before whose lights the encircling gloom retreats.

So when any one of us lights a candle today or in the coming weeks, he ought not to do this mechanically, just because it is the thing to do or because it is so emotionally appealing. Rather let him—I plead with him to do it—let him do it with a thought in his mind, a little sacrifice of his spirit. And the thought I mean and which I commend to you runs something like this: This small candle is only a sign. It points to the light of that harbor toward which I am moving through the darkness. And this little candle is at the same time a question, addressing itself to me: Has the lamp of my life gone out? Am I drifting? Am I cruising without lights in the night—or is there a burning and a shining within me? Am I sending out blinks of light that I may be found of him? Have I (and this is the ultimate question) grasped the meaning, the theme, of my life? Am I on the point of missing it, even though I go on writing the story of my life line by line and day by day? Am I remembering the *theme,* the meaning?

Watch, therefore, for you know not when the fateful hour will come!

XVI

The Parable of the Marriage Feast

And again Jesus spoke to them in parables, saying, "The kingdom of
heaven may be compared to a king who gave a marriage feast for his son,
and sent his servants to call those who were invited to the marriage feast;
but they would not come. Again he sent other servants, saying, 'Tell those
who are invited, Behold, I have made ready my dinner, my oxen and my fat
calves are killed, and everything is ready; come to the marriage feast.' But
they made light of it and went off, one to his farm, another to his business,
while the rest seized his servants, treated them shamefully, and killed them.
The king was angry, and he sent his troops and destroyed those murderers
and burned their city. Then he said to his servants, 'The wedding is ready,
but those invited were not worthy. Go therefore to the thoroughfares, and
invite to the marriage feast as many as you find.' And those servants went
out into the streets and gathered all whom they found, both bad and good; so
the wedding hall was filled with guests.

"But when the king came in to look at the guests, he saw there a man who
had no wedding garment; and he said to him, 'Friend, how did you get in
here without a wedding garment?' And he was speechless. Then the king
said to the attendants, 'Bind him hand and foot, and cast him into the outer
darkness; there men will weep and gnash their teeth.' For many are called,
but few are chosen."

—MATTHEW 22:1–14

This parable strikes a note and presents to our imagination a
picture that immediately commands our attention.

It was not only the listeners in the long past who pricked up their
ears because they were intensely expectant of the end of the world and
the coming of the messianic kingdom. On the contrary, the dream of
the kingdom of God has moved men's minds in every age. It extends
all the way from the thought of the millennial kingdom in the last book
of the Bible to Karl Marx's classless society and workers' paradise.

And always it is the same deep yearning that is reflected in it: Someday the mystery of suffering, the mystery of madhouses, mass graves,

182

the mystery of widows and orphans must be illuminated. Someday must come the "hereafter," when we shall learn all the answers. Someday the paralyzing contradiction between justice, on the one hand, and life's blind game of chance, on the other, must be reconciled. Someday the tension between rich and poor, between the sunny side of life and the gloomy zones of horror, must be equalized. Every great political and cultural ideal has in it something of the hope and the light of this final fulfillment.

But it is precisely when we put it in this way that we become aware of that altogether different world that emerges with the very first words of our parable.

The first thing that strikes us as altogether different in our parable is this, that the kingdom of God is not a state or condition of this world, not an ideal order of nations and life, but that it centers about a *person:* The king, God himself, is, in a way which we must consider later, the source and sustainer of everything that happens. This king gives a wedding banquet. This in any case makes one thing clear from the very outset and that is that the kingdom of God has nothing to do with the reformatory and revolutionary efforts of man, who wants to realize social and political programs and is out after utopias. It is *God* who acts. It is *he* who prepares the royal banquet. We must therefore take cognizance of something that no man could assert by himself: God wants to prepare a feast for us. He wants us to be his free guests. He wants us to have fellowship and peace with him.

No man could ever fairly arrive at this idea by himself. For this God has no reason whatsoever to take us seriously or even to "love" us. The very fact that this God should invite us to his table is in itself a great miracle. It is something that needs to be told to us by those who have experienced it. For there are no indications whatsoever that would give us reason to imagine such a monstrous thing (for it is nothing less than that). Actually, the indications would point to an altogether different conclusion.

Nietzsche once characterized humanity as "vermin on the crust of the earth." This may be a bit strong but nevertheless it does express the pitiful diminutiveness of the human being who presents a picture of childish pathos standing there with his high claims and pretensions. And God should interest himself in such a thing? Frederick the Great was capable of saying—and this statement was not among the least of his insights into life—that men are canaille, a pack of dogs. And we are to believe that God would lavish anything so magnificent as his plan of salvation upon such a dubious species? Stage the drama of Calvary and trouble his head about the idea of divine grace for such as that?

I have expressed all this in somewhat extreme language. But this way of putting it may point up a deep and fundamental problem.

One of the most puzzling questions with which our Christian education confronts us from our youth up is the fact that it is constantly depriving us of this sense of wonder and amazement. The longer we are Christians the more commonplace does this unheard-of thing become; the miracle is taken for granted and the supernatural becomes "second nature." We are even a bit spoiled and coddled with this grace that is so easily piped into us by way of baptism and confirmation in the midst of our respectable Christian lives. And therefore we can hardly appreciate the tremendous blessedness of that invitation. But Christian satiation is worse than hungry heathenism. It is not for nothing that the saying about those who hunger and thirst appears in the Sermon on the Mount. And if there are any among us who have this hunger and do not know how to satisfy it and yet would be glad to know how to begin becoming a Christian, they should be glad at any rate that they even feel this hunger. For those who hunger are promised that they shall be filled and not be the least in the kingdom of God. "Blessed are those who are homesick, for they shall come home" (Jean Paul).

It is very important, then, to see what this unhoped-for invitation really means. In the first place we must see that it is a real "invitation" and by no means an order to report for service. The message does not come as a "thou shalt," a categorical imperative. It does not come to us as a duty and a law. Rather, God addresses us as a friend and host. He comes to us as a royal donor, the giver of every good gift and joy. For this is an invitation to a wedding feast.

Perhaps it is just at *this* point that we Christians always get the thing wrong. When, in a pause in our work or an evening conversation, somebody asks us, actually plucks up the courage to ask us: "Tell me, how does one really get that inner steadiness that you have, so that a man can have some kind of peace and be able to face this dirty business of life with cheerfulness and confidence?" We often give a very wrong answer. All too frequently we say something like this: "Now first you must do this and stop doing that. Dancing and amusements are out. And, besides, there are some dark spots in your life; first you will have to set this straight. And you must really want to change and then make a complete about-face."

None of us who have given or received such a miserable answer has ever been helped one bit by this kind of moralizing appeal. It only breaks a man down and takes away from him the last spark of courage he may have left. When we are facing the worst things and wrestling with the most secret bondages in our lives the real menace by no means lies only in the fact that our will is too weak to achieve our goal but rather that we cannot even *will* to do it with our whole heart. This is undoubtedly what Luther meant when he said that the Law may well point the way but that it is far from being the strength in one's legs. Therefore the Law only makes us more miserable.

In any case, God proceeds quite differently. True, he demands of us obedience. We must even turn our whole life around, and we must pay for our Christianity with all that we are. But first he *gives* us something, first he simply invites us to come.

So we ought to learn quite simply from this message of the wedding heralds that the job of a disciple of Jesus is to attract and invite and offer the gospel, that he can never speak too highly and glowingly of the royal banquet and the peace and security of the Father's house, whose joy he has himself been permitted to taste. Then later, when the guest is inside the bright halls of that house, when he has really entered the joy and festivity of being a Christian, he will see how great was the darkness and gloom from which he has been so mercifully rescued and he will be sorry and repent.

Shall I say something that sounds altogether heretical?

Repentance and remorse always come soon enough, but joy can never come too soon. We who know Jesus Christ have only to proclaim joy. We need only to remember how the King does it. He invites and calls and gives. Or let us remember how the Sermon on the Mount begins. Nowhere else in all the Scriptures are we so called into question at the innermost core of our existence. Nowhere else are such piercingly radical demands made upon us. Nowhere else are we exposed to a light so consuming that we are ruthlessly compelled to see ourselves at the absolute end of our tether. And yet that chapter begins with the words, many times repeated, "Blessed are . . ."

Jesus can mean nothing but this: Come unto me, all of you; I have something to tell you. And what I have to say is certainly very hard. It will expose the innermost crisis of your life and your absolute helplessness before God. But first, before I speak of that, you must know that I am among you as your Saviour and that, because I am with you, nothing can snatch you out of the Father's hand, not even that utter darkness and that absolute shortcoming of which I am about to speak to you. First I can say to you: Blessed are those in whose midst I am; blessed are those who hunger and thirst; blessed are those who are poor in spirit and those whom I may call my brothers. And now that you have been given this blessedness, now that you know this imperishable peace with the Father, now listen to what is required of you; now hear what it is that may bring you to shipwreck.

And then, when the messengers of the king had delivered the joyful message of that invitation, the response of those who were invited was nothing less than monstrous: they rejected it.

It is easy enough to understand why someone may reject an excessive demand. Many of us have burdensome demands made upon us. How many there are who are always wanting something from us; wanting us to give money, wanting us to support this cause or that, wanting us to provide dwellings and jobs and so forth. We can understand, then, why a person who has excessive demands made upon him sometimes loses his temper and finally says, "That's the end of it; let me alone!"

But here the situation is different. Here an invitation is being refused. Have we ever known what it is like to try to do something for somebody and be given the cold shoulder? It is just this kind of hurt that was inflicted when these people brusquely dismissed the messengers of the king and "made light" of the invitation.

This is very hard to understand. *Why* did they react so strangely?

In the Lucan parallel of our text other expressions are used. There it says not that "they made light of it" but that they "began to make excuses" (Luke 14:18 ff.). One has bought a field, another a yoke of oxen, and a third has married a wife. In other words, these people are putting the everyday concerns of their life, whatever happens to be immediately at hand—the business letter they have to write, the important transaction they have to settle, the cocktail party they have to attend, the garden work they do for their pleasure—they are putting all this *before* the call from eternity, before the great joy that is being offered to them.

In themselves none of these things and activities are bad. After all, writing business letters and settling transactions are part of our duty. Actually, there is not the slightest objection that can be made to these things. But this is just the trouble. As a rule, the road to hell is paved not with crimes and great scandals but with things that are quite harmless, with pure proprieties, and simply because these harmless proprieties acquire a false importance in our life, because they suddenly get in our light. The people in our parable certainly had within them that hunger and expectancy of which we have spoken; otherwise they would not have been human beings. They too wished to get away from the everlasting routine of life and work and yearned for fulfillment and peace. They too dreamed the dream of light. But now, at the moment when all this was at hand, ready to touch their life, they failed.

But is all this really so utterly incomprehensible as it may seem at first glance? It is incomprehensible only to those who do not have enough love to put themselves in their shoes or who no longer remember how they themselves felt before they had accepted the Lord Christ. That was the time when they still refused to take the risk of accepting that great joy and giving up their own indulgences and ties in order to have it. And they refused to risk it simply because they still did not know the promised joy, because it was impossible to judge beforehand to what extent each sacrifice and each departure from the past would be rewarded. They did not understand, and at that point they could not possibly have understood, that this, which they, with their natural eyes, considered to be letting themselves in for a binding and therefore burdensome allegiance, is actually the greatest freedom of all. They had no idea that what they considered a state of renunciation, in which one is always having to say no, in which never again can there be any joy and youthful exuberance, is actually peace, is actually the abundant life.

Haven't all of us at some time had an associate or friend who honestly regretted that we were Christians, since, after all, we were quite decent chaps, humorous, lively fellows, real guys?

I fear, however, that in this respect we Christians often represent our Lord very badly. The glum, sour faces of many Christians, who frequently enough look as if they had gallstones (all those who really have them will excuse me!) are poor proclaimers of that wedding joy. They rather give the impression that, instead of coming from the Father's joyful banquet, they have just come from the sheriff who has auctioned off their sins and now are sorry they can't get them back again. Nietzsche made a true observation when he said, "You will have to look more redeemed if I am to believe in your Redeemer."

The reason why many refuse the invitation is just that they do not know and also that we Christians all too often withhold from them what it is that is being given to them. For probably everybody has regretted almost everything once in his life, but never yet has anybody regretted having become a disciple of this Lord. It is really a pity that the theme of that rather mawkish hymn verse,

> If people only knew
> The joy of Jesus' way,
> Then surely more than few
> Would Christians be today . . .

has not found a greater poet who would help people to see that not only would their skepticism vanish but also that their boldest expectations would be surpassed once they crossed the threshold of that royal house in which the Father awaits them and welcomes them to a happy Christian life. There must be something festive and happy in our whole Christian life, otherwise people will not believe that we are the messengers of the King. When a person has to struggle with inferiority feelings when he is obliged to talk to his neighbor about Jesus, he may speak like an angel from heaven but a certain tone of voice belies him. And then he ought not to talk himself out of it by saying that it is the message that is offensive. He found no faith only because he himself was not convincing, not worthy of being believed.

In any case, the better people refuse. They have more important things to do than to jump up forthwith and forsake their business to go chasing after some hypothetical bird in the bush. After all, every one of us has certain areas in his life which he will not give up and hand over. It may be my ambition in my job, which brings me into a bad relationship with my colleagues and competitors and makes it impossible for me to sit down with them at the King's table. It may be the jealousy or the prejudice that exists between me and my neighbor and therefore also between me and the King. Perhaps it is my business practices, which the King must not know about and which, quite rightly, cannot bear the light of the festal hall. Perhaps what I hold back lies in the area of sex: God can have everything else, but *not* this! At some *other* point in my life I'm willing to let him in, but not *here,* not at *this* point. After all, I am good-natured; I don't wish anybody any harm; I have a tender heart; I have many good qualifications, and so he can have my brotherly love. I am idealistic, I have enthusiasm and a great willingness to work; so he can have my activity. But this *one* thing he cannot have!

And now the very strange thing is that God is not interested in getting into my life at any other point, that he has taken it into his head to come into my life only by way of this most difficult terrain. It is characteristic of the kingdom of God that it never follows the path of least resistance, but always seeks out the thickest concrete walls in my life in order to enter there and only there. If I do not allow it entrance there, it turns away from me altogether, and this most assuredly. Do we know where in our lives the thickest walls have been built up? It is worth thinking about.

Presumably this is just what the invited guests in our parable said. "Some other time we will be glad to accept your invitation; but not right *now.* I have no use for you in what I plan to do *today;* here you simply cannot butt in and get in my way."

But here too the rule applies: If they do not open the door to him *today,* at the point where it is hardest for them to do so, God turns away and goes elsewhere. True enough, it is perhaps much simpler to become religious after the "second heart attack," since then, as Wilhelm Busch said, you have "everything behind you" (though even in old age and in this condition people may be crotchety). But the point is that God wants me now, when I am on the rise or at the high point of life, and where my work and my struggles and my passions will clash with much that God commands and demands of me. I have no promise that God will come to me again if I make an appointment to meet him later in the pleasant pastures of retirement; and who knows whether they will be so pleasant after all?

There is still another important feature of our parable that must be noted at this point.

These invited guests did not stop at mere refusal to come along. The parable says that they seized the messengers of the king, treated them shamefully, and killed them. And this touches upon a profound mystery of the kingdom of God and that is that one can never take a passive attitude toward the message of Christ. Eventually one must actively oppose it. Here is the root of all of Israel's hostility to the prophets and here too is the root of all the fanaticism and radicalism of modern anti-Christians. One must simply get Christ and his followers out of sight because they are a permanent reproach and because they make it so obvious to us that we want our *own* life. One cannot live in continuing tension with the message of Christ. One cannot be exposed indefinitely to the necessity of having to prove that it is valid and at the same time prove to oneself that one has no need for it. To say no to Christ in the attitude of tolerance (which means rejecting him as far as we ourselves are concerned but letting other people keep their faith), the kind of tolerance which is cultivated by those who advocate a so-called democratic freedom of religious confession is merely a passing calm. Anybody who knows the secret of the kingdom of God knows that one day the storm will break loose again. One need not even conjure up the example of the Third Reich (which *also* began so tolerantly!) to know the course these things take.

But then, when the better people failed and rejected the invitation, the messengers of the king were sent out again. This time they went out to the people in the highways and hedges. And among them are good people and bad ones, honest people and rascals. So God carried out his plan—no matter what happened. The great antagonists from Nebuchadnezzar to Judas and the modern representatives of anti-Christianity cannot queer God's plans, for they themselves are part of the plan.

So his banquet did not fall through. When the geniuses fail, God turns to the nobodies. When the bearers of the Christian tradition, the church Christians, walk out and descend into dogmatic hairsplitting or church politics, he turns to the neopagans and rejoices in the freshness of their new-found Christianity. For God has no prejudices. A man can come as he is, even as an utterly poor, utterly sinful, and utterly unlovable person who cannot understand what God can see in him. The fact is that he cannot see anything in him, but he makes something of him; he makes him his beloved child.

So there they were, all seated around the table: the beggars and the prostitutes, swindling bankrupts and broken-down geniuses, poor wretches whom nobody takes seriously, and artful dodgers—all in all a nice gang of people.

And then the king appeared.

This is the main thing—to see him and to be able to speak to him. This is the real end and aim of the invitation—to be with him—not the heavenly crowns and the palms and the golden streets or the crystal sea or any kind of pious or half-pious talk of kingdom come.

When the father of Adolf Schlatter, the great theologian, lay dying a friend consoled him, telling him that he would soon be tarrying in the golden streets of the heavenly Jerusalem and gazing upon the crystal sea. Thereupon the dying man turned upon him in anger and cried out, "Away with such rubbish! All I want is to be in the Father's bosom." In other words, heaven does not consist in what we "get" but in what we shall "be." Then we shall no longer be limited to faith and hope, and therefore subject to temptation and doubt. Then we shall live in love alone, and in loving will be permitted to see what once we believed.

Then at its close our parable takes a dramatic turn. One of the guests got into the worst kind of trouble because he was not wearing a wedding garment and was thrown out of the banquet hall. What is the meaning of this wedding garment?

To be sure, we can accept the call to come into the Father's house just as we are. We need not be ashamed of the highways and hedges from which we have come. It is our very pitiableness that proves the Father's pity. We can come just as we are.

But this by no means implies that we can *enter* the Father's house as we are. And this is precisely what the parable means by this metaphor of the wedding garment. We seat ourselves at the banquet table without a wedding garment when we allow our sins to be forgiven but still want to hang on to them. We do this, in other words, when we say to ourselves, consciously or unconsciously, "This is great stuff; a man can remain in his sins without worrying, since this God of love can never be really angry; he shuts both eyes; he will let it pass." Thus in all artful innocence I can apply for forgiveness every day without having to abstain from a single dubious thing to which my heart clings. Did not Heine say of God's forgiving, *"C'est son métier,"* this is God's business. Report at the service department and God's grace will be supplied. Even the church has its service department.

And right here is where God's warning comes in: the person who comes without the wedding garment, the person who permits the fact that he can come as he is to make him shameless instead of humble, who, instead of being concerned with sanctification and discipline, allows himself to play a frivolous game with the grace of God, that person is just as badly off as the people who refuse *altogether,* who, indeed, kill the messengers of the king.

Even Christians, not only pagans, can be cast into outer darkness. Even the grace of God can become our doom. This is why there is such great sense in the custom of making confession and setting various things to rights before going to Holy Communion. This is comparable to our putting on the wedding garment.

But even in this grievous thought, which we cannot contemplate without anxiety, the message of joy still breaks through. And this is the last point that we shall consider. For joy remains the real theme of our parable, despite all its dark and somber features.

How, then, can even the analogy of the wedding garment constitute a message of joy? When Jesus speaks here in these figurative terms of sanctifying and preparing oneself, he is by no means thinking of somber penitential exercises and agonizing starvation cures. On the contrary, the very imagery he uses for all this is the festive image of the wedding garment, the image of joy. Who ever thought it a sacrifice and a burden to change his clothes and put on festive garments in order to go to a banquet he has looked forward to for weeks? This dressing up and preparing for the occasion is itself a part of the celebration and is full of joy and anticipated excitement. It is the joy of the bride who is waiting expectantly. She knows for whom it is she is adorning herself. And this lends joy to the preparations and the dressing up, even though it takes time and effort.

And that, in plain and practical terms, means that when I make an effort to establish a new relationship with my neighbor, when I combat the spirit of care within myself or the vagaries of my imagination, or jealousy and envy, this is not morose rigorism, but rather joy, because I know for whom I am doing all this, and because the joy of heaven over one sinner who repents simply communicates itself infectiously and makes this act of repentance itself a thing of joy.

Repentance is not a woebegone renunciation of things that mean a lot to me; it is a joyful homecoming to the place where certain things no longer have any importance to me.

After all, the prodigal son did not moan over the fact that now he would have to leave that interesting, fascinating far country, the great adventure of his life. On the contrary, he saw the lighted windows of his father's house, where a fervent welcome awaited him, and suddenly the far country became a gloomy dream that dissolved behind him.

How, then, do you go about becoming a Christian in order to enter that lighted, festive hall, into this fulfillment of life?

My answer would be this: We shall enter it only if we start out by simply allowing someone to tell us that there is One who rules the world with a father's heart; that he is interested in me; that I am not too paltry or too vile for him to love; and that he wants to love me out of the terrible loneliness and alienness and guilt of my life and bring me to the Father's house.

Perhaps someone will reply, "I hear the message but I lack the faith; it's all too good to be true." And there may well be such a thing as a voice of inner scruple that warns a person to be on guard against such siren songs.

Jesus would certainly understand such hesitation. One day there came to Jesus a young man (he became known as "the rich young ruler," one of the classical figures of Christianity). He too gave an account of his fruitless efforts to find peace and get straight with God. And the record says that "Jesus looking upon him loved him" (Mark

10:21). It is a comfort to know that he knows me and is looking at me, even though I go helplessly searching for him. He has seen me and loved me long since—even in my doubt and despair.

So, if anyone is too honest to give credence to the message of divine joy at first go, if he is afraid of himself and afraid that he may slip because of weakness, then he ought at least to be willing to make an *experiment* with Jesus. Even the most strict intellectual honesty is capable of this. Even the scientist who is dedicated to hard-boiled realism does this.

So I challenge you to start with this working hypothesis—"as if" there were something to this Jesus and "as if" that invitation to come to the table of the King actually existed. And then in the name of this working hypothesis venture for once to be confident and joyful in everything that happens to you today and tomorrow because it is designed for you by a higher hand. Just talk to God—about your sin and that difficulty in your life which you cannot manage—"as if" he existed. Say a good word to that colleague who gets on your nerves or that person in your house who annoys you, but do it in his name and at his behest, "as if" he existed. Just make an experiment with this working hypothesis, Jesus, and see whether you are met with silence or whether he actually shows you that you can count on him. But *do* something.

God is no piker; and he has said that he who comes to him will not be cast out. But you *must* come to him, you must beseech and besiege him and find out whether you meet with any resistance.

Why shouldn't you try this for once? This is not a Faust-like search for meaning that carries you down endless unknown roads; what is at stake is the joy of homecoming.

You understand and catch the secret of the Christian life only in so far as you understand and catch its *joy*. And it is not at all as if it were only you who were always waiting and longing. There is another who is waiting for you, and he is already standing at the door, ready to come to meet you.

The deepest mystery of the world is that God is waiting for us, for the near and the far, for the homeless waif and the settled townsman. The person who understands this and takes it in is near to the blessedness of the royal wedding feast. Already there shines about him the flooding light of the festal hall even though he still walks in the midst of the valley of the shadow. He may be sorrowful, and yet he is always rejoicing; he may be poor, and yet he makes many rich; he may have nothing, and yet he possesses all things.